OFFICIAL REPORT

OF THE

THIRTIETH INTERNATIONAL

CHRISTIAN ENDEAVOR CONVENTION

Held in Portland, Oregon

July 4 to 10, 1925

First Fruits Press
Wilmore, Kentucky
c2015

First Fruits Press
The Academic Open Press of Asbury Theological Seminary
204 N. Lexington Ave., Wilmore, KY 40390
859-858-2236
first.fruits@asburyseminary.edu
asbury.to/firstfruits

The Story of the Portland Convention

The Official Report

of

The Thirtieth International

Christian Endeavor Convention

Held in Portland, Oregon
July 4 to 10, 1925

Boston United Society of Christian Endeavor Chicago

Copyright, 1925, by the United Society of
Christian Endeavor.

CONTENTS

Foreword	5
Officers of the United Society of Christian Endeavor	6
Trustees of the United Society of Christian Endeavor	7
Denominational Trustees	7
Convention Committees	8
Westward, Ho!	9
The First Day, Saturday, July 4	13
The Second Day, Sunday, July 5	27
The Third Day, Monday, July 6	39
The Fourth Day, Tuesday, July 7	72
The Fifth Day, Wednesday, July 8	87
The Sixth Day, Thursday, July 9	98
The Morning Conferences	115
The Intermediates Loom Large	121
The Juniors Score	126
The Denominational Rallies	137
Resolutions	140
Christian Endeavor Society Standards	147
Convention Snap-Shots	152
Looking Backward	156
Dr. Clark's Retirement	158

FOREWORD

This report of the Portland convention covers practically all the major meetings, but it does not begin to give an idea of the number of excellent addresses that were delivered in conference halls, at luncheons, and before Junior and Intermediate workers. These were legion. The aim of the writer was to give a broad picture of the convention, a consecutive description of the main meetings and events from beginning to end. Hence the report has been divided into "Days," making it easy to follow the course of affairs.

The convention was one of the best International Christian Endeavor conventions ever held in this country. The arrangements made by the convention committee were perfect in every detail. The courtesy of the people of Portland was unfailing. The speeches were full of inspiration. The meetings were enthusiastic and well attended.

It is a pity that we cannot reproduce in these pages the practical ideas thrown out in the sixteen or seventeen conferences that were held each morning. The effect of these conferences will be felt in the home societies of the delegates.

The bulk of this report was written in the various sessions of the convention. Grateful acknowledgment is here made to Dr. John F. Cowan, of San Diego, Cal., for his account of the Alumni Banquet, to Paul C. Brown, of Los Angeles, for the account of the Intermediate programme, and to Mildreth Haggard, of Minneapolis, Minn., for her full report of the splendid Junior programme.

This record of Portland, 1925, will keep fresh in our memories the happiness of those days spent in the City of Roses. It will recall pleasant hours, delightful hosts, and an unforgettable trip. Portland furnished a thrill even to old convention-goers. It renewed our faith in young people. It gave to us new pledges for the future of the Kingdom of God.

ROBERT P. ANDERSON.

Boston, Mass.

LIST OF ILLUSTRATIONS

	Page
Officers of the United Society of Christian Endeavor	8, 9
All from Dixie	32
The Covered Wagon	56
Arizona, First in the Parade	56
The Massachusetts Crowd	80
The Ship-shape Iowa Delegation	96
Dr. Clark and Dr. Poling	112
Christian Endeavor Society Standards Chart	147

OFFICERS OF THE UNITED SOCIETY OF CHRISTIAN ENDEAVOR

REV. FRANCIS E. CLARK, D.D., LL.D.
President Emeritus

REV. DANIEL A. POLING, LL.D., Litt.D.
President

REV. HOWARD B. GROSE, D.D.
Vice-President

REV. WILLIAM HIRAM FOULKES, D.D.
Vice-President

EDWARD P. GATES
General Secretary

ALVIN J. SHARTLE
Treasurer and Field Secretary

REV. STANLEY B. VANDERSALL
Assistant Treasurer and Alumni Superintendent

CLARENCE C. HAMILTON
Publication Manager

REV. ROBERT P. ANDERSON
Editorial Secretary

REV. IRA LANDRITH, D.D.
Extension Secretary

CHARLES F. EVANS
Southern Secretary

PAUL C. BROWN
Pacific Coast Secretary

R. A. WALKER
Manager Western Office

FREDERICK A. WALLIS
Citizenship Superintendent

REV. S. C. RAMSDEN
Army and Navy Superintendent

TRUSTEES OF THE UNITED SOCIETY OF CHRISTIAN ENDEAVOR

Life Trustees

Mrs. Francis E. Clark—Sagamore Beach, Mass.
Rev. M. Rhodes, D. D.—St. Louis, Mo.
William Shaw, LL.D.—Boston, Mass.
Mrs. William Shaw—Boston, Mass.
Rev. J. Z. Tyler, D. D.—Richmond, Va.

Trustees at Large

Rev. R. P. Anderson—Boston, Mass.
Rev. I. W. Bingaman, D. D.—Quincy, Ill.
Rev. Bernard Clausen — Syracuse, N. Y.
Mr. John R. Clements—Binghamton, N. Y.
Rev. A. E. Cory, D. D.—Kinston, N. C.
Rev. William Hiram Foulkes, D. D.—Cleveland, Ohio.
Mr. E. P. Gates—Boston, Mass.
Mr. O. F. Gilliom—Berne, Ind.
Mr. Clarence C. Hamilton—Boston, Mass.
Mr. Charles H. Jones—Boston, Mass.
Rev. Orvis F. Jordan—Park Ridge, Ill.
Rev. Daniel A. Poling, LL. D.—Litt. D., New York City.
Rev. E. L. Reiner—Chicago, Ill.
Mr. A. J. Shartle—Boston, Mass.
Mr John T. Sproull—New York City.
Mr. Charles G. Stewart—Winnipeg, Canada.
Rev. Stanley B. Vandersall—Boston, Mass.
Prof. Amos R. Wells, LL.D., Litt. D.—Boston, Mass.

Special Trustees Representing Denominational Young People's Work

Prof. Aaron Brown—A. M. E. Zion, Varick League, Pensacola, Fla.
Rev. O. T. Deever—United Brethren, Dayton, Ohio.
Rev. Walter Getty — Presbyterian U. S., Richmond, Va.
Rev. William Ralph Hall—Presbyterian U. S., Philadelphia, Pa.
Rev. J. E. Harwood—United Brethren in Christ (Old Constitution), Huntington, Ind.
Miss Helen Hawkins — Secretary, Board of Young Friends Activities, Richmond, Ind.
Rev. A. B. Kendall, D. D.—Christian, Springfield, Ohio.
Mr. Charles R. Matlock — Cumberland Presbyterian, Cleveland, Tenn.
Miss Catherine A. Miller—Reformed Church in the United States, Philadelphia, Pa.
Rev. S. S. Morris, D. D.—Allen Christian Endeavor League, African Methodist Episcopal, Norfolk, Va.
Mr. H. L. Pickerill—Disciples of Christ, St. Louis, Mo.
Rev. E. W. Praetorius—Evangelical, Cleveland, Ohio.
Rev. E. A. Sexsmith — Methodist Protestant, Baltimore, Md.
Mr. Moses M. Shaw—United Presbyterian, Chicago, Ill.
Mr. Harry Thomas Stock—Congregational, Boston, Mass.
Rev. H. L. Streich — Evangelical Synod, St. Louis, Mo.

Denominational Trustees

Rev. J. Lambert Alexander—Northern Congregational, Hamilton, Ontario, Canada.
Rev. Ernest Bourner Allen, D. D.—Congregational, Oak Park, Ill.
Rev. B. W. Arnett, D. D.—African Methodist Episcopal, Philadelphia, Pa.
Mr. John Willis Baer, LL.D.—Presbyterian, Pasadena, Cal.
Mr. Fred L. Ball—Congregational, Cleveland, Ohio.
Rev. David James Burrell, D. D.—Reformed Church in America, New York City.
Rev. J. Whitcomb Brougher, D. D.—Baptist, Los Angeles, Cal.
Rev. W. W. Bustard, D. D.—Baptist, Cleveland, Ohio.
Bishop A. J. Carey—African Methodist Episcopal, Chicago, Ill.
Rev. G. C. Carpenter — Brethren, Hagerstown, Maryland.
Rev. Ora W. Carrell—Friends, Central City, Neb.
Rev. James L. Hill, D. D.—Congregational, Salem, Mass.
Prof. James Lewis Howe, Ph.D.—Presbyterian in the U. S., Lexington, Va.
Rev. Elijah Humphries, D. D.—Primitive Methodist, Billerica, Mass.
Rev. Albert W. Jefferson, D. D.—Free Baptist, Lawrence, Mass.
Dr. B. F. Johanson—Seventh Day Baptist, Battle Creek, Mich.
Mr. Elmer E. S. Johnson—Schwenkfelder, Hartford, Conn.
Rev. W. T. Johnson, D. D.—Colored Baptist, Richmond, Va.
Bishop Lynnwood Westinghouse Kyles, A. M., D. D. — African Methodist Episcopal Zion, Winston-Salem, N. C.
President Henry Churchill King, D. D., LL.D. — Congregational, Oberlin, Ohio.
Rev. Ira Landrith, D. D., LL.D.—Presbyterian, U. S. A., Chicago, Ill.

Mr. George W. Coleman—Baptist, Wellesley Heights, Mass.
Rev. James A. Cosby, D. D.—United Presbyterian, Ellwood City, Pa.
Rev. J. C. Cummins—General Baptist, Oakland City, Ind.
Rev. H. A. Denton, D. D.—Disciples of Christ, Altoona, Pa.
Rev. J. Stanley Durkee, D. D.—Congregational, Washington, D. C.
James W. Eichelberger — African Methodist Episcopal Zion, Chicago, Ill.
Rev. J. H. Garrison, LL.D.—Disciples of Christ, St. Louis, Mo.
Rev. Gilbert Glass, D. D.—Presbyterian, U. S., Richmond, Va.
Rev. Howard B. Grose, D. D.—Baptist, New York City.
Rev. Joseph F. Gross—Evangelical, Wilkes-Barre, Pa.
Rev. G. W. Haddaway, D. D.—Methodist Protestant, Baltimore, Md.
Rev. W. C. Hallwachs—Evangelical, Cleveland, Ohio.
Rev. P. A. Heilman, D. D.—Lutheran, Baltimore, Md.
Rev. Floyd W. Tomkins, S. T. D.—Episcopal, Philadelphia, Pa.
Bishop W. T. Vernon, D. D.—African Methodist Episcopal, Nashville, Tenn.
Rev. Hugh K. Walker, D. D.—Presbyterian, Los Angeles, Cal.
President E. A. Watkins, D. D.—Christian Convention, Albany, Mo.
Bishop W. M. Weekley, D. D.—United Brethren, Parkersburg, W. Va.

Rev. Cleland B. McAfee, D. D.—Presbyterian, Chicago, Ill.
Rev. W. A. MacTaggart—Canadian Presbyterian, Toronto, Ont., Canada.
Rev. Arthur Meilicke — Moravian, Grand Rapids, Wis.
Rev. Rufus W. Miller, D. D.—Reformed Church in U. S., Philadelphia, Pa.
Rev. Samuel M. Musselman—Mennonite, Bluffton, Ohio.
Rev. P. O. Orrt—Christian Union, Excelsior Springs, Mo.
Rev. MacLeod M. Pearce, D. D.—Reformed Presbyterian, Geneva College, Beaver Falls, Pennsylvania.
Rev. W. F. Richardson, D. D.—Disciples of Christ, Los Angeles, Cal.
Rev. James G. Ryder—Union American M. E. Church, New York City.
Rev. H. F. Shupe, D. D.—United Brethren, Dayton, Ohio.
Rev. Egbert W. Smith, D. D.—Presbyterian in the U. S., Nashville, Tenn.
Rev. Frank Snavely—Church of God, McMechen, W. Va.
Rev. Erie Wilfley, D. D.—Disciples of Christ, Washington, D. C.
Rev. Herbert L. Willett, D. D.—Disciples of Christ, Chicago, Ill.
Rev. Samuel H. Woodrow, D. D.—Congregational, Newton Highlands, Mass.

All presidents of State Christian Endeavor Unions are trustees of the United Society of Christian Endeavor.

In office at the opening of the convention.

CONVENTION COMMITTEES
The Executive Committee

Chairman—Judge Jacob Kanzler.
Vice-Chairman — Rev. Lloyd R. Carrick.
Executive Secretary — Rev. Charles T. Hurd.
Treasurer—Mr. S. C. Pier.
Badges—Walter R. Dimm.
Banquets—W. A. Eliot.
Decorations—Jacob Kanzler, Elaine Cooper.
Finance—E. C. Sammons.
Halls and Exhibits—A. J. Bale.
Hotels and Housing — Charles T. Hurd.
Information—A. P. Patten.
Intermediate—Mrs. J. Hunter Wells.
Junior—Mrs. B. I. Elliott.
Mailing—Miss Faye Beery.
Motor Cars—Rev. E. C. Farnham.
Music—Dr. J. W. McMichael.
Pages and Guides—Rev. C. P. Gates.
Parade—Rev. W. S. Gilbert.

Members at Large—G. Evert Baker, E. D. Geiger, Rev. W. S. Gilbert. Miss Mary Gulley, S. W. Lawrence. William McMurray, J. W. Palmer, Warde W. Robinson, J. J. Ross, James Henderson.
Park and Street Meetings—Jas. W. Palmer.
Press—Ernest W. Peterson.
Program—Fred W. Nelson, Royce McCandliss.
Publicity—Rev. L. R. Carrick.
Pulpit Study—Dr. H. L. Bowman.
Reception—Warde W. Robinson.
Recreation—Ray Conway.
Registrar—Donald Nelson.
Registration Promotion (out of city) —Miss Frankie Coykendall.
Registration Promotion (Portland) —E. Earl Felke.
Speakers' Bureau—G. Evert Baker.
Supplies—Miss Emma Rehwalt.
Ushers—C. Jay Walker.

The Convention Council

Secretary of this Council—Warde W. Robinson.
Assistant Secretary of this Council—Miss Bonnebelle Kent.
President of the Oregon Christian Endeavor Union—Miss Mary Gulley.
Secretary of the Oregon Christian Endeavor Union—Miss Viola Odgen.
President of the Portland Christian Endeavor Union—James Henderson.
Secretary of the Portland Christian Endeavor Union — Miss Helen Hunt Jackson.

OFFICERS OF THE UNITED SOCIETY OF CHRISTIAN ENDEAVOR

E. P. Gates
General Secretary

A. J. Shartle
Treasurer and Field-Secretary

Rev. Francis E. Clark, D.D., LL.D.
President Emeritus

Rev. Daniel A. Poling, LL.D., Litt.D.
President

Rev. Howard B. Grose, D.D.
Vice-President

Rev. William Hiram Foulkes, D.D.
Vice-President

OFFICERS OF THE UNITED SOCIETY OF CHRISTIAN ENDEAVOR

IRA LANDRITH, D.D.
Extension Secretary

CLARENCE C. HAMILTON
Publication Manager

STANLEY B. VANDERSALL
*Assistant-Treasurer and
Alumni Superintendent*

Rev. ROBERT P. ANDERSON
Editorial Secretary

R. A. WALKER
Manager Western Office

CHARLES F. EVANS
Southern Secretary

PAUL C. BROWN
Pacific-Coast Secretary

WESTWARD, HO!

Christian Endeavor Crosses the Continent.—Portland Pilgrims on the Way

Once again it was the privilege of large crowds of Endeavorers to cross the Rocky Mountains and the great plains to attend an International Christian Endeavor Convention. Portland, Or., proved a great attraction. For a week before the opening day, July 4, special Christian Endeavor trains speeded westward. There were special trains from New York, Pennsylvania, Ohio, Dixie, New England, and other States. Some States which had no specials for themselves came to Chicago to join some other group in a special from that gateway of the West. Maryland and Delaware, for instance, brought sixty-one delegates, quite a remarkable showing for so small areas.

Happy youth! There are no dull moments in a Christian Endeavor crowd. We are with the New England-Maryland groups, which are augmented here and there on the way. On this train, as on all the others, the journey is a time of fun, fellowship, and friendship. A happy bridal couple are aboard on their honeymoon, and are the occasion of floods of good-natured and hilarious merriment. Coming from breakfast, they find their section decorated with paper garlands and a printed announcement to the effect that they must not be disturbed.

Arrangements on this train, by which Dr. Francis E. Clark and Mrs. Clark travelled, were excellent; and a daily programme was prepared in advance that made dullness impossible. General Secretary Gates was the leader, and his genial personality contributed a great deal to the success of the trip. It takes both good humor and tact to be "papa" to a train-load of nearly two hundred persons.

ENDEAVOR IN WONDERLAND
First Stop, Minneapolis

Early Tuesday afternoon the special train reached Minneapolis, Minn., where the State convention was in session, the first stop after Chicago. The Portlanders were whisked in red-and-blue taxicabs to the convention church and then in private automobiles on a long afternoon trip that showed the beauty spots and milling interests in a delightful city.

All the Portlanders were royally entertained at an Alumni banquet in the evening, a unique affair in a tent, with open sides and ends, in the court of Hotel Curtis. Greetings were brought by the field-secretaries and officers of the United Society, including Dr. Clark. Three outstanding guests were Governors Gifford Pinchot of Pennsylvania and Theodore Christianson of Minnesota and Mr. James Kelly of Scotland.

Governor Christianson brought the welcome and greetings of the churches. He pointed out that the State owes much to the Church, and it is doubtful whether the State could exist without the Church. He spoke warmly of Christian Endeavor and its work of laying spiritual foundations for the social structure, and he pledged himself and his office to help Christian Endeavor in this task.

Governor Pinchot was on his way to address the Christian Endeavor Convention in Portland. He started his brief talk at Minneapolis by saying: "What I think of Christian Endeavor may be expressed by saying that I am crossing the continent to address a great Christian Endeavor Convention in Portland. I know by personal experience something of the work that you are doing. What this country needs is men and women, boys and girls, who will stand up and be counted, and not be ashamed of what they stand for, heads high, and a glory in their eyes. We have to fight spiritual wickedness in high places, and especially contempt for the Constitution of the United States, particularly the Eighteenth Amendment." The address was a ringing challenge to aggressive and whole-hearted endeavor.

Next morning we were crossing North Dakota, an immense green plain with possibilities for agriculture that seem limitless. In the early morning a group of Jamestown, N. D., Endeavorers boarded the train, and on the breakfast-tables in the diner the delegates found a deep container with honey, the gift of the First Congregational Endeavorers of Jamestown. For Mrs. Clark they brought a beautiful bouquet of orchids, roses, and sweet peas.

Then Came Bismarck

Bismarck is the capital of North Dakota, and is a little more than half-way across the continent. To be exact, it is 1,439 miles from Portland. Here the State Christian Endeavor convention was in session; and of course the special had to stop and "look in" at the meetings. The Bismarck Juvenile Band was at the station, and headed the procession from the station to the city auditorium. Drs. Clark and Poling made the principal speeches, and a little girl brought to Mrs. Clark a bouquet of roses expressing the love of the North Dakota Endeavorers.

Dancing Indians

Fifteen minutes at Mandan gave us a chance to see five Indians, gala-garbed with colored beads and abundance of feathers. Four of them, two women and two men, danced to the beating of a tambourine played by a fourth Indian. The dance was a slight hop in time to the music, a performance that was manifestly hot under a bright sun.

And Bucking Bronchos

For the first time, probably, in Christian Endeavor history a round-up was especially staged for the delegates on the New England train. It was at Medora, in the centre of the famous "Bad Lands" of North Dakota. Medora has gained fame as the one-time home of the late President Roosevelt. The town, which in 1920 had 212 inhabitants, is on the Little Missouri River, and not far distant is the ranch where Roosevelt lived and gained some of the health nature had at first denied him.

Here were gathered a score of cowboy farmers to show the delegates something of the wild life of the West. The stage was a fenced field. From various stalls opening on the field horses and their riders were introduced. The horses came tearing into the inclosure, leaping, jumping, throwing up forefeet, flinging up vicious heels, and snorting hoarsely in the excitement of trying to throw their riders. Some of them twisted their bodies suddenly as they bucked, threw up their heads, pulled them down, and did everything a horse could think of except roll over. Yet the men stuck on, and brought the horses first to an even gallop and then to a canter. One twelve-year-old boy was as clever as any, and knew how to throw himself clear off the horse if it tried to break through the fence.

There were exhibitions of steer-throwing and of lassoing, an art amazing in Eastern eyes; and it was noticed that when a wild steer made for the fence at a gallop, the spectators retired quickly to a safe distance. These "rough riders" gave a convincing and interesting exhibition of the fact that horse and man are one and that a well-trained horse knows as well as its rider what is expected of it. The hour and a half at Medora reproduced scenes that Roosevelt must often have witnessed and in which in private he must often have taken part; anyhow, the Endeavorers got a thrill out of a unique experience.

Helena: Across the Great Divide

Snow-capped mountains looked toward us with shining faces as we rose Thursday morning in Montana.

At Logan, Mont., we saw the first evidence of the earthquake that took place a week or ten days before. It was a schoolhouse, a large, square, brick structure, the roof of which had been pretty well shaken down.

A little farther on, at Lombard, where the rocks rise almost perpendicularly above the town, we could see where parts of them had broken off and fallen into the river or across the railroad track. The marvel is that the place was not wiped out. In other near-by towns some of the buildings were ruined.

Helena, the capital of Montana, was the next stop. It is a fine city of twelve thousand, nestling among the mountains, whose dark tops rose above white clouds.

Automobiles carried the Endeavorers on a tour around the city—unfortunately in rain—to the Broadwater Natatorium, the largest and surely the most beautiful indoor swimming-pool in the world. The water, which is warm, comes from a natural hot-water spring a mile distant. Most of the officers of the United Society, including Dr. Clark, and many of the delegates, enjoyed a plunge and swim in the tempting pool.

Then came breakfast in the hotel and a trip by car to the train. Not far from Helena the Portland Pilgrims (travelling in unpilgrim-like luxury) crossed the Great Divide, the backbone of the continent.

Spokane and Yakima

The mountains of Montana are wonderful to see, great shaggy giants that they are; but they are even more wonderful in the riches they hide in their secret heart—gold and copper, lead and iron. Here and there one sees a tiny hole in the mountain-side where some eager prospector, no doubt, has sought for hidden gold, and one feels how difficult it must be to strike a vein of gold in the immensities of these massive ranges.

All day long, then, through gorgeous scenes until in the late evening—half past ten—we arrived in Spokane, Wash., where a crowd of Endeavorers waited to welcome us.

Thursday evening was stunt night. The dining-car was cleared of tables and filled with chairs. It was a jolly crowd that met in it. Maryland sang its famous gesture song, "Beneath the spreading chestnut-tree," and Massachusetts gave a perfectly side-splitting presentation of a Ford car crossing the Great Divide. Gates, Poling, Shartle, Brown, Paterson, Hamilton, and Anderson kept the audience convulsed with laughter with their funny stories until the train rolled into Spokane.

Next morning, Friday, found us at Yakima, where a great host was assembled to greet us.

The Charm of Puget Sound

The next stop was Seattle, Wash., at 1.30 P. M. With clockwork precision we were loaded into automobiles and busses and taken on a sightseeing trip around one of the most beautiful cities in the United States. Seattle is a city of boulevards, lakes, and ocean. In the distance Mt. Rainier lifted itself into the sky, a giant more than fourteen thousand feet above the sea.

Then came an hour and a half's boat-ride on Puget Sound to Tacoma, dinner in the great dining-hall of the Tacoma Hotel, a beautiful evening service in the moonlit garden, and so to the train for the last lap of our journey to Portland, Or., only a few miles, comparatively speaking, across the line.

THE FIRST DAY

SATURDAY, JULY 4, 1925

The Delegates Arrive.—Portland Pennants Flutter.— A Glorious Welcome.—The Convention Opens.— The First Mass Meeting

A big reception committee of Portland Endeavorers was on the platform at seven o'clock on Saturday morning, July 4, ready to welcome to Portland the delegates as train after train came in. The point of special interest was the reception of Dr. and Mrs. Francis E. Clark. It was unique. Not because there were flowers and pretty speeches, but because of signal honor done to Dr. Clark such as no other Convention city ever did him before. Among a host of local Endeavorers there stood Judge Jacob Kanzler, chairman of the convention committee, smiling, genial, radiantly happy as Dr. and Mrs. Clark stepped from the train; and there was Mayor Baker of Portland, a stalwart, strong and happy Christian gentleman; and there was Mr. Jenkins, chief of Portland's police force, resplendent in his full gala uniform, ready to do anything and everything to make the visitors comfortable. And more than even that, the chief of police invited Dr. and Mrs. Clark into his own automobile, and drove them in triumph through decorated streets to the convention headquarters in Multnomah Hotel.

Never have Christian Endeavor delegates had a warmer welcome to a city than the delegates received in Portland. Talk about Western hospitality! Here it was true to its best form. Shining eyes, smiling faces, hearty hand-clasps, and cheery, happy words!

Manifestly all Portland knew that the Endeavorers were coming, and equally manifest was it that the Endeavorers were welcome. The Christian Endeavor monogram was everywhere in evidence. Flags—American flags for the most part—fluttered in arches across many streets as far as the eye could see. Ample provision in the shape of automobiles was made so that every delegate (with his luggage) was carried to the hotel headquarters and assigned a room with no confusion and no delay.

Members of the reception committee were everywhere not merely willing but eager to serve every delegate. The great lobby of the hotel was the scene of many hilarious meetings the first forenoon, as batch after batch arrived. Such firm hand-clasps! Such genuine joy! And such picturesque color! Iowa in flaming red shirts or blouses, Ohio in charming white, and other States with colors of various hues.

Young people are irrepressible, and the tendency of Endeavorers on occasions like these is to break into song. Said one of the elevator girls as the sound of fresh young voices rang through the lobby, "It is not often we hear that kind of music." It did one good to listen to it, for it was literally good will set to music.

And so, when friendships have been renewed, we come to

The First Meeting

The first meeting of the convention was a pre-prayer meeting in the Multnomah Hotel at three in the afternoon on Saturday, July 4. It was led by Dr. Clark, and to it were especially invited the trustees and field-secretaries.

It was a noble company that gathered, men and women in the freshness of early maturity, to turn their hearts to God, seeking His blessing on this day and all the Convention days to follow.

Dr. Clark, reading Psalm 103, urged that this might be a singing convention, as some of our early conventions have been, that the people of Portland may learn the triumphant and happy spirit of Christian Endeavor. How fully this was achieved may be judged from the fact that the people in the hotels spoke of the singing hosts of youth, and the newspapers remarked in various editorials on the happy type of Christianity that Christian Endeavor represents.

All parts of the country were represented, workers from the Southland, workers from the East, workers from the West, and workers from our sister nation, Canada, and from regions beyond the seas.

Some of the State presidents told of good things done in their States, and how snappy and encouraging talks they were! The spirit of Christian Endeavor is so genuinely optimistic that there is no room for pessimism. Ohio, Utah, Pennsylvania, Massachusetts, Georgia, Florida, Oregon, and other States started off. The Utah president pointed out that Christian Endeavor is making a truly valuable contribution to the Protestant life of the State, for without Christian Endeavor it would be hard to keep the young people true to the faith of their fathers. But every testimony was an inspiration. It is impossible not to rejoice when we learn, for instance, that Oklahoma organized one hundred new societies in the past year, making nine hundred societies in the State. Every speech recorded advance movements, both in America and in Great Britain; and we learned that Christian Edeavor is aggressive and progressive, going from strength to strength, to new visions and new achievements.

At the same time in the Alazar Temple, near the main auditorium, Paul Brown was leading a pre-prayer meeting that packed that beautiful meeting-place, while more than one hundred stood in the aisles. The Convention thus started in prayer, a most auspicious fact. It began in the spirit of consecration.

At half past five there was a luncheon in the beautiful grill room of the hotel for field-secretaries and officers and trustees of the United Society of Christian Endeavor. The idea was to give an opportunity for getting acquainted.

IN MULTNOMAH FIELD
Saturday Evening, July 4

The Ohio delegation is out for the 1927 International Convention. Cleveland, O., has issued an invitation, Atlantic City putting in an equally earnest plea to win the Convention. Both delegations are pushing their claims, using buttons and badges; but Ohio has brought several hundred delegates to Portland, and can make both a showing and a noise.

An Ohio parade, for example. It was an impressive sight to see the procession of radiant young people march through the streets to Multnomah Field, headed by a fife-and-drum band. Around the field they marched, a triumphant throng prophetic of the future of America; for good and righteousness, and not evil and iniquity, are going to win the world at last.

A great audience estimated at fifteen thousand was present well before the opening hour. Iowa was there, like Ohio, a great red-clad group, singing the song that has made them famous in previous International Conventions, the song of Iowa, "Where the tall corn grows." But many other delegations stood out clearly, among them Dixie's 103 young people with their attractive Christian Endeavor fezes.

The meeting opened with Judge Jacob Kanzler, the Convention committee chairman, presenting to Dr. Clark a gavel made from the wood of fourteen different kinds of trees, all of which are connected with the development of the State of Oregon and of the Northwest.

What a mighty, colorful throng rose in response to Percy Foster's invitation to sing! It was twilight, but one has to see such a sight to appreciate the tremendous hold that the religious and worshipful spirit has on human life. Of course Percy Foster is a superbly magnetic and wise leader. He gauges the spirit of an audience with uncanny accuracy, and he shifts from song to song with charming taste. After a few hymns and Julia Ward Howe's "Mine eyes have seen the glory of the coming of the Lord," he has the audience singing in sections the Ohio delegation one line, the Endeavorers of Idaho the next line, and so on. He is witty, and he can make people sing, even in sections; but when they all sing together, it is like the sound of many waters. When Mr. Foster finishes the song service, everybody is transformed in spirit; the mind is captured and the heart is prepared for the messages to come. It should be added that there are two grand pianos and a Christian Endeavor orchestra, which render magnificent service.

Rev. Charles C. Poling, D. D., father of Associate President Dr. Daniel A. Poling, dedicated the opening meeting and the whole Convention to God in a prayer of remarkable spiritual power.

The Official Welcome

Governor Walter M. Pierce of Oregon was the first speaker. He welcomed especially Governor Pinchot, who was to speak later, because of his activities in seeking the enforcement of the prohibition law, and welcomed the Endeavorers because of their contribution to the prohibition crusade.

The welcome of Portland was voiced by Mayor George L. Baker, whose first ringing words were: "Welcome to the city of Portland. Because we have long awaited the hour to extend to you young men and women a hearty welcome and because tonight we see a fond dream come true." He urged with great force and eloquence the necessity of more religious training in the home. Parents, he said, too often neglect the privilege of giving religious training to their children. He pleaded that at least two hours a week be given to the teaching of religion in the public schools. Much of the crime of the country is committed by young people under twenty-four years of age, and things will never be otherwise until the children of the country are taught the principles of Christian living.

The churches of Portland spoke with the eloquent voice of Dr. E. H. Pence. He vividly painted the type of men who were the pioneers in Oregon, whose children are now speaking their welcome. The foundation for the new age and the new time is now, as it was in old days, religion. We must show that being a Christian is the finest thing, the noblest thing, and the only thing that can save the country and the world.

Judge Jacob Kanzler, chairman of the Convention committee, won a great reception. He voiced the welcome of his committee, which numbered more than two thousand workers. They were on a worth-while task, he said. It was a magnificent thing for them to be laboring together for more than nine months in preparing for the Convention. The results would surely be an increase in the spirit of service, and on this spirit depends the whole future of our race.

Citizenship with a Sword

It was a voice from the other side of the continent that next addressed the meeting. Governor Pinchot of Pennsylvania was introduced by Dr. Clark, and received a great ovation, a host of Pennsylvania Edeavorers singing in his honor and giving him a real Pennsylvania "yell." Gifford Pinchot is a tall, spare man with winning presence and a gift of real eloquence. Dr. Clark welcomed him for what he is in himself, for the work he has done for conservation, for the enemies he has made, and for the host of friends, the best in the nation, that have gathered around him in ardent support.

Dr. Pinchot declared that the best proof he could give of the joy he felt at speaking to this meeting was the fact that he had crossed the continent to do so. The speech, which we give here, was a fighting speech, a clarion-call to militant Christianity.

COUNT FOR YOUR COUNTRY

By the Hon. Gifford Pinchot, D. Sc., LL. D., Governor of Pennsylvania

There is no good cause but is worth fighting for, and no cause that is worth fighting for but is worth being beaten for. You and I are Christians. What Christ stands for we stand for. But unless we are willing to fight for it, and even to be beaten for it, our standing for it is nothing better than an empty sham.

Our country has many troubles, but none greater than this, that in matters that have to do with the common good so many of the people who believe rightly, whose personal lives are blameless, and whose action if they acted would be on the right side, refuse to act at all. Because so many of them leave undone their clear duty as citizens, a huge part of the blame for the evils which exist in our body politic rests squarely on the churchgoing people of America.

That great burden of duty undone rests upon them, not because their hearts are wrong, not because their principles are bad, but because, as Roosevelt said, "they mean well feebly." They are content to let others bear the brunt of battles which over and over again are won by the forces of evil for no other reason than because the good people refuse to fight.

Take my own State of Pennsylvania, and in particular the city of Philadelphia, which is in complete control of one of the worst political machines in the United States. At every election in Philadelphia there are enough people—people who, if they voted, would vote right—who stay away from the polls to carry the election the right way. And there is hardly ever an election in that city that is not carried the wrong way just because these people do not vote.

Philadelphia is dominated, exploited, and made a byword of corrupt politics, primarily because the good people of that city are too supine to use their power. The gang in Philadelphia, like the gang in every city, is a minority. Everywhere there are more good people than bad. But it is a melancholy fact that in matters which affect the common good the power of political plunder keeps the gangsters unrestingly at work, while the obligations of Christian citizenship do not drive the people who recognize them in theory to meet them in practical fact.

In Philadelphia hundreds of thousands of men and women who have the right to vote, who have the duty to vote, and who, Heaven knows, have the need to vote, refrain from voting for no other reason than their blindness to the obligations of Christian citizenship. The result is gang control, and the responsibility for one of the worst-governed cities in the United States falls directly upon these citizens who do not vote.

Pennsylvania until recently has been a byword for the worst type of politics in the United States. She has been so not because she lacks in God-fearing men and women, not because her people are worse than those of other States, but because the servants of God in the great cities, and to a less degree throughout the commonwealth, have refused to respond when the need to fight and the call to fight was put squarely before them.

A few years ago I asked one of the chief leaders of the Sunday-school movement in Pennsylvania why he stood for Penrose, then boss of the Republican machine and the perfect representative of everything that a Christian citizen was in honor bound to stand against. His answer was, "Well, I always figured that Penrose was good for business." There is also the answer to the question why Pennsylvania was for so many years corrupt and contented.

What Philadelphia needs, what Pennsylvania needs, what our whole country needs, is boys and girls and men and women who not only hold high their heads because they are Americans, but who make themselves count for the honor of their country on the right side.

Centuries ago the Master said, "He that is not with me is against me." He who does not count on the side of Christian citizenship counts against it. A vote withheld for righteousness is a vote for evil. It is the votes that are not cast that keep corrupt politics alive.

Moral questions are always the most important questions, for they go to the heart of every problem. One tremendous moral question stands out above all others to-day.

The greatest danger to our Government, the most immediate threat to the welfare of our people, and the greatest moral question before our nation, all lie in the matter of law-enforcement. There is no other attack on our Constitution so serious, there is no other burden of crime so heavy, there is no other source of misfortune so abundant, as that which comes from the flood of illegal drink in many parts of the United States.

If there is any call for Christian men and women to take arms, this is that call. If there is a cause which cries aloud for the fighting backing of those who believe in God, who believe in the law, and who accept the obligations of Christian citizenship, this is that cause.

The criminal elements of our population, actively aided and abetted by tens of thousands of those who think themselves respectable, are banded together from one end of this country to the other to pour poison into the mouths of our people, to instill disrespect of the law in the souls of our people, and to hold up the hands of every anarchist, Bolshevist, or other enemy of our institutions from the Atlantic to the Pacific and from Canada to the Gulf.

No such wide-spread defiance of the will of the people has ever been known in America; and no such flood of poverty, crime, disease, and death has ever before flowed from such defiance.

This question has passed far beyond the issue of wet or dry. Whether you believe as I do that the Eighteenth Amendment is right or whether you do not, your obligation to support it is just as clear and rests on exactly the same foundations as your claim to American citizenship. If you do not obey and support it as a part of the Constitution of the United States, you are not a good American.

The responsibility for this open defiance of law rests first upon the citizens who have tolerated it when they could have stopped it, for in such matters the people have all power. It rests next, to our shame and disgrace, upon the officials of our national Government. The bootleggers are bold because they know that the Government of the United States has never yet determined to put an end to their criminal traffic. They know, you know, and I know that the Treasury

Department could have set its foot down at any time and have removed this scandal from the good name of the United States.

Secretary Mellon has for four years had the power and the money, and by driving politics out of the enforcement service he could at any time have had the men. He has refused to carry out the duties of his office, and far too many of the good people of the United States have openly or tacitly supported him in that refusal, for precisely the same reason as the Sunday-school man in Pennsylvania supported Penrose, because they figured that Mellon was good for business.

Secretary Mellon, for the better part of a generation a whiskey-distiller and whiskey-distributor, and only within the last few weeks divested of his interest in millions of dollars' worth of whiskey, was chosen to enforce this law, and accepted the responsibility for enforcing this law. The result, and the natural result, is known to every man and woman who cares to think.

I hope most earnestly that the appointment of General Andrews as head of the law-enforcement service of the Treasury Department means that this abominable situation, this scandal which by the shameful failure of the Government itself has outgrown every measure, is about to be taken in hand honestly, vigorously, and with the intention of getting results. When that happens, the day of the bootlegger will rapidly draw to its close.

I do not overlook the responsibility of the States. Pennsylvania for the last two years and more has used to the full every weapon against bootleggers that was at her command, and she will continue to do so to the last day, hour, and minute of the present State administration. But while the national Government lies down, the States are badly handicapped. The Christian citizens of America should demand that the national Government shall do its duty; and when they do, it will.

There is another problem as overwhelming in another field as that of law-enforcement in the field of morals. It is the problem of giant power.

The story of mankind on the earth is mainly, on the material side, the story of a few great conquests over nature and their results. For example, the domestication of animals for the service of man, the application of tools to the needs of man, the harnessing of falling water for power, and the discovery of the use of steam.

Our civilization to-day is a steam-made civilization. Our people live in cities, most of them, because steam-power can be used only where it is produced. The food, the shelter, and the clothing of our people; our economic problems; the relations of capital and labor; our material troubles and our material blessings; and even to a very large degree the human mind itself, are all to-day what steam has made them. The soil of the United States to-day can support 110,000,000 people instead of the 300,000 Indians who occupied it before the white man came, mainly because of steam.

When steam came, it changed the life of men, the thoughts of men, and the relations of men to each other. It is one of the greatest facts in the whole history of the human race.

But steam is not the end of the story. Just as steam came to supplement or take the place of the power of human muscle, animal muscle, of wind and of falling water, so electricity is coming to supplement or take the place of steam. We are just at the beginning of a new electrical civilization, which we can already foresee will be as different from that of steam as that was from the ages which went before it.

What its development will be no man can yet foretell. But we are all familiar with electric light. We all know that work can be done hundreds of miles from the source of power by the transmission of electricity. Every housewife uses or wants to use the new electrical conveniences which are capable of taking from her shoulders the larger part of the drudgery of her daily tasks. We know already something at least of what electricity has in store.

Human life in America is already largely dependent on the electric current. The time is clearly in sight when practically all people, at least in North America, can be supplied with electric servants at their work and in their homes, servants whose coming may become the greatest material blessing in human history or the greatest curse.

You may fairly ask how this great forward step in the conquest of man over nature can ever become a curse. It can become a curse only if the common good is forgotten in the hunger for exorbitant profits to the electric companies.

In nearly every portion of the United States there is spreading out a vast network of electrical wires, which will before long merge into a single great system or monopoly covering every portion of our country with electric service, and running into practically every home. Already these wires extend from, or will soon extend from, the Gulf of Mexico to Niagara Falls in a single interconnected system under a single control. The leaders of the electric industry do not hesitate to look forward to the time when a single unified electric system will cover, from border to border, the whole United States. The coming of such a system is already inevitable.

A single system in America means a single monopoly, and a monopoly so powerful in wealth and political influence, covering so large a territory, and having so much to do with the success of every business and the comfort of every home, that nothing like it was ever known in the world before.

This great monopoly is certain to come. Under proper regulation by the people it is necessary for the common welfare that it would come. Like the telephone, the supplying of electricity is a natural monopoly. The advantages and economies of a single control are so great, and the benefits to the people, if that monopoly is properly controlled by them, are so vast, that it would be foolish to attempt to prevent it. Indeed, this gigantic concentration of electrical ownership cannot be prevented. But it can be controlled.

Just as every cloud has a silver lining, so every possible benefit has its corresponding abuse. We are already getting a foretaste in a small way of what such a monopoly as this might do to the people in the absence of adequate and effective public control.

The concentration of ownership of water-power and steam-plants which produce electricity, and of the transmission and distributing lines of wire over which it travels from the producer to the consumer, is all bringing about enormous economies, which the companies are keeping almost entirely for themselves. There is little or no reduction from the war-time rates of electric service, and from these gigantic savings the consumer is getting little or nothing.

Moreover, in addition to the large profits which the companies are distributing to their stockholders they are realizing huge sums from the rise in price of their stocks. So enormous is the value of this rise in stocks to the companies that *The Wall Street Journal* computes the profits of only ten companies within eighteen months from this source alone at more than $250,000,000. All this means that the companies are taking in more than they ought, and the consumers are paying out more than they ought, for electrical service.

The gradual building up of this monopoly, mainly for the profit of the companies, is the Super-Power Plan. The gradual building up of a nation-wide system of electric service, mainly for the benefit of the people, is the Giant Power Plan.

The Giant Power Plan proposes that electrical energy for all purposes shall be made available to every one far more cheaply than at present, and without unfair discrimination as to rates or service.

To realize these purposes there must be, first of all, a just and effective public control of the growing monopoly, and this control must be exerted partly by the States and partly by the nation. When I speak of public control, I do not mean public ownership, but public regulation and control. The Giant Power Plan does not even raise the question of public ownership, but deals with things as they are.

In the second place, the growth of the great network of electric wires over the United States must be planned not mainly for the profit of the companies, but mainly for the service of the public.

Third, vastly more electricity must be produced in larger central stations, than ever before in the history of the world.

Fourth, the electric current thus cheaply produced must be poured, as it were, into a great pool of power out of which electricity for all users will be taken, thus reducing the cost to the consumer.

Under such a plan as this the regulation of rates and service, while giving the companies neither less nor more than a reasonable profit, will immensely reduce the cost of current to the user. It will thus not only lighten his bills, but multiply the electric service he is receiving now by many times, and it will reduce the cost of living and immensely increase the convenience and satisfaction of daily life. But none of this will happen unless the great mass of consumers get a square deal.

At present the companies are serving great power-users, such as large mills and street-car companies, with current below cost, at cost, or at a very slight increase over cost, and charging five, ten, or even fifteen times as much for current supplied to the domestic consumer. There is no reason for this great spread between the price charged to one consumer and to another except that the traffic will bear it. It represents a great and unfair advantage to the few large users of current at the expense of the many small users; and it is one of the best illustrations I can give of what a great unregulated electrical monopoly would do to the household consumer, to the business men, both great and small, and to the vast majority of our manufacturers.

This overcharge to the great body of consumers for the benefit of the few greatest consumers has worked out naturally in the failure or refusal of the companies to supply current to our farmers, most of whom, because of unfair rates, are still without electric service of any kind. One of the great purposes of Giant Power is to see that a wire shall bring cheap and abundant electric current to practically every farm in America.

Electricity is a servant of our material wants, and it may be contended that this threatened unregulated monopoly of it is purely a material question. There could be few greater mistakes. Injustice is always and everywhere a moral question. The poor man who is forced to pay excessive monopoly prices for the necessaries of life is thereby compelled to forego, and his family is compelled to forego, things urgently needed for the body, like food, shoes, and clothing; like doctors and dentists. But he and his family are also cut off from countless things of the spirit, like teachers, books, music, and the thousand and one other things which educate and expand the mental and spiritual nature of men, but which cost money to get.

This vast monopoly of power is advancing to completion by leaps and bounds. When it is here, and that means soon, nothing but effective regulation will keep it from dealing with all but a few great consumers under the rule of fang and claw. Giant Power, on the contrary, proposes that the vast coming electrical developments shall take place in accordance with the Golden Rule—that this boundless economic fact in the whole world, and the most significant, shall work out on the principles for which the Christian Endeavor Society definitely stands, shall be governed by the precepts of Christian citizenship, shall be handled for the greatest good of the greatest number, and not simply for the profit of a few.

And so ended the first day of the Convention. It was a beautiful day, sunlight without, sunshine within. It was a successful day, a glorious day, a day prophetic of all the days to come.

THE CONVENTION CHORUS

It was late—and chilly—when the great Convention chorus of five hundred voices was called upon to sing. This lateness, be it said softly, was a mistake; for the chorus was an excellent one, splendidly led by Dr. T. W. McMichael, a dentist of Portland. It proved its real worth, for it held the great audience until the next speaker was called. It proved to be

A VOICE FROM OREGON

Poling Captures an Audience

Dr. Daniel A. Poling, born in Oregon within a mile of the spot where Multnomah Field is located, is always and everywhere a welcome and delightful orator. He was the very spirit of youth and of the West as he stood before the audience, who warmed toward him in spite of the chilly air; and he held them rapt by the power and magic of his words. His theme was

CHRISTIAN ENDEAVOR

By Rev. Daniel A. Poling, Litt. D., LL. D., Minister of the Marble Collegiate Church, New York City, and President of the United Society of Christian Endeavor

In the opinion of the speaker Christian Endeavor, by any test that may he applied to a religious organization, is the most strategic and important young people's society in the Christian church. Numerically it is great, more than four million young women and men being enrolled in its membership. In a practical sense it is universal, being represented on all continents, in all lands, among all races, and in all Protestant denominations. In the genius of its organism it seems to those who, though not officially connected with it, have been for a long time intimately associated in its activities to be unsurpassed. Its societies, Senior, Young People's, Intermediate, and Junior, with yet other divisions to meet the requirements of a comprehensive programme of religious education in very large congregations, enroll all ages and always both sexes. In the speaker's opinion—and he speaks as an Endeavorer who has passed through all the grades, and is now the minister of a church which maintains them all—Christian Endeavor is the most important co-educational enterprise for youth in this generation. Girls and boys, young women and young men, are always associated as comrades and partners in the great Kingdom enterprises of the church. In a score of departments, prayer meeting, good citizenship, Bible-study, mission-study, vocational study, the Tenth Legion or systematic and proportional giving, etc., they are introduced to, and trained and exercised in, a task that can succeed only in unity. Scientifically, the internal organizational scheme of Christian Endeavor is sound. Practically, the least that can be said for it after forty-four years of demonstration is this: It is effective. Also in the genius of Christian Endeavor emphasis is placed upon volunteer leadership and service. It enrolls more than 350,000 unsalaried officers, who serve in national, Provincial, State, district, county, and city unions; a million more who serve in local societies and on local committees; and it has fewer than fifty salaried executives in all the world.

The total budget of the interdenominational world organization of Christian Endeavor is many times less than that of the Y. M. C. A. in this or any other city of like size. It is this genius for the association and training together of young women and young men, this genius for selecting and engaging leaders, that has made Christian Endeavor the West Point of the church. To-day few of the denominational executives at home and abroad were not first identified with the Young People's society, and practically every clergyman received his first opportunity for religious expression under its auspices. In the genius of Christian Endeavor an organization composed of the representatives of more than a hundred denominations is found supporting strengthening, and vitalizing the programme of each denomination and of every local church. This vast and inspiring movement has literally fulfilled the text, and has found its life by losing it. To-night and through these days that will never be forgotten we mingle and we unite as Methodists and Presbyterians and Baptists and Congregationalists and Disciples and Friends and in fourscore other denominational relationships; but we *do* mingle and we *do* unite. Mingle and unite without prejudice to the fundamental principles and tenets of any of us, and with information, inspiration, and enrichment for each of us.

This genius of organism is accompanied by a programme which has been developed and adapted through the years until a great publicist said of it recently, "For young people it is in its practical features the most sound and comprehensive in the entire field of religious education." The programme begins first with the individual youth, begins by laying primary emphasis upon his innermost life, but goes forward to enlist all of his life. Christian Endeavor dreams of a new, a better world; Christian Endeavor has visions of the new, the Christian order, but in all her teaching and in all her practice is committed to the proposition that there can be no such consummation without new men and new women, men and women made new in Jesus Christ. Christian Endeavor as a ministry to youth seeks to lead young people to Christ, to strengthen them in the Christian life, to train and engage them in service for and with Christ.

The undergirding principle of the movement is found in its great covenant, "Trusting in the Lord Jesus Christ for strength, I promise Him that I will strive to do whatever He would like to have me do." It is well that we should begin with the acknowledgement of our own inadequacy and the statement of our source of power, "*Trusting in the Lord Jesus Christ for strength.*"

Trusting in the Lord Jesus Christ for strength, now, "*I promise*"; that declaration, that commitment, has been vindicated in many millions of lives. "*I promise*"; only eternity has the answer for my question, "What fateful issues, what gracious ministries, have rested on that 'I promise—trusting in the Lord Jesus Christ for strength'?" Ay; and this promise is to God, this covenant is with Him, with the One who is able, with the One who on His part has pledged to keep that which is committed unto Him. Trusting in Him for strength, we promise Him. I am sure that Dr. Clark's pen when it wrote those words was divinely pointed.

And now comes the intimate understanding of the nature and relative station of youth, "I promise Him that I will strive to do whatever He would like to have me do." "*I will strive to do*"—words altogether appropriate for an Endeavor society! This is an organization of those who are trying, endeavoring. Now, to endeavor, honestly to try, implies two things. It implies success. It implies success, success in spite of difficulties, success in spite of handicaps, success in spite of stammering lips and stuttering tongues and shaking limbs, but success. Yes, to endeavor, honestly to try, implies success; but in the second place it implies *success after failure*. This is not a Christian Perfection society! This is a Christian Endeavor society. And because it is as it is, it has in all lands and for more than two generations taken uncouth lads and ungainly girls, and made out of them kings and queens in Christ's service. This very principle has led hundreds of thousands to say, "In spite of what I am, trusting in God, out there in front of me is what I may become."

Finally, this principle reaches a climax in its application. "Whatever He would like to have me do"; here is Christian Endeavor's "beginning at Jerusalem"; here is her "multum in parvo."

Whatever—I will pray and read the Bible; I will teach a Sunday-school class; I will attend the midweek service; I will sing in the choir; I will visit the sick; I will turn the ice-cream freezer; I will lead the meeting.

Whatever—I will begin now. I will be on call for the pastor; I will honor the talent God has given me; I will not hide it in a napkin; I will use it and it shall grow.

Whatever—I will go to China; I will go to Arabia; I will go to India; I will go to Africa; I will go to Alaska; I will go to the Southern Seas.

Whatever—I will serve my city; and I see Winnipeg Endeavorers building a fountain, and Cleveland Endeavorers icing fountains; I see Brooklyn Endeavorers and many others leading hundreds of undernourished little children out to summer camps; I see playgrounds opening and hear many voices raised in foreign-language classes; I find doors of evil closing before youthful hands; I hear songs of patriotism, and I have a vision of a community sturdily striving toward the moral dimensions of the City of God.

Whatever—I will serve my country. And my ears are still ringing with the echoes of more than one hundred and fifty thousand pairs of feet marching toward flaming skies and steel-shod death. Christian Endeavor has not only the right, Christian Endeavor has the moral obligation, to be heard for peace; for her sons bled and died in brutal war. I will serve my country, and I see California organizing her amazing chain of coffee-houses; I hear William Shaw challenge the brutal and debasing prize-fight; I watch Chicago Endeavorers win a Sabbath of rest for post-office employees, and in winning there set in motion a force that moves on to win as much for the letter-carriers of the nation. I find the United Society establishing a Good-Citizenship Day and initiating a correspondence that brings together, after a hundred years of separation and misunderstanding, the temperance forces of the continent. Ay, and I find myself in the midst of a vast company of young men and young women, a company not unlike this; but where we gather to-night on the Pacific, they stood that day on a mighty pier above the blue waters of the Atlantic, and louder than the roar of the tide they brought forth a shout that has girdled the globe and that echoes now in the most remote regions of organized society, "A saloonless nation by 1920."

Whatever—again we are at the conclusion of the whole matter, "Whatever He would like to have me do." God's will in the individual life, God's will in church and city and nation and unto all the world. That "whatever" has issued in the lives of members of the Cabinet, governors of States, presidents of banks and of colleges, farmers and teachers and missionaries and preachers and preachers' wives.

Whatever—but I find myself, as Paul found himself in the eleventh chapter of Hebrews, out of breath; and I exclaim, "What should I say more? for time would fail me to tell."

Perhaps the developing of initiative, the locating of responsibility, the honoring, the dignifying of personality, has been a chief ministry of Christian Endeavor to youth. What I might say somewhat at length, were there time, is suggested by the number already referred to as enlisted unsalaried leadership positions. Personally, I fear any centralization in a programme of religious education that eliminates in a local church the young people's society as such, a society with its own name, its own officers, and its own programme correlated with the whole programme of the church. For my young people a department in any general programme would be an utterly unattractive substitute for Christian Endeavor. I have found that there may be a theoretical efficiency which in practice is quite inefficient, and that there may be a concentration that scatters. I must be quite frank and say that we do not give to Christian Endeavor the place that it has in the Marble Collegiate Church because of sentiment—and we will replace it whenever something better appears; always the church must stand with eyes front; but Christian Endeavor remains to-day for us the most efficient agency for the enlisting and training of young people. We have clubs for girls and young women, four of them; a club for boys; a Boy Scout troop; a fully organized Sunday school with several organized classes; and there is an institutional mission; but without Christian Endeavor, which ministers to them all and is supported by them all, we should be in our programme of religious education for young people like an educational institution of many beautiful appointments and properties, but lacking a central heating and power plant. And beyond all this our Sunday-evening evangelistic service would be without the nearly forty trained personal workers who are very largely responsible for any measure of success that has been achieved.

A supreme element in the success of Christian Endeavor has been its adaptability. I joined a Junior society in Lafayette, Or. That society in a little Willamette Valley village, under the leadership of a consecrated, talented woman, was a success. From its membership have come up Christian mothers, teachers, business men, a college president, preachers of the gospel, and at least one missionary. I have belonged to a college Christian Endeavor society. I have served as a Junior superintendent. I have known Christian Endeavor in a small industrial city. I have seen it flourish in an Ohio country community; I have visited it in a thousand centres on both hemispheres; and over a period of thirty years I have found it unfailingly doing two things: placing emphasis in church, in home, in school and State always upon first things, and everywhere adapting itself to the circumstances of its environment and the requirements of its particular setting. Christian Endeavor is not an automatic machine. It may be used, and it may be abused. Neglect will cause it to decline, but it is an instrument that lends itself to the need and purpose of a Christian leader with youth in any generation more readily and effectually than any other I have ever known. This, then, very hurriedly and very inadequately stated, is the ministry of Christian Endeavor to youth. What is its message to the world?

The message of Christian Endeavor to the world is supremely, "Have faith in youth." With more than forty years of history behind her, with the children of her first generation now the fathers and mothers and grandparents of this generation, Christian Endeavor comes to the grave anxiety and disturbed questioning of 1925, declaring, "Have faith in youth."

Surely the times in which we live are full of peril for youth, and certainly vast numbers of young people are doing recklessly and living riotously; but this I know, that even these are more sinned against than sinning; that our good holdings are far beyond the investment we have made; that for every youthful flapper there is an adult flapper, and that for all young people who sell their birthright of health and chastity for the pottage of pleasure there are hundreds of thousands who hold fast their virtue and faith. Many others there are who, swept from their feet by sudden tides of temptation, struggle back again to gain at last the guarded heights.

All honor to them. By those of us who are older let it be remembered that when we find ourselves out of sympathy with youth, then is our work in this world done.

Also in the twentieth century fathers and mothers must face the fact that discipline without example is disaster. Booth Tarkington in an article published by *Collier's* asked the question, "Will you please tell me how a child can respect its parents after it has seen them turkey-trotting?" We criticise the young people's hair, their skin, their shoes, their skirts, their manners. "I suppose," says a great bishop, "that when we were young, to hear some of us talk, we were gentle angels sitting around on horsehair sofas with piously folded hands. We forget banged hair. We forget balloon skirts and bell sleeves that crowded innocent citizens into the street and blocked the entrance to public buildings. We look upon 'Yes, we have no bananas' as a sign of degeneracy, but who was it, what generation if you please, that sang,

> "Pharaoh's daughter on the bank,
> Little Moses in the pool;
> She fished him out with a telegraph-pole,
> And sent him off to school"?

Stop slandering youth! Let the adult generation first set its own physical and moral and spiritual house in order. One of the All-American football stars of last year said to me in speaking of his great university: "Following our undergraduate campaign for law-observance student drinking became negligible. The fellow who encouraged it was in disgrace. Fraternity, athletic, and class leaders united for a thorough law-enforcement programme. But when the alumni came back for commencement and for the functions preceding commencement, the campus went drunk again." What an indictment of the adult! Stop slandering youth. Live decently before him. Give time and attention to him, and have faith in him. This is the message of Christian Endeavor to the world.

Have faith in youth, for youth is instinctively loyal: loyal to God and Jesus Christ, for he is instinctively religious; loyal to his country, for he is instinctively patriotic; loyal to all of life, for he is supremely alive. He will take the flag of his State to the most dangerous battle salient and the standard of his church to the last missionary frontier. He will give his body to be burned for a righteous cause, and the love with which he journeys to the stake will leap higher as a beacon to the world than the flames that clasp him there. Within recent months I have seen more than twenty thousand young people in religious conferences and conventions. A finer, cleaner, more normal lot of young men and women no generation has ever produced. In my whole life as a minister I have never known young people to fail when appealed to on the plane of sincerity and honor. Stop slandering youth, and give them your confidence. Trust youth to be progressive, to be progressive always; but, given sane leadership, given sound parental example and comradeship, trust youth to reverence ancient worthy things, to serve with concentration and abandon, but to serve as those who stand in the highest places of moral and spiritual discovery, crying to all the winds that blow, "We believe; make way for truth." Another name for youth is faith.

Finally, the message of Christian Endeavor to the world is ministry in Christ to bring the world to Christ. What a spectacle, what a demonstration of unity, unity in essentials and in the gracious fellowship of unity, these forty-four years of Christian Endeavor have been! Certainly more than two hundred thousand summer gatherings have been held, ranging from tiny village conferences to international conventions attended by more than twenty thousand delegates; gatherings bringing into one masterful purpose literally millions of young people and their trusted leadership. From Portland, Me., in 1881, to Portland, Or., in 1925, is a long trail, and it leads by the fairest and the farthest cities of the Old World as well as of the New. It hesitates for the Crystal Palace of London and the Taj Mahal of India, but it finds its youthful travellers as fresh and fit to-night as when their fathers and mothers began the journey nearly half a century ago. Were there nothing beyond this to add, an international demonstration of the Christian unity of Christian youth such as this meeting is would entirely justify a world movement. And the simple statement that in Portland, Or., in July, 1925, we fold our banners to unfurl them in London, England, in July, 1926, is a more adequate statement of the fellowship characteristic of our organization than many addresses.

Ours is a message of unity, unity in the spirit supremely, though we labor, too, each in his own place, true to his own church and responsible to its leadership, for that unity of programme and for that organic union of like communions which shall, in the good providence of the One who prayed that we all might be one, make the old hymn. "Like a mighty army moves the church of God" more than a poet's fancy and marching-song.

Ours is a message of unity, world unity, that unity in brotherhood which shall at last perfect the peace, that brotherhood which shall make wars to cease "where'er the sun does his successive journeys run." Nor is this an easy sentence from a convention address. Our English Christian Endeavor cousins are even as I speak entertaining in their prophetic Holiday Homes the Christian Endeavorers, not only of Europe in general, but of Germany in particular. Men who were by a cruel and brutal fate launched as deadly engines of destruction against each other walk now side by side across the quiet moors, and muse together of a better way that shall bring us at last into a new era of the soul.

This is the ministry of Christian Endeavor to youth, and this is her message to the world. May we to-night rededicate ourselves to our world programme of service, and let us rally to its ideals of peace with the spirit of the prayer:

> I do not ask, O Lord, a life all free from pain;
> I do not seek to be in this vast world of sin
> Without my load of care.
> For this I know: The present cross is my eternal gain,
> And he who, struggling, battles on at last shall enter in
> And be a victor there.
> Dear God, then keep me clean within,
> And give me strength to fight;
> And I shall follow through the din
> From darkness up to light.

THE SECOND DAY

SUNDAY, JULY 5, 1925

Morning Services.—Great Meetings in Multnomah Field

More than sixty of the delegates were assigned to as many pulpits in the city and suburbs to preach in the morning church services. Automobiles were at the hotel to take the speakers to their assignments. The day after the Fourth of July is not a particularly good day for large church attendance, since so many persons are away from home over the holidays; but the Christian Endeavor churches were crowded, some of them to overflowing. Names of nation-wide reputation were on the bulletin-boards, and attracted great audiences. Portland is a city of churches. Its people are religious and supporters of righteousness. But beyond the value of the preachers' messages to the people these hours of morning worship prepared the minds of the delegates for the services of the coming week.

MULTNOMAH AGAIN
The Thrill of Evangelism

Sunday afternoon is not the best time to hold a meeting in so large an amphitheatre as Multnomah Field, but thousands of persons turned out at half past two to hear a trio of speakers whose addresses touched high-water marks of eloquence and feeling.

Our Friends for Christ

was the first phase of the general topic "Evangelism," which was on the programme; and no better man to interpret it could have been found than Rev. Lapsley A. McAfee, D. D., of Berkeley, Cal. Dr. McAfee began by humorously repudiating the title of "Doctor" in Christian Endeavor, and he made the California delegation tell the great audience what his proper Christian Endeavor title is. "Daddy" came the vigorous response. "Which," said Dr. McAfee, "will soon have to be changed to granddaddy." But nobody believes it. He has the secret of eternal youth.

Dr. McAfee is a man of commanding presence, and there is music in his voice, which carries with delightful distinctness, so that not a syllable of his message is lost. The audience he faced this afternoon numbered thousands, who hung on his words with eager attention. They were simple, eloquent words, pungent, direct, happily chosen. For Dr. McAfee has sympathy. He understands what people are interested in, and what things he should say to help them.

"Christianity," he said, "begins with salvation. It has its doctrines, of course. Every Christian believes definite things. But Christianity does not begin in doctrine. It begins with salvation. Christianity has a great fellowship, and great friendships; but it does not begin in friendship; it begins with salvation. Christianity calls for sacrifices, and Christians make sacrifices; but Christianity does not begin with our sacrifices; it begins with salvation."

The speaker told graphically of a visit to the Sea of Tiberias in Galilee, where he saw the very scenes that Jesus saw in His day, women gossiping at the well, men in groups talking, fishermen mending their nets. On his telling this to Sunday-school boys one of them said, "Then it's sure enough." "Yes," said Dr. McAfee, "the story of the Bible is sure enough, for I've been there." This is the normal thing for men to do—to tell the things they know; that is, to testify. This is the way to win "Our Friends for Christ," which was Dr. McAfee's specific topic. Tell them about Jesus. This is our work. The plan that Jesus followed and history has approved is to have every Christian as a normal thing talk about the Master. This is conversational evangelism, which grows like a snowball, each one winning one until all the world is won.

We can do this, as Brother Lawrence did while he worked among mean things in the monastery kitchen. With him we can "practise the presence of God."

It was a winning, an appealing speach that Dr. McAfee delivered, a speech that will surely result in new interest in personal evangelism.

The Community for Christ

Dr. Poling, who presided, introduced Dr. A. Ray Petty of New York, who was to speak on another phase of the subject, "The Community for Christ." Dr. Petty is powerful of frame, powerful of voice, and powerful in personality. As Dr. McAfee dealt with the winning of individuals, Dr. Petty dealt with the winning of men in masses. His church, led by its vigorous and social-minded pastor, has thrown itseelf into the vortex of New York's slum life in sacrificial service. He is among the poor who are hungry, body and spirit; and he sees that ordinary methods of evangelism never will reach them. They can "see Jesus" only through the evangelism of service, and we can never win some men to Christ until we can show Christ to them in our ministries.

Surely out of the heart of a real minister of Jesus came those stirring stories of the poor of New York slums that thrilled the audience almost to tears. There was the story of Mario. He was three and one-half years old when the church nurse discovered him in the slums. He was terribly undernourished. He had grapevine rickets, with the bones of his legs between the hip and knee bent in one direction, and the bones between knee and ankle bent in the other. Mario was taken to the hospital; his legs were broken in six places and were reset and placed in casts. He was in the hospital for seven months, and returned home tremendously helped. Later the casts were taken off, and the child cured.

Dr. Petty's plea for the children of the poor was a moving one. He deplored the loss of the child-labor amendment, for Christ cannot come into the slums, where sweat-shop and child labor still exist, as long as children are delivered into the hard hands of industry. Christ must be shown to the whole community, Christ for labor.

There was wit in Dr. Petty's address, which helped to relieve the darkness of the picture the speaker was painting. But people gasped when he cried: "The person I am most afraid of is the one-hundred-per-cent American. . I don't know what a one-hundred-per-cent American is," he continued, and told the amusing story of a man who put a sign in his window: "I am a two-hundred-per-cent American. I hate everybody." There is something wrong with our Christianity when it is possible for eighteen automobiles to pass on the road a Negro bleeding to death after an accident, before one would pick him up and take him to a doctor, simply because he was a Negro. We must learn that we are brothers. The blood of a common Father flows in our veins. When we see this and believe it and live it, the kingdom of God will have come.

The World for Christ

Dr. A. W. Beaven of Rochester, N. Y., is a man who has made a great name for himself in the ministry of the word in his home town. Dr. Poling introduced him as a man without a peer on the platform in America, and his first few sentences showed that Dr. Poling was not mistaken. He spoke with ease and eloquence. He spoke with feeling. And he spoke with understanding and power.

Dr. Beaven is an Oregonian. He told the story of his English father who came long ago to this country as one of the pioneers, and who wandered away from God. Before she died the boy's mother wrote to her son in America, and told him that it was her daily prayer that he might become a minister. She told him that she had saved a little bit of money, which she wished should be used to help to build the first church of which he should become the pastor. She died, and the money was brought to her boy in America. When he received the gift and her letter with it, he went out into the night, and there in the silences he found again the Lord he had forgotten. For forty years or more he preached the gospel in the Western country.

Dr. Beaven's address was on "The World for Christ." Christianity is an imperial religion. It is a religion for every race. This was the Master's view. "God so loved *the world.*" "Go ye, therefore, into *all the world.*" The method of Jesus was to win men one by one; but the ultimate aim of Jesus was to win the world. The missionary influence is at the very heart of Christianity; it can never be at its circumference. Salvation is not for the individual alone; it must be passed on by them to others, and so to all the world.

It is impossible to reproduce the thrilling power of Dr. Beaven's torrential argument and tremendous plea. The stories he told of actual sacrifices that men have made to bring the gospel to the world gripped the audience and held it fast. He contrasted lives controlled by spiritual ideals with those controlled by material ideals. An automobile, for instance, must have brakes and steering-gear capable of controlling the power of the engine. A set of Ford brakes cannot control the driving force of a Peerless. Control and driving-force must be balanced. Low control and high power in man lead to moral destruction. Men have power. The question is: "What controls a man's life? What ideals dominate him?" If our control is low and our power is high, we shall end in destruction. To control our power we must raise our ideals. The greatest danger to our nation lies right here. America does not need more wealth or more power; what she needs is more men who will allow God to fill their lives with Himself.

Speaking of prohibition, he exclaimed: "If America can win the fight for prohibition, the whole world will have to follow. But if America loses the fight, the world will not get rid of the liquor curse for five hundred years."

With convincing eloquence, Dr. Beaven spoke of disarmament. He pointed out that the nations have always asked the question, "Who's biggest?" but America has now the greatest opportunity of all time to ask the Christian question, "What's right?" If we can spend billions of dollars for war, we can surely spend millions for peace. "If we can have a secretary of war, which we don't want, in God's name, why can't we have a secretary for peace, which all declare they do want?"

During this speech the audience was seeing visions. It was brought face to face with great problems. It was challenged with great questions. It was pointed to great opportunities. The youth of to-day are on the threshold of opportunity. Shall we count? Shall we achieve? If we are to count, we must see Jesus Christ in our souls, pledge ourselves to His service, and bring Him to all the world.

Dr. McMichael then led the chorus in the beautiful choral "Jehovah Reigns." The service of the choir cannot be described except by saying that the singing is thrilling and exquisitely delightful. Its contribution to the Convention programme and the faithfulness of its five hundred members are beyond all praise.

THE PARENTS' HOUR

Older Folks Learn Something of Their Duty

From Multnomah Field part of the Sunday-afternoon crowd flowed like a river in the direction of the First Methodist Church where at five o'clock a meeting for parents was scheduled. The splendid Junior programme was prepared by Miss Mildreth Haggard, who was the moving spirit behind the Junior sessions of these stirring days.

This meeting was opened with prayer by Mrs. Francis E. Clark, and was continued by a speech by Rev. William Hiram Foulkes, D. D., of Cleveland, O. "Can the Church Do It All?" was his suggestive theme. There can really be only one answer to this question. The church cannot do it all. Parents have done something, great things, indeed, in the education of the child. Many voices belabor the church, said Dr. Foulkes, because of the things she has not done, not realizing that in a sense they are accusing their own mother. Yet, no matter how much the church does in Sunday school and in Christian Endeavor societies, the responsibilities of parents can never be evaded. Whatever is done or left undone, the main work in the Christian education of the young lies at the door of the church's manhood and womanhood. God will not permit us to dodge our duty toward our own children.

Something of the Home

Dr. A. Ray Petty's theme was "The Home God Meant." The theme was a challenging one; and it received cogent, wise, and even witty treatment. Dr. Petty listed various elements that God meant should enter into our home life. He spoke of companionship, which youth craves and must have; of sympathy, without which it is sure to go astray; of tolerance, without which home is a den of strife; and of loyalty to one another. One story is worth repeating. It was used to illustrate tolerance. A college boy came home from school. All the colors of a jazz rainbow were in the ribbon on his hat; he had a flashy handkerchief and socks to match, and perfume that went with the boy. When he came home, he threw his bag into a corner, and rushed over to his father with "Hello, Governor! I'm glad to see you." The father rose, and looked at him sternly. "You're a fool," he said. The boy subsided. By and by a neighbor came in, and said: "Hello, Jack, I'm glad to see you home. You're just like what your father was twenty years

All from Dixie

121 Delegates, whose travel-mileage totalled 125,800 miles. Southern-Secretary Evans and Mrs. Evans are the second and third persons in the front row at the left

ago." "Yes," returned the lad; "he's just told me that."

Well, Dr. Petty told the older folks some things hard to bear, but good to know.

"Forbid Them Not"

Dr. Daniel A. Poling was at his own eloquent best in a topic with so exquisitely tender suggestions as the words of Jesus, "Forbid them not." He had been speaking to Juniors immediately before, on his own experience as a Junior boy; and doubtless he was thinking of the woman who was superintendent of the Junior society of which he was a member, and who told of that host who to-day are saying, "Suffer the little children to come unto me, and forbid them not." He spoke of the sympathy that we must feel for children, of the eagerness with which children respond to leadership, and of the duty that is ours to take the children to our hearts and see in them clearly the generation of the future. We are in a deep and real sense the makers of to-morrow, since the molding of the character of childhood lies entirely in our hands.

Junior Convention Number One

The first of the three conventions for the Juniors themselves, held in connection with the International Convention at Portland, was held in the First Methodist Church on Sunday afternoon, July 5, at five o'clock. This session was simultaneous with the Parents' Hour held in the main auditorium of the same church and the nursery conducted in the basement.

The theme of the Junior convention was the beautiful thought, "For Christ and the Church, I Would Be True." Miss Mamie Gene Cole, All-South field-secretary for Junior Christian Endeavor, presided, and Miss Bessie Dunn, the new State Junior superintendent for California, played the piano.

The Scripture lesson read by the presiding officer was the story of "Jesus the Junior Boy," Luke 2: 40-52.

The message of the afternoon was given by Dr. Daniel A. Poling, who told in his own inimitable way the story of his own life as a Junior Christian Endeavorer in Lafayette, Or.

Dr. Poling told of the day the society was organized in the church where his father was pastor; of the boys and girls who were members of that society, and what they are now doing "for Christ and the Church" because they are "true" to the training they received in that little Junior society.

The feature of the afternoon was a beautiful pageant, "Tidings of Great Joy," written by Dr. Louise A. Dorman, assistant superintendent, week-day Bible school, First Presbyterian Church, Seattle, Wash., which was presented by thirty Juniors of the Seattle Junior Christian Endeavor Union, under the capable direction of their city superintendent, Mrs. Dailey.

These Juniors lived the Bible before us. They told the story, using only Bible verses, from the fall of man to the ascension of Jesus. Then as a climax they gave a practical missionary interpretation of the great commission, "Go ye." In this scene children from all nations appealed to "Evangel" or "Love" for Christ, who could bring to them "Tidings of Great Joy."

SUNDAY EVENING AT MULTNOMAH FIELD
Glorious Fellowship

The immense gallery at Multnomah Field was solidly crowded for the Sunday-evening service, the theme of which was "Fellowship."

Visualize a large, high platform at one end of the great bowl. In front of this platform, but considerably lower, stands another, broad as the first one, on which sits the choir of five hundred voices. Immediately in front of that the orchestra and pianos are situated. Then, sitting on the level field, solid ranks of eager listeners. These ranks form a wide semi-circle around the platforms. They would be far away indeed from the speakers' table, were we to depend on the power of the human voice to reach them clearly; but in these days of amplifiers the farther away you are, the better you hear.

But look beyond these rows of eager faces on the level field. Behind them rise the sides of the bowl, an enormous bank, or rather banks, of humanity. Not a seat seems empty. Thousands are seated there. And they hear as well as those that sit on the platform. Those marvelous amplifiers do it.

But the song service, led by Percy Foster, is over on the stroke of the hour, and Dr. Clark takes charge of the session.

Europe Talks to Us

The first speaker was Rev. James Kelly of Glasgow, Scotland, who brought to the Endeavorers of America the greetings of the Endeavorers of Europe. "International Fellowship" was his specific theme.

Mr. Kelly is tall and thin. He speaks with a slight accent, rolling his r's like the Scotchman he is; but his speech is plain, his language is well chosen, and his burning earnestness carries conviction on wings of flame.

He spoke only of the religious conditions of Europe. He told of the miseries that have followed the war, and pointed out that religious animosities are bitter in many places, and that Protestantism is fighting for its life.

The authorities in some countries on the Baltic Sea have put many hindrances in the way of Protestant teaching. Some time ago a Christian Endeavor convention was held in one of the cities in that section. For three days delegates from all these countries met in long conferences and public meetings. No fewer than 1,100 persons were present at every public meeting, and no evening closed before eleven o'clock, and often after the benediction had been pronounced three times.

With stirring eloquence Mr. Kelly told of the struggle of Protestantism in Poland, where the Roman Catholic hierarchy does all it can do to hinder all Protestant work.

The story of Czechoslovakia, that new kingdom composed of Bohemia, Moravia, and other small states, was outlined in brief and cogent sentences. In days before the war Protestantism was hampered and persecuted and often stamped out in many towns and villages. So bitter was this persecution that when the war closed and the people were freed from the control of the Catholic Church, the fate of Roman Catholicism in that region was sealed; and people left the church of Rome by the thousand, forming churches of their own.

Hungary, too, is Roman Catholic, but there is a vigorous Protestant and evangelical minority in the land. Here Christian Endeavor is remarkably strong, and is doing great work among the people.

For many years Rumania was oppressed, and one would have thought that when the war brought liberty she would not persecute alien races within her borders. But although the Allied treaty set up religious freedom, Rumania is deliberately and harshly coercing all who are of other faiths than the state.

Turning to Russia, Mr. Kelly lashed the Bolshevik régime. Bolshevism, he said, is seeking to root out religion. How can a child in Russia learn about God when parents are prohibited by law from teaching religion to their little ones? Bolshevism has committed many crimes, but this crime against the souls of children is the most heinous and unforgettable. Christian Endeavor has little foothold in Russia, but among the thousands of Russian refugees in other lands Christian Endeavor societies have been formed; and there is a young Russian, trained in Christian Endeavor, who stands ready to go back to his own people with the Christian Endeavor message when the psychological hour arrives.

Mr. Kelly drove home the truth that the hope of the world is youth and the gospel. Wars will cease only when the young people of the world are fed the principles of peace. "The youth of the world is knocking at the doors to-day. They are calling for life. And it is our mission to bring that life to them to the uttermost parts of the earth."

The Next World's Christian Endeavor Convention

That the great audience grasped the significance of this great speech was shown by the warm applause that greeted Mr. Kelly's announcement that a World's Christian Endeavor Convention will be held in London, England, July 16-21, 1926. The object of the convention will be to give an opportunity to express international good will, to bring the churches of Europe together on a platform of love and service, and to help to cultivate the spirit of interdenominational fellowship.

Mr. Kelly made it plain that Europe is too poor to send delegates to London. He challenged the Endeavorers of America to raise $2,000, the Endeavorers of Britain raising a similar amount, the money to be used to pay the expenses of European delegates to the World's Convention in London. The Endeavorers of Great Britain and America will thus be the hosts of these people, who will see a practical demonstration of real Christian fellowship.

Mr. Kelly's speech made a great impression, and the collection that was taken immediately afterward will go entirely to this $2,000 fund for Europe.

Interracial Fellowship

It was a man of another race who gave the next talk, the subject being "Interracial Fellowship." Rt. Rev. Lynnwood Westinghouse Kyles, D. D., bishop of the African Methodist Episcopal Church, was the speaker. Dr. Clark, introducing Bishop Kyles, pointed out that Christian Endeavor is interracial as well as international. Bishop Kyles is a Negro, educated, efficient, with a happy knack of saying tersely just what he means. He is a stocky, deliberate man, evidently possessed of a great fund of both physical and spiritual force.

He modestly disclaimed being an expert on the subject of interracial fellowship, but hoped that he might be considered a student of it; and apt quotations from many authorities showed that he had given earnest thought to his theme.

He dealt first with the possibility of fellowship combating the theory that calls for segregation of the races. He argued for fellowship on the basis of our common humanity, and because the marks of our fundamental unity as human beings are far more than the marks of difference. Christianity is based on the unity of all men.

Bishop Kyles called in witnesses from science to prove that mankind came from a common stock in the dim days of the past. "The races may be as diverse as the fingers, but humanity is one as the hand."

The argument the speaker presented would be hard to overturn, even if one had a desire to controvert it. It was a clear argument based on science and on witnesses whose word cannot lightly be set aside. Bishop Kyles showed that interracial fellowship is actually now in operation between Negroes and white folks in many of the activities of life. He drew from the wide field of literature to indicate that the best thought of the world clearly sees the unity of man and recognizes the transitory character of all our differences.

Interdenominational Fellowship

Before Dr. William Hiram Foulkes' talk on "Interdenominational Fellowship" the choir rendered one of its superb anthems, whose glorious music filled the amphitheatre with praise to the King of glory.

Dr. Foulkes, new pastor of the Old Stone Church of Cleveland, O., was at one time head of the New Era Movement in the Presbyterian Church. He is one of the great leaders of American religious life, a strong man intellectually and spiritually, and beloved by a great multitude.

Dr. Foulkes said in part:

It is one of the tragedies of our faith that in a day when great union movements are sweeping through our organized social life there are also divisive influences within the Christian church. Every time church union is consummated between any of the denominations a split takes place.

Yet denominationalism marks a definite stage in the development of our Christian life. It has for the most part worthy historical traditions. It is not destitute of great strength. The Christian bodies are usually bound together by unity of purpose, a common plan, a similarity of outlook, and by a practical capacity to work together. Denominationalism has served a true purpose in marshaling many units of power in many places.

Interdenominational co-operation of the proper sort does not require us to surrender our identity. It involves making a common survey of our task. We ought to remove the denominational blinders from our eyes and to look out upon the whole field as though it were one field for one united church. In addition to a co-operative survey of our task we must also have co-operative planning.

In the midst of all the co-operative agencies of the church the Christian Endeavor movement is second to none. From its beginning it has been an open channel of spiritual power. At times people have tried to divert it into devious ways. Others have been willing to try to muddy its clear waters, and still others to clog up the channel. It is a tribute to its divine origin that it has gone on its inspired way, breaking down artificial barriers and becoming a mighty torrent. While I would not belittle such worthy movements I know of no one of them all whose roots go deeper down into the soil of our Christian activities than those of the Christian Endeavor society.

We are faced to-day with a real challenge to be true to our historic traditions and to carry on our enterprise without losing its purpose. There are those who say the Christian Endeavor movement is a spent force. Not a few denominational leaders seem to be actuated by a new denominational urge. Summer conferences, programmes of study, the obligations of denominational missionary support, are all elements in a new appeal for denominational loyalty. It is our proud boast as Endeavorers that we have always manifested such loyalty, and we will continue to do so as long as our society remains true to its principles; but we must also see that the channels of interdenominational understanding and co-operation are kept wide open.

We have in our hands the key to the largest opportunity that has yet confronted the Protestant Church. We can promote interdenominational co-operation by demanding it where it needs to be demanded, by embracing it where it is offered to us, by interpreting it where it is misunderstood, and by preaching and practising it in our individual and in organized society life. The leaders of denominationalism may decline to listen to the counsels of groups of young people gathered in conference from time to time and in isolated places. They may be justified in thinking that such periodic gatherings are not warranted in making demands upon the church. They will not resist, and in my judgment they do not desire to resist, the appeal that is voiced by the rank and file of their own young people, by those who do their work, who teach their Sunday-school classes, who form the very sinews of their church life.

The end of this fine meeting came in a glorious declaration expressed by the Endeavorers in song, one stanza of "Onward Christian soldiers." The audience sang with the thought of fellowship in their hearts.

> Like a mighty army,
>   Moves the church of God;
> Brothers, we are treading
>   Where the saints have trod.
> We are not divided,
>   All one body, we;
> One in hope and doctrine,
>   One in charity.

These words took on a new meaning after Dr. Foulkes' powerful address, and the familiar "Blest be the tie that binds" seemed to ring with a new and holy sincerity.

THE THIRD DAY

MONDAY, JULY 6, 1925

Around the World in Eighty Minutes

Eight o'clock in the morning is an early hour at which to hold religious meetings, but it is not too early for Endeavorers.

On Monday morning, July 6, the Convention got down to its conference work. The three great meetings in Multnomah Field, already described, gave the Convention an inspirational start that no other Convention has had in years. Every speech delivered at these meetings struck twelve. In fact, if the Convention had closed on Sunday night, it could have been pronounced successful. The hearts of the delegates were lifted. Their courage was renewed as they saw—what they could never have seen in the local societies—the greatness of the movement, the worldwide sweep of it.

Quiet Moments in Meditation

Monday morning, then, at eight, hundreds of delegates trooped out to the beautiful civic Auditorium where the main sessions of the Convention were to be held till the close on Thursday evening. Here, in the great hall which seats five thousand, morning by morning, the week through, devotional services were held to start the day aright.

Dr. A. W. Beaven of Rochester, N. Y., was the speaker at the first meeting on Monday morning. Tuesday morning the speaker was Rev. J. Whitcomb Brougher, D. D., of Los Angeles, Cal.; on Wednesday morning Dr. Poling led the meeting; and on Thursday morning Rev. James Kelly of Scotland delivered the address. Those gatherings gave a spiritual tone to the whole day. They led us to the source of power in Christ Jesus our Lord.

One story told by Dr. Beaven, will suggest the gripping power of these meetings. A man and some companions went on a hunting-trip to the mountains. One night in the hunting-lodge the group wanted to play cards. One of the men knew it was wrong to play, and he declined. He went to the radio receiver, and tried to tune in a station; but not a sound came. The others urged him to come along and play, and he yielded. In the midst of the game suddenly there came from the mouth of the radio loud speaker the words, "Our Father, who art in heaven," etc. The game ceased. The men knew they were in an impossible situation. The voice stirred their consciences. They swept away their cards; they threw their liquor out of the window, and gave themselves to better tasks. Young people listen avidly to the experiences of others, and such incidents touch the heart and move the will.

Morning by morning, too, the Intermediates held their Quiet Hour services in one of the Convention halls. Dr. William Hiram Foulkes; Dr. Royal J. Dye, former missionary to Africa; Rev. William Ralph Hall of Philadelphia; and Rev. R. F. Kirkpatrick, D. D., chairman of the All-South Christian Endeavor Committee, were the leaders of the Intermediate meetings on the four mornings, beginning on Monday. These speakers opened up many avenues of thought for the Intermediates, and the numbers present and the readiness with which they listened to the messages are proof of the real seriousness of adolescent boys and girls.

IN THE FORENOON

The conferences from nine to half past ten being over, the Endeavorers met for a general mass-meeting of delegates in the main hall of the civic Auditorium, which was gayly decorated with flags of all kinds and with the Christian Endeavor colors, red and white. When the meeting opened, the entire floor of the Auditorium was filled with attentive listeners, and many were in the galleries.

Percy Foster, superb song-leader, was on deck again and in great spirits. He is a tonic for the pessimist, full of fire and vigor and an entertaining wit that carries wisdom on the wings of laughter. Some song-leaders bore the audience by lecturing, not to say hectoring, them; but Percy Foster never lectures, and he certainly never bores; he just talks with the utmost familiarity and friendliness and with scintillating humor. He always gains his point, the undivided attention of the audience, which he puts with great skill into the right spirit for the messages to come. It is not a mere audience that is before him, but a crowd of participants, who feel that they are really taking part in the meeting.

At this session Alvin J. Shartle, treasurer of the United Society of Christian Endeavor, presided in his usual interesting and telling way.

The Place of Christian Endeavor

The first speaker was Rev. William Ralph Hall of Philadelphia, whose subject was "The Place of Christian Endeavor." Dr. Hall is leader in young people's work in the Presbyterian Church, U. S. A., and his connection with Christian Endeavor for many years makes him an authority on this subject.

In a clear-cut talk he pointed out that every life should have a goal worth striving for, and that Christian Endeavor supplies both a goal and the inspiration to achieve it. The goal is Christian character, and in the attainment of it Christian Endeavor sets before us definite ideals and seeks to embody these ideals in our lives. You can always guarantee character when it is based upon such ideals as Christian Endeavor brings.

Christian Endeavor has a place in the individual life because it gives us that training which we all need. It begins this training at the point of development where we happen to be—perhaps able only to read a verse of Scripture. In many ways it trains us to be Christian leaders, and it opens to us the door of opportunity to the larger work of the Kingdom.

Christian Endeavor is not the only agency in the church for the upbuilding of our youth, but it has a very clear place in the church's programme of education, and it does not conflict in any way with any other agency in the church. Christian Endeavor has a place in the church because it fits with admirable flexibility into the church's plan. Mr. Hall said that he had been working for more than a year on a comprehensive programme of education for Presbyterians, and into this programme he had written the Christian Endeavor society as one of the church's agencies for training the young.

Further, he added that Christian Endeavor has a place in the church because of its interdenominational relations. He briefly sketched the chaotic conditions that would result if no railway train could pass beyond the border of its State and passengers had to change trains every time they reached the border. Christian Endeavor is like an interstate railroad. It sets up standards and a programme for all denominations, and in doing this serves a useful service in the church.

More Junior Societies

Dan Poling is interested in Junior societies. He has never forgotten the fact that he was a member of one of the first Junior societies organized west of the Rocky Mountains. His speech therefore, which followed William Ralph Hall's, dealt with the topic, "More Junior Societies." He told the story of that early society and of how its influence had remained with him throughout all the intervening years. In that society Dr. Poling got a vital part of his training. The Scripture passages that come most readily to his lips to-day, he said, are those that he learned when he was a member of the Junior society. He made a striking and eloquent plea for more societies, and the practical results of Junior work, exemplified in himself, will certainly lead some of his hearers to go back home and organize a Junior society as part of the organization of the church.

Dr. Poling made a strong plea for a graded society and for a comprehensive educational programme for all the young people of the church. He objected to an all-inclusive organization on the ground that young people do not wish to belong to a department of some other organization, but wish an organization of their own. He recited convincingly his own experience with the society in his own church in New York. The all-inclusive *programme* idea works. The all-inclusive *organization* has failed so often that its value is greatly to be doubted so far as the ordinary church is concerned.

Let Us Meditate and Pray

A new feature of these forenoon sessions was a closing meditation designed to tie together in moments of worship the thoughts and ideas that had been thrown out in the forenoon sessions. Dr. William Hiram Foulkes beautifully led this meeting, lifting the delegates into the very presence of the Eternal. The morning thus began in prayer, and was rounded out by a period of prayer and meditation at noon. Dr. Foulkes spoke on the first day on following Jesus. On the second day his theme was following Jesus in the way of the cross. His third meditation was on following Jesus wherever He wants us to go; and his fourth talk was on following Jesus to victory.

THE BUSY BASEMENT
Subterranean Christian Endeavor

If the main auditorium was busy, the basement underneath was busier still, if that were possible. The basement was a large hall practically of the same size as the auditorium. At one end was a fully equipped cafeteria, where one might get an excellent meal at any time of the day for a very reasonable sum. This feature was a necessity, as lunch-rooms in this district are almost as scarce as hen's teeth, and it would have been difficult for the delegates to go down-town between meetings.

Some of the churches within easy walking-distance took advantage of the situation, or the organizers of the Convention did, and arranged special luncheons for various kinds of workers—Junior workers, Intermediates, Life-Work Recruits, and so on. As excellent speakers were present at these luncheons, they proved exceedingly attractive, and were attended by many hundreds. This helped to take care of congestion in the cafeteria in the basement.

The Booths

Around the walls of the basement were all sorts of booths, tastefully furnished, decorated with flowers, and each booth had one or two attendants. Some of the larger denominations had booths there for the convenience of their own people—the Congregationalists, Disciples, the Evangelical Church, the Presbyterians, and so on.

The booths on one entire side of the basement were given over to the committee in charge of registration. Here one might register. Here one might be assigned to a room in a private home. Here was an information section, where questions of every imaginable kind were asked and answered. Here were attendants ready to explain all about the numerous after-Convention tours, and give friendly, and often valuable, advice. And here at one end was a fully equipped United States post-office that took care of mail addressed to persons at the Convention. Here, too, went on a brisk sale of tickets for tours or luncheons or banquets; and here, towards the end of the Convention, the official photographer displayed his wares, and did a roaring trade. This section presented a busy scene with telephones in constant operation and stenographers at work with their clicking machines.

Literature Booth

In the centre of the basement a large square booth was erected for the publication department of the United Society of Christian Endeavor, and here Mr. C. C. Hamilton and Mr. R. A. Walker were kept exceedingly busy. Delegates had here a chance to look over books dealing with all phases of Christian Endeavor work and to purchase or order these as they chose. The new Christian Endeavor society Standards Chart, costing one dollar, was on sale here, and found many purchasers. For the first time in many years a Christian Endeavor Bible was on sale. This is a beautiful edition of the Bible with many readers' helps, and with special articles by officers of the United Society. Dr. Clark was kept busy autographing these Bibles, and the name of Daniel A. Poling in his books was also sought. "The Furnace," his new novel, was especially in demand.

The Amusement Question

More than seven hundred young people met in the Al-Azar Temple for a mid-day conference on amusements. This conference was conducted by Carlton M. Sherwood, New York State field-secretary. It was announced that no one above thirty years of age would be admitted, and the conference was therefore confined to the young.

Emphasis was laid on the fact that Christian Endeavor is a religious organization whose aim is to uphold the ideals of Jesus. "What would Jesus do?" is a helpful question to ask one's self with regard to amusements.

On a large blackboard the conference listed amusements that are unqualifiedly bad, gambling, prize fighting, intoxication, and so on; those that are good, such as socials, hikes, and so forth; and those that are in the twilight zone, or doubtful.

The young people freely expressed their opinions on all sorts of amusements. Dancing received a good deal of attention.

Some maintained, for example, that the dancing foot and the praying knee cannot go together; others maintained that they could. Sunday amusements were discussed from various angles. The Endeavorers were urged to remember that their example affects others, and to see that it does not lead any one astray. "Amusement should be recreation, not wreck-creation," said Mr. Sherwood. "Most of the problems lie with the individual, and the great danger is not that the Endeavorer will chose the bad as opposed to the good, but that he will be satisfied with the average instead of the best."

AROUND THE WORLD IN EIGHTY MINUTES

Monday afternoon the main auditorium was again filled for the foreign session, over which Stanley B. Vandersall presided. The idea of this meeting was to bring to the delegates a glimpse of Christian Endeavor in many lands, and this purpose was finely accomplished. The foreign touch was given to the meeting by the presence of ten Pima Indians from Arizona, all of them Endeavorers, who were enabled to come to the Convention through the generosity of American Endeavorers.

The Indians, led by Rev. Dirk Lay, D. D., their missionary, were first on the programme. Mr. Lay referred at the outset to an appeal he had made two years ago in Des Moines to the Endeavorers to help the Indians to get back their water rights on the Gila River, rights which the white man had taken away from them. Mr. Lay told of going to Washington to ask that a bill might be passed giving the Indians their rights, which meant life or death, prosperity or poverty, to them. Everywhere he was repulsed until he found one Senator who was ready to introduce the bill. The thing, however, that ultimately influenced the Senators most was the number of telegrams, mostly from Endeavorers, that poured in upon them. Opposition melted slowly, directly in answer to prayer, until the bill was passed the Senate. All the Senators seemed to have heard about it from their constituencies.

But it had still to pass the House. In the last week of Congress the case seemed hopeless. The matter was put before President Coolidge, who said when he had read the statement on the bill, "I shall do everything in my power to get that bill passed." The opposition, seemingly insuperable, melted away, and the bill finally got by. It was a direct answer to prayer.

Seldom does any group get the ovation that these Indians got when they rose to thank the Endeavorers for what they have done to help the Indians win back their water rights. To understand the Indians' feeling we must remember that robbed of their water this tribe could barely exist, while with water from the Gila River they can raise their crops and prosper in the arts of peace.

An Eskimo from Alaska

The farthest north Christian Endeavor society in the world is in Alaska. Its representative at this gathering was Rev. E. O. Marsden, an Alaskan Eskimo, whose first contact with Christian Endeavor conventions was made as far back as 1892. He told the story of Alaska, its needs, its hopes, and its promises, and put in a strong plea for the native Alaskan race. Only about one thousand of these people have accepted Christ as their Saviour, leaving perhaps twice that number in the darkness of sin.

The Christian Endeavor society has been a help to the Eskimos in the north, enabling the church to reach some of the race that could not otherwise have been reached. Christian Endeavor has helped to break down tribal barriers, and it has also helped to train the young people to live the Christian life.

Mr. Marsden told of the needs of his people, which include help in their industries, the establishment of schools, and the teaching of the ideals which the church brings. It was a powerful appeal, coming as it did from the stocky middle-aged man who has given his life to God and his people.

Japan

Rev. Seizo Abe brought the greetings of the Endeavorers of Japan. The speaker told briefly the beginnings of Christian Endeavor in Japan, and outlined its present-day progress. For some years the movement has been weak; but a field-secretary has been appointed, and the societies have taken on new life and vigor. Mr. Abe suggested that an International Christian Endeavor Convention like the present one be held in Japan, and closed by bringing to the Convention the love of his people.

Rev. Seijiro Vemur, another Japanese, also spoke of Christian Endeavor among his people in their home land.

China

Once more it was the privilege of Endeavorers to see and hear the man who organized the first Christian Endeavor society in China. His name is Rev. George H. Hubbard of Foochow, China. He is yet virile in spite of the passage of the two-score years that have run their course since he formed the first society in his church. He is a man of sterling Christian character and of gracious personality. He told of the recent celebration in China of the fortieth anniversary of the founding of Christian Endeavor there. At that time a ten years' increase programme was inaugurated, and a slogan was adopted, "Ten times as many societies in China by 1935 as there are to-day." At the time this slogan was adopted there were 1,200 societies in China. To-day there are 2,325 societies, which is a very good beginning for their ten years' plan.

Dr. Hubbard described the symbolism of the Chinese star,

which has eight points. This star has in it the cross on which the Saviour died, the St. Andrew's cross, which is the symbol of brotherhood, and the Chinese symbol for love. How beautiful a star that tells of these three supreme things, sacrifice, brotherhood, and love!

It caused many poignant feelings when Mr. Hubbard told of the death of his wife just ten days before they had planned to leave for America. A little personal touch brought out the fact that it was Mrs. Hubbard who led Mr. Hubbard to devote his life to China.

Mr. Hubbard spoke in warm admiration of Rev. and Mrs. E. E. Strother, Christian Endeavor secretaries in China, whose home is in Shanghai, where they come into contact with many missionaries and are doing a wonderful work for Christian Endeavor in the new republic.

Syria

Above the platform a long banner was stretched which proclaimed in large letters something of the record that Columbia, S. C., did last year for Golden Rule Sunday. This city won the prize offered by the Near East Relief for the city that made the best campaign for Golden Rule Sunday, and as a reward was permitted to send an Endeavorer to the Near East. The Endeavorers of Columbia went out in teams and enrolled 25,000 persons out of a population of 40,000; and this great army observed Golden Rule Sunday, making Columbia, S. C., the Golden Rule city of America.

Mrs. James H. Grauel of Columbia, S. C., and of Syria, eloquently told the story of this successful campaign, and read a letter of thanks and greeting from Sidon, Syria.

"Christian Endeavorers, as one of you I bring to you from a land of the Master Himself a greeting, a message, and a challenge. First is this message from Barclay Acheson, speaking for the orphans in the Near East.

MAY 25, 1925.
SIDON, SYRIA.

Dear Endeavorers, I have been requested to send a greeting to the great International Christian Endeavor Convention which is to convene in Portland. This request has been made by orphans in the Near East who met the Christian Endeavorer, Chester Alexander, who visited them last summer as the national Golden Rule ambassador of the young people of America.

They request me to say for them: "We thank the Christian Endeavorers for their co-operation in the Golden Rule Sunday campaigns especially, and have been glad to hear that last fall the Christian Endeavorers of Columbia, S. C., made such a great record. We are so thankful for the opportunity which we orphans have to live and to be trained in the body and in the mind and in the soul. We are all determined that we will prove worthy of the help that has been given us in the spirit of the Golden Rule. We ask you to pray that all orphans inside the orphanages, when they must leave at sixteen, may be great workers for the cause of Jesus Christ, the Saviour of us all. We ask also that you would pray very much for the orphans who are still in dirty and filthy refugee camps, who cannot be taken in because there isn't enough money for all. May our Father in Heaven bless your big Convention."

In behalf of the orphans,

BARCLAY ACHESON,
Overseas General Director.

Mrs. Grauel continued:

"In behalf of the children of the Near East, homeless and friendless but for you and me, I present to you this gavel made in our orphanage at Nazareth of olivewood from the sunny slopes of Palestine. With it goes the hope that wherever it shall be wielded there will go up to God a prayer for the safety and salvation of those suffering little children. It is for their sakes as well as your own that I have travelled four thousand miles, hoping that I may bring to you something of the vision of their need that came to the Christian Endeavorers of my home city, Columbia, S. C. May I say here that I am not here as an official of that splendid organization, the Near East Relief, but simply as a Christian Endeavorer who directed and led the 530 young people in that crusade. It was those young people, representative of every young people's church society in the city, but led by the Christian Endeavorers, who led America last year in the observance of Golden Rule Sunday and won for us the proud title 'Columbia, the Golden Rule City of America.' I know of no other group who could reach such an achievement as this but young people, and most of those Christian Endeavorers.

"They engineered such a crusade as our city had never seen before. Organized into teams with captains, colonels, and a general, this army of Columbia's youth went out and enrolled 25,000 observers of Golden Rule Sunday in our little city of 40,000, and made the day one of 'plain living and high thinking' indeed. As their leader I can gratefully testify that more good came to the hearts and souls of those young people than came to the minds and bodies of the children overseas. And so I appeal to you, not only for the sake of the children of the Near East, but for the sake of your societies and yourselves, to enlist one hundred per cent for the furtherance of the Golden Rule programme this fall. During this Convention definite plans will be launched by Mr. Gates and Dr. Poling for the December, 1925, programme of the 'World Fellowship of the Golden Rule.' This programme is being made prayerfully with the hope that one million observers of Golden Rule Sunday (December 6, 1925) will be enrolled through the work of Christian Endeavorers.

"In Dr. Poling's words, 'let us do a great and gracious thing; let us make the occasion one of physical and spiritual giving, measuring ourselves as we do by the one Golden Rule. 'Whatsoever ye would that men should do to you, do ye even so unto them.'"

Mrs. Grauel also read the following letter from the governor of South Carolina to Dr. Poling, as the national chairman of the Young People's Golden Rule Committee:

DR. DANIEL A. POLING,
National Chairman of the Young People's Golden Rule Committee,
and
To THE CHRISTIAN ENDEAVOR CONVENTION,
Portland, Or.

Christian Endeavorers, It gives me great pleasure to extend a greeting to you as governor of the State which has twice had the great honor of having the city which has been designated the Golden Rule City of America. Both in "Chester, the 1923 Golden Rule City of America," and in "Columbia Unlimited, the 1924 Golden Rule City of America," I have heard that the Christian Endeavor societies were at the forefront in the promotion of the campaigns. We are proud of what the young people of these two cities and others which I might also mention have done, and also of the wonderful co-operation which they have secured from and by all the women's and men's organizations in these communities.

We of South Carolina, the members of the State Golden Rule committee, issue a friendly challenge to all other States to equal the record which every city, town, and hamlet in this State is preparing to make in the promotion of the third international Golden Rule Sunday, December 6, 1925. May we all do our utmost that the unfortunate orphans who came out of Turkey may have the same opportunity which we would wish for our children if their places were exchanged.

Yours faithfully,

THOMAS G. McLEOD,
Governor of South Carolina,
Honorary Chairman, State
Golden Rule Committee.

Europe Once More

The last speaker was Rev. James Kelly of Scotland, president of the European Christian Endeavor Union. He told of the efforts of British Endeavorers, after the war, to get into touch with the Endeavorers of Germany. At first it seemed hopeless, feeling being so bitter. But this antagonism died down; a European Christian Endeavor Convention was held; and now, this year, when Mr. Kelly was passing through Germany, great crowds of German Endeavorers met him on the platform of the railroad stations at several places along the route. They brought with them brass bands and banners and gifts by which to express their Christian love and fellowship.

Mr. Kelly told of Christian Endeavor in France, in Switzerland, in Hungary, where a great work is being done. In Jugo-Slavia work is going on in spite of many difficulties. There are societies in Norway. In Poland our cause is in a very healthy condition. In Esthonia the work is well organized. There are fourteen societies with a full-time secretary and two or three deaconesses. In Lithuania, too, there are Endeavorers, and there is hope for a large development of the work there. In Russia there are but few societies, but there is a young Russian ready to enter that country with the message of Christian Endeavor.

Mr. Kelly made an earnest plea for peace and good will on earth. With passionate eloquence he told of having seen with his own eyes the wreck and the agonies of war; but in spite of all, he said, we must learn to forgive. If we do not forgive, how can we ever expect to be forgiven?

General-Secretary Gates did not read his report, but handed printed copies to the delegates. The time of such a convention is precious and no one realizes this more than Mr. Gates. It seemed to him unnecessary to read a report which delegates might read for themselves. The report follows:

CHRISTIAN ENDEAVOR IS GROWING

[*Report of E. P. Gates, General Secretary of the United Society of Christian Endeavor, to the Thirtieth International Christian Endeavor Convention, Portland, Oregon, July 4-10, 1925.*]

Christian Endeavor is growing. Nine thousand seven hundred and thirty-two new Christian Endeavor societies have been organized during the past two years. More than six thousand of this number have been reported during the past twelve months. Fifteen thousand four hundred and twenty-seven Comrades of the Quiet Hour have pledged themselves to set aside a definite time every day for prayer and Bible-study. Four thousand three hundred and sixteen young people have promised to contribute to the extension of the Kingdom at least one-tenth of their incomes. One thousand and twenty-eight have volunteered for full-time Christian service as ministers of the gospel, missionaries on the home and foreign fields, or in other ways.

Christian Endeavor is growing in large churches. In an increasing number of churches there are now five, six, seven or eight Christian Endeavor societies, and Christian Endeavor is more and more recognized by these churches as a vital factor in their programme of religious education for young people of all ages. Graded Christian Endeavor has come to stay. While the question of the number of age groups will always depend upon the size of the church and its own special problems, and while no absolute uniformity of nomenclature can be expected, the evident tendency is in the direction of a considerable increase in the number of Christian Endeavor societies in the local church and in the number of young people who will be reached by the Christian Endeavor programme.

Christian Endeavor is growing in union churches. In communities all over America churches of different denominations are uniting in a common programme, and almost invariably the interdenominational fellowship of Christian Endeavor makes it the logical young people's organization for the united church.

Christian Endeavor is growing in difficult places. From Alaska comes the news of many new societies. In country churches, in city churches, in churches with few young people and churches with many, Christian Endeavor has been found adaptable to the needs of the young people. Christian Endeavor is the nearest approach to a self-operating group yet developed within the churches.

Christian Endeavor is growing in foreign lands. From China comes the glorious news of the organization of more than a thousand societies. India, Japan, and Korea send equally glowing reports. In Great Britain, Germany, and nearly every other European country the movement is making remarkable progress.

Christian Endeavor is growing wherever there is a desire to hold up a definite spiritual standard for young people. Christian Endeavor believes that young people need to accept the Lord Jesus Christ as a personal Saviour and to witness for Him in the home life, the community, the nation, and the world. Christian Endeavor believes in the importance of daily prayer and Bible-study to equip persons for life's task. Christian Endeavor exalts the church. Christian Endeavor challenges young people to a programme of Christian living and Christian world service. Only where the church has this ideal for its young people can Christian Endeavor prosper.

The New Campaign

Dr. Francis E. Clark, with his usual vision of the needs of the movement, proposes at this Convention a campaign for fidelity to Christian Endeavor principles. In the promotion of this campaign as outlined by our great leader we suggest the following points of emphasis for the coming year:

1. Promote hearty co-operation with denominational leaders and with all agencies seeking to serve young people. Our whole organization must seek to emphasize in every possible way that interdenominational fellowship means increased denominational loyalty. Much of the wonderful progress of Christian Endeavor in recent years has been due to the enthusiastic support of the young people's secretaries of many of the denominations. There are no fewer than a thousand national, State, and district denominational field-workers who are continually carrying the message of Christian Endeavor to the groups with which they work. Christian Endeavor has a definite obligation to promote the programmes of these denominations. Just as far as our funds permit we should keep every church leader in this country and on the foreign field in touch with the programme of Christian Endeavor.

Within the past year the United Society of Christian Endeavor has accepted membership on the executive committee of the International Council of Religious Education. We look forward to the opportunity to co-operate with this great organization and with all others in whose programmes Christian Endeavorers can properly participate.

2. Undertake intensive instructions in the principles of Christian Endeavor. The only people who do not believe in Christian Endeavor are those who do not know about it. Even the best-informed of our leadership need to be reminded of what Christian Endeavor stands for and of the place of Christian Endeavor in the modern church programme. To meet this need, we offer at this Convention a new book from the pen of Amos R. Wells, "Progressive Endeavor." We shall strive to organize classes in this new text-book of Christian Endeavor principles in every society and union. Seminaries and other training schools will be asked to use the book in the study of young people's work. To those who study the book and pass a satisfactory examination will be given the degree of "Progressive Christian Endeavor," with a certificate of honor awarded by the United Society of Christian Endeavor.

3. Extend graded Christian Endeavor. Christian Endeavor is adaptable, and any church is at liberty to group its young people as local conditions seem to require, and to call these groups by such names as it considers appropriate. It is neither possible nor desirable to propose hard and fast age-limits for Christian Endeavor societies or to insist on certain names which must be used everywhere.

Christian Endeavor leaders everywhere should look with favor on the age groups and nomenclature generally recognized in the field of religious education, and so far as local conditions make possible Christian Endeavor societies in the local church should be so graded as to correspond in age-period and names to other departments of the church.

4. Emphasize new society standards. To meet a very general demand from the field we are offering at this Convention standards for Intermediate and young people's societies. These standards have been planned to suggest a full programme of Christian Endeavor activity. They have been made sufficiently general so as to be completely adaptable to the particular needs of every society. They give abundant opportunity for the promotion of both the denominational and the interdenominational programme. Recognition for work done will be given by the United Society of Christian Endeavor, not for reaching a required number of points or a required percentage, but on the certificate of the pastor of the church that in his opinion his Christian Endeavor society has attained a satisfactory standard.

MONTHLY SERVICE PLANS FOR CHRISTIAN ENDEAVOR UNIONS AND SOCIETIES
1925-1926
SEPTEMBER
Practice World Fellowship in Prayer and Bible Study

Enroll 500,000 young people to memorize great passages of scripture and to pray daily for a world revival of religion, for world peace and international friendship.

A list of suggested scripture passages will be published. Enrollment blanks for Comrades of the Quiet Hour may be secured at nominal cost. To encourage daily use of the Bible, special Christian Endeavorers' editions of the Bible and of the New Testament have been published and will be sold by the United Society of Christian Endeavor.

The campaign for memorization of Bible passages will be launched in September and will continue throughout the year. Bibles will be awarded as recognitions to the societies in each State reporting the greatest success in the campaign. Details of the awards will be announced in the columns of The Christian Endeavor World.

Recognition in the campaign will be given to all local, city, county and district unions reaching a minimum goal of 100 enrollments in the Quiet Hour and 100 participating in the Bible memory campaign. Additional recognition will be given for each hundred additional enrollments.

Helpful suggestions for carrying out these plans will be found in the columns of The Christian Endeavor World in connection with the treatment of the following Christian Endeavor prayer meeting topics: Young People's, September 6, "Learning how to Pray"; September 20, "Getting Strength from God"; Intermediate, September 6, "Prayer, the Greatest Power in the World."

OCTOBER
Organize for World Service

Present to fifty thousand Christian Endeavor societies in the United States and Canada the new Christian Endeavor standards with the programs of their own denominations and communions. Urge every society to plan a program of its own, adapting these standards to the needs of its own church and community.

Emphasize Graded Christian Endeavor—Enough Christian Endeavor societies of the proper age groups to offer training to all young people of the church and community.

Introduce The Christian Endeavor World to every Christian Endeavorer. While this campaign will be begun in October, it will continue until every union has reached every goal.

Available material, sent free on request, will include a leaflet describing the new society standards, leaflets outlining the young people's programs of the various denominations, a leaflet on Graded Christian Endeavor and Christian Endeavor World blanks and advertising material.

Recognition in the campaign will be given to all local, city, county, district unions reaching the following goals:
  a. The national standards presented by visitation, correspondence or in union meetings to at least three-fourths of the societies.
  b. Not less than ten new subscriptions to The Christian Endeavor World.
  c. A Junior superintendent, an Intermediate superintendent and a union Christian Endeavor literature representative elected or

appointed. Names and addresses to be reported to the General Secretary of the United Society of Christian Endeavor.

Helpful suggestions for carrying out these plans will be found in connection with the treatment of the regular Christian Endeavor prayer meeting topics: Young People's topics: October 4, "How Can Our Society Benefit Our Community?"; October 11, "They First Gave Their Own Selves." Intermediate: September 27, "How Can We Serve Our Neighborhood?" October 4, "How Can Our Society Help Other Intermediates?"

NOVEMBER
Study World Christian Citizenship

Enlist 500,000 young people to face world problems in study and discussion groups.

"Adventuring in World Co-operation" has been published by the United Society of Christian Endeavor as the text-book of the campaign. Copies may be secured at twenty-five cents, post-paid. It has been written especially for Christian Endeavorers. For those who do not desire a special study book, the regular Christian Endeavor prayer meeting topics will afford excellent material for discussion of world problems. Young People's topics: October 18, "What is expected of a Christian Citizen?" October 25, "Our New Americans"; November 1, "Can We Live by the Golden Rule?" November 8, "What can Young People do for International Friendship?" November 15, "How can we overcome the Spirit of Lawlessness?" Intermediate topics: October 18, "How can Intermediates Help Enforce Law?" November 1, "World Peace Sunday"; October 25, "How can we show our friendship for the Jews?"

In addition a special Christian Endeavor programme will be suggested for November 11, 1925, (Armistice Day).

Recognition in the campaign will be given to all local, city, county and district unions enlisting at least one hundred Christian Endeavorers to consider world problems, either through the use of the regular Christian Endeavor prayer meeting topics or in society or union study classes. Recognition will also be given for each additional hundred reported.

DECEMBER, 1925
World Service Through the Golden Rule

Enroll one million adult church members and other friends for the observance of Golden Rule Sunday, December 6, 1925.

A Golden Rule committee in every union and society to promote the plan. Special awards to successful societies and unions. Available material sent free on request includes a leaflet explaining the plan for society and union co-operation, enrollment blanks and descriptive literature.

Recognition in the campaign will be given to all local, city, county and district unions reaching a minimum goal of 2,000 Golden Rule enrollments. Recognition will also be given for additional enrollments.

Helpful suggestions for carrying out these plans will be found in the columns of The Christian Endeavor World, especially in connection with the treatment of the following prayer meeting topics: Young People's: November 22, "God's Bounties—How Can We Share Them with Others?" December 6, "How Can We Translate Christmas into Service?" Intermediate: November 24, "How Can All Intermediates Be Missionaries?"

JANUARY, 1926
Educating in Christian Endeavor Principles

Study Christian Endeavor principles, and methods in every society and union.

Inform every adult church member about Christian Endeavor, during Christian Endeavor Week, January 31 to February 7, 1926.

"Progressive Endeavor," a new text-book of Christian Endeavor principles, has been published by the United Society of Christian Endeavor and sells for $1.00, postpaid. To those who study this book and pass the required examination will be given the degree of "Progressive Christian Endeavorer." Fifty thousand young people will be enrolled for the study of this text-book or its companion volume, "Expert Endeavor."

Available material for Christian Endeavor Week will include programmes for Christian Endeavor Week and Christian Endeavor Day (ready November 1, 1925) and a new Christian Endeavor Pageant, "Christ Exalted."

Recognition will be given to all local, city, county, and district unions reaching a minimum goal of fifty graduates of "Progressive Endeavor" or "Expert Endeavor" between September 1, 1925, and June 1, 1926.

Helpful suggestions for carrying out these plans will be found in connection with the treatment of the regular Christian Endeavor prayer meeting topics: Young People's topics: January 17, "Great Ideas That Have Spurred People to Action"; January 31, "The Call, the Claims, and the Conquests of the Church"; February 7, "What Does Christian Endeavor Mean to Me!" Intermediate topics: January 31, "The Call, the Claims, and the Conquests of the Church"; February 7, "What Does Christian Endeavor Mean to Me!"

FEBRUARY and MARCH, 1926
Christ for the Young People of the World

Seek to win 100,000 young people for Christ and the Church membership.

Enlist 10,000 Christian Endeavorers to train under the direction of the churches for Sunday-school teaching, leadership of Junior or Intermediate Christian Endeavor societies or other groups of boys and girls.

Encourage increased support of denominational missionary enterprises, and increased church attendance.

Organize new Christian Endeavor societies.

A leaflet, giving suggestions for evangelistic work through Christian Endeavor will be available after November 1, 1925.

Recognition will be given to unions reporting two or more new Christian Endeavor societies and at least ten Christian Endeavorers enrolled to train for leadership. Recognition will also be given for additional societies and enrollments.

Helpful suggestions for carrying out these plans will be found in the columns of The Christian Endeavor World, especially in connection with the treatment of the following Christian Endeavor topics: Young People's: February 14, "What Is Faith and What Does It Do for Us?"; February 21, "Lives Transformed by Christ"; February 28, "Neglected Areas in the Country"; March 7, "Persevere: In What!" March 21, "What Does Jesus Mean by Cross-Bearing?" April 4, "Thoughts Suggested by Easter." Intermediate: February 28, "What Missionary Work Is Needed in America?" March 7, "How Do Christian Principles Help in Business?" March 14, "The Importance of Good Comrades"; March 28, "Jesus'

Triumphal Entry into Other Lives through Me"; April 14, "What Is Easter's Greatest Message to Me?"

APRIL, MAY and JUNE, 1926
Victory Months

A follow-up campaign to make every union an honor union and every society an honor society. Suggested plans will be ready February 1, 1926.

JULY, 1926
World's Christian Endeavor Convention, London, July 16 to 21, 1926

Christian Endeavorers from all over the world will attend this great gathering. The report of the year's campaign will be presented. Recognitions of Honor Societies and unions in America will be announced in London and mailed from the convention.

Special Christian Endeavor tours to London with after-trips to European countries have been planned by the United Society of Christian Endeavor.

RECOGNITIONS

Honor Banners will be awarded to local, city, county and district Christian Endeavor unions reaching the minimum goals suggested for four of the six monthly themes. A ribbon of honor will be added to the banner for each 100 per cent increase over any monthly goal.

The **Francis E. Clark** ribbon of honor will be added to the banners of union reporting a ten per cent increase in the number of societies in the union between July 1, 1925, and July 1, 1926.

State Honor Banners will be awarded to State and Provincial Christian Endeavor unions reaching the following goals:

1. List of Christian Endeavor societies in the State with names and addresses of their correspondents, and list of all local, county, city, and district union officers and department superintendents reported to the General Secretary of the United Society of Christian Endeavor, 41 Mt. Vernon Street, Boston, Mass.
2. Evidence of hearty promotion of the Monthly Promotion Programme outlined above.
3. Minimum attainment as follows:
    For States with less than 100 Intermediate and Young People's societies: Twice the numerical goals suggested for district unions.
    For States with less than 500 Intermediate and Young People's societies: Five times the numerical goals suggested for district unions.
    For States with less than 1,000 Intermediate and Young People's societies: Ten times the numerical goals suggested for district unions.
    For States with more than 1,000 Intermediate and Young People's societies: Fifteen times the numerical goals suggested for district unions.
4. At least seventy-five per cent of financial quota for national and world-wide Christian Endeavor paid in before May 1, 1926.
5. At least fifty per cent of the State goal for Christian Endeavor World subscriptions reached before May 1, 1926.

Honor Societies: Those certified by their pastors to have maintained worth-while work on the basis of the new Christian Endeavor standards over a period of six months. Special recognition (to be announced later) to societies reaching certain monthly goals.

Correspondence in regard to details of the campaign should be addressed to

EDWARD P. GATES,
General Secretary,
United Society of Christian Endeavor,
41 Mt. Vernon St., Boston, Mass.

A Musical Good Time

Part of the audience went to attend the Washington and Oregon State conventions, but many remained to hear "a musical good time" under the leadership of Percy Foster. The idea was to show the young people how they may have a good time singing at their socials or other gatherings. Mr. Foster made the crowd sing all sorts of things, serious and comic; and every one took part with great gusto. "Mary had a little lamb," went over *big*. It was amusing indeed to hear one-half of the audience singing this song and the other half singing "Three Blind Mice." Try it and see the effect. The half-hour period was soon gone; but the audience, like Oliver Twist, demanded more, and had to get a half-hour extra.

HIGH NOON
Lunch with Life-Work Recruits

Paul Brown presided Monday noon at the luncheon for Life-Work Recruits, when between two and three hundred sat down to a delightful meal in the First Christian Church. In meetings like these the thing that impresses a visitor is the superb quality of the young people of the churches—young, joyous, overflowing with life, full of pep and faith and courage, lovers of home, lovers of country, lovers of God, and lovers of all the world. In all the meetings it has been my privilege to attend I have never seen anything like the equal of these charming young men and women. There is something in religion that makes for beauty and peace.

While the majority were eating, Paul Brown called the roll, making the ministers and workers at the tables rise and tell who they were and what they are doing. A great crowd rose when Mr. Brown asked the Life-Work Recruits to stand. Surely the church is safe with this quality of young people in it! These were not callow young people, but young men and women who knew what they were doing when they offered themselves to God in the work of His ministry.

After a brief talk by Rev. H. L. Pickerill of St. Louis, Mo., Dr. Royal J. Dye, one of the great missionaries of the Christian Church (Disciples) to Africa, was called upon to address the gathering. Dr. Dye was stationed at Bolenge, Africa, where he found the people savages; but before he left the country, on account of his health, practically the whole community had turned to the Lord, and his church housed the largest Christian Endeavor society in the world, for every church-member was an Endeavorer.

In spite of the fact that Dr. Dye has behind him years of memorable achievement he is still a man who appears to be on the sunny side of middle life. He talks with that simplicity and tumultuous earnestness that grip the audience. Speaking to this group of Life-Work Recruits, he doubtless felt himself at home. The atmosphere was favorable to anecdotal illustration of work for "witnesses of Jesus." With varying instances he drove home the truth that there is work for every Recruit at his own door. We need not look to distant lands for our field; we can begin to serve just where we are. If God wants to send us into larger work, He will make the work at home the stepping-stone to higher things.

An illustration will indicate Dr. Dye's method. A young girl went to live in a town where many foreigners lived. The churches in that town were lifeless; and the Christian Church, to which the girl belonged, had quit and closed its doors, and the key was in the hands of a saloon-keeper. The children of the place were neglected, and this young girl saw it. She set to work, and succeeded in getting the key of the idle church, and invited the children of the community to come into the Sunday school she opened. Her work with these children opened the way to a position as head of a community survey committee. So God leads His workers on step by step.

Dr. Dye has vision. The instances he related showed not merely the magnitude of the task, but the greatness of the opportunity that challenges the young people of to-day. Big jobs are awaiting us. The question is not whether there are big jobs for us, but whether we are big enough for the jobs.

Dr. Dye's description of how the native African rises gradually out of his filth and his pagan life was exquisitely humorous. We saw the native wash himself and realize that he was naked. We saw his desire for better clothing emerge from his mind, and how he began to build better homes and better furniture.

This view of missions brought new ideas to many. A big job that calls for big souls! A challenge, nothing else! A challenge that makes no appeal to selfishness, but that stirs to its depths the heart that loves the suffering world.

THE JUNIOR SUPERINTENDENT'S CONCEPTION OF HER TASK

At the dinner conference for Junior leaders on Monday, Walter D. Howell, of Philadelphia, Field Director, Presbyterian Board of Christian Education, gave a thoughtful address, here condensed.

The Junior superintendent must conceive her task as one among several educational tasks in the local church's work with children under twelve. Her task is related to the others and must not duplicate the others. She must work in close and complete understanding with the superintendent of the Junior Department of the Sunday school, the leaders of children's missionary organizations, the head of the Daily Vacation Bible school, and the leaders of the Week-Day Church school, if there is one.

She must recognize that hers is a task that requires a special type of preparation. This special training should include at least

THE COVERED WAGON
This was in Oregon's Section of the parade

ARIZONA, FIRST IN THE PARADE
Arizona won the right to march at the head of the parade. The picture shows the delegates at the reviewing stand

three major elements: A psychological knowledge of the child and how he develops from infancy to adolescence; a knowledge of the broad fundamental principles of how to teach, since she is to help the children in a process of learning through their own activity; a knowledge of how to apply the general principles of religious instruction and training to the particular age groups with which she works—the younger children in the group six to eight years old and the older group who are nine to twelve.

She must perceive the fact that her task is distinct from that of every other children's leader in the church, different from them all. Her task is to develop within the children the ability to express and to use the knowledge of Christianity that they get elsewhere. To train boys and girls to be "doers of the Word and not hearers only,"—this is the distinctive task of the Junior Christian Endeavor leader.

She must understand that her task is vital to the whole programme of the church and the kingdom of God. There can be no strong leadership for the church a generation ahead unless the children of this generation start their training in expressing and applying their knowledge of Christianity while they are still children. After twelve is far too late to begin learning how to express one's religious belief and ideas in words; too late to begin to pray in the presence of others; too late to get the first experience in leading meetings, working on committees and helping others to do simple tasks of Christian service. If the life is to be most fruitful and forceful in the work of Christ, the start in acquiring the ability to do these things must be made in the plastic years of the Junior period.

THE BUSINESS OF THE KINGDOM
Annual Meeting of the United Society of Christian Endeavor.—Dr. Clark Resigns.—A $100,000 Fund Proposed to Honor Him

Monday afternoon at half past four the United Society of Christian Endeavor held its annual meeting in one of the large rooms of the Multnomah Hotel. Mr. John T. Sproull of New Jersey opened the meeting with prayer, by invitation of Dr. Clark, who presided.

The most impressive item on the programme of this meeting was the resignation of Dr. Clark as president of the United Society of Christian Endeavor. A number of times in the past Dr. Clark has been anxious to resign, but it did not seem the wise thing at any time in the past to grant the president's request. He has served as president for thirty-eight years, giving in service the very best that was in him. He pointed out that a man was now ready to step into his place, and that the organization would not be a single day without a head. Strangely enough on this very day, July 6, thirty-eight years ago, Dr. Clark entered upon his office. In simple words, on this anniversary, then, he presented his plea for release from the burden of service as president of the society.

The proposal manifestly came as a great surprise to some, but Dr. Clark made it clear that his action was final; and therefore, with great regret, yet with sympathy and understanding, his resignation was accepted.

It should be said that Dr. Clark remains president of the World's Union of Christian Endeavor, and will continue to direct the work of Christian Endeavor in foreign lands; and his influence and counsel will, of course, be available to the movement as long as he lives.

Dr. Poling spoke feelingly of the honor Dr. Clark wished to confer upon him, of the overwhelming nature of the work, and of the hesitation he naturally felt as he was asked to step into the place of a man that can never have a successor.

The nominating committee presented its report with a resolution of appreciation of Dr. Clark and his work, as well as that of Mrs. Clark. The committee proposed that Dr. Clark be elected president-emeritus of the United Society of Christian Endeavor, and that a fund of $100,000 be raised, to be called the Francis E. Clark Recognition Fund, the interest of which should go to Dr. and Mrs. Clark as long as they live. On their passing the interest will go to the world-wide work of Christian Endeavor.

The committee's proposal was unanimously approved.

Other reports were presented, the treasurer's and the nominating committee's, making Dr. Clark president emeritus, and Dr. Poling president, of the United Society of Christian Endeavor. Rev. H. B. Grose. D. D., was elected vice-president, as was also Dr. William Hiram Foulkes. E. P. Gates was re-elected general secretary; treasurer and field-secretary, A. J. Shartle; assistant treasurer, Stanley B. Vandersall; editorial secretary, Robert P. Anderson; publication-manager and clerk, Clarence C. Hamilton; extension secretary, Dr. Ira Landrith; Pacific coast secretary, Paul C. Brown; Southern secretary, Charles F. Evans; army and navy superintendent, S. C. Ramsden; and citizenship superintendent, Frederick A. Wallis of New York.

KNIGHTHOOD IN FLOWER
Dr. Clark Made a Knight of the Rose

It is sometimes the things that are not on the printed programme of our conventions that make the sessions interesting and often picturesque. This was true for the evening meeting on Monday, when the great hall was crowded from floor to the uppermost reach of the balconies.

The hall had a colorful effect with flags of all sorts draped around the front of the galleries. The civic Auditorium is a "playhouse," with a real stage and scenery that is used in drama. In front of the curtain, above, hung a row of radiant flags illuminated from behind. A little farther back hung another row of flags, and in the centre a large Christian Endeavor monogram made of colored electric lights, the "C" a brilliant red, and the "E" inside, white. Behind, where the scenery should be, hung yet more flags and a banner with the Christian Endeavor monogram, and the word "Welcome."

While the delegations were assembling, there were the usual songs and "yells" that make Christian Endeavor conventions different from all others. Many of the delegations wore special uniforms whose massed colors made a striking effect; others had only special caps and arm-bands or sashes; while a great many wore fanciful, colored head-dresses. From the platform the hall looked like a great garden with flowers of all varieties moving in the breeze. Musical flowers, of course, such as nature never produces!

The surprise of the evening came at the very beginning when a delegation of Royal Rosarians appeared and took their places on the platform in front of the choir with the intention of conferring on Dr. Francis E. Clark the distinguished honor of the Knighthood of the Rose. It is the custom of Rosarians to select every year one distinguished person who for his work's sake is considered worthy of this high honor of knighthood, and this year Dr. Clark was the man selected.

The officers of the Rosarians sat in a row on the platform, and after a brief talk by their chief explaining the symbolic meaning of the order, the leader conferred on Dr. Clark the order of knighthood, and solemnly declared him.

Sir Francis E. Clark, Knight of the Order of the Rose

The Royal Gardener then presented him with a basket of beautiful roses; another officer, the secretary of State, handed to him the parchment of the order establishing his knighthood; and the chaplain placed him under the obligation of the order, Dr. Clark declaring his consent to it. The order makes much of the symbolism suggested by roses and rose gardens, a beautiful and tender symbolism that arouses deep sentiments that slumber in the soul.

The members of the order arose, and Dr. Clark delivered to them one of those charming and tactful speeches which have made him both famous and loved. Dr. Clark is a lover of nature, and his reference to his old farmhouse on Cape Cod, where the roses bloom all around the house in summer-time, brought out his affection for all beautiful things. Was it not a happy touch to have Dr. Clark made a Royal Rosarian in Portland, the city of roses?

Dr. Clark Gets Pictures

Mr. Lloyd Carrick, associate chairman of the Convention committee, brought another delightful surprise by presenting to Dr. Clark two beautiful large pictures of Oregon scenery, a picture of Mt. Hood and one of Multnomah Falls, while to Mrs. Clark was given a basket of flowers with a book in which are inscribed the names of those that contributed to these beautiful gifts. For these gifts Dr. Clark spoke his thanks with his usual, or rather with even unusual, graciousness.

THE CAPTAIN OF THE HOST
The Message of Dr. Clark

Dr. Clark received an ovation when Dr. Poling introduced him as "the captain of the hosts of youth in America." Beginning his speech in firm and resonant voice, he contrasted the beginnings of Christian Endeavor in Portland, Me., with the Christian Endeavor of to-day, holding its Convention in the Portland of the West.

In the meeting of the trustees in the afternoon Dr. Clark had resigned his position as president of the United Society of Christian Endeavor; but his public announcement came as a surprise, and took away the breath of the audience. But the tension was relieved when with his unfailing instinct for saying the right thing he turned to Dr. Poling, and said, *"The president has resigned; long live the president."* The audience applauded to the echo when Dr. Clark further proclaimed Dr. Poling as "a man born in Portland," and declared that he wanted to hug him as his good friend. Again came a loud salvo of applause as he carried out his desire to hug the new president; and only his Yankee reticency, he said, prevented him from kissing "Dan" on both cheeks, as he would have done, had he been French.

Dr. Clark's speech follows. It is entitled

A CAMPAIGN OF FIDELITY TO PRINCIPLES
Biennial Message of Rev. Francis E. Clark, D. D., LL. D., President of the United Society of Christian Endeavor, at the International Christian Endeavor Convention, Portland, Oregon, July 6

In Portland, Me., on the Atlantic shore, Christian Endeavor began its career, something more than forty-four years ago. In Portland, Or., on the Pacific shore, it to-day holds its chief Convention for the year.

From Portland to Portland overland is a long three thousand miles of mountain and meadow and forest and farm. In a very few years from its beginning Christian Endeavor made this long journey, following westward the "star of empire."

But Christian Endeavor went east as well as west, and it went north and south, bounded by no lines of latitude or longitude, and has found a home in every land on the globe. Going east also from the eastern Portland, across the Atlantic, across Europe, across Asia, across the Pacific, and stopping at every port by the way, Christian Endeavor is holding its greatest Convention to-day in the beautiful western Portland of the coast.

A Personal Note

Allow me here to interject a personal note, a note which has hitherto been absent from the Convention messages of the president. For nearly forty years you have elected and re-elected me as the president of the United Society of Christian Endeavor. I appreciate the fact that for an ordinary lifetime you have allowed me thus to serve the cause which has brought us together to-day.

But now at the close of this Convention I shall lay down the tasks which you have put upon my willing shoulders as president of the United Society of Christian Endeavor. Military men in army and navy are retired at the age of sixty-four. I have passed by nearly ten years the age when these officers must relinquish their commands and write "retired" after their names. In the Lord's army, too, there comes a time when for the best efficiency a man should resign his post and place the standard of office in younger hands. Some months of serious ill health, as well as advancing years with their inevitable handicaps, compel me to do this now.

I will not weary you with the story of these forty years. I can at least say that during these years I have never sought yours, but you. I will not at this time tell you how many miles I have travelled, nor how many addresses I have made, in the interests of Christian Endeavor. I do not know, myself. I will only say that I have seen the societies increase from a single one until they are to-day numbered by the tens of thousands and their members are counted by millions.

Not a Swan-Song

I shall indulge in no further figures. This is neither an arithmetical problem nor a swan-song. I am giving up my office in the year when Christian Endeavor is largest in numbers, strongest in its personnel, and widest in its influence of its whole history. There was never a time, take it the country over and the world around, when Christian Endeavor was so flourishing and blessed of God as now.

Nor will the office you have allowed me to fill so long be vacant even for an hour. The president has resigned; long live the president! A beloved friend of mine and of yours, the associate president of the United Society, Dr. Daniel A. Poling, has already been chosen as my successor. A secretary unexcelled for efficiency, a well-equipped and well-tried treasurer, publication-manager, editorial secretary, secretary of the Alumni, editors of *The Christian Endeavor World,* and other officers remain in the posts they have so ably filled. Christian Endeavor at the peak of prosperity is going forward to new victories and a larger influence.

I still hope to serve in the ranks, and perhaps for a season as president of the World's Christian Endeavor Union.

I wish to thank you all who are present, and through you the Endeavorers of all North America, for your unfailing love and personal loyalty. You have filled the cup of my official life with kindness and undeserved appreciation. Indeed, my cup runneth over. No one has ever had greater assurances of devoted affection than I, and now I make one more request and offer one more prayer. It is that throughout all the future years Endeavorers may be loyal to the principles which God in the past has so greatly prospered. Fidelity to our principles shall be the theme of this my last message to you as president of the United Society of Christian Endeavor.

Backward, Upward, Forward

It is well for us at such a time as this to look not only north and south and east and west, as we have done, but in three other directions—first, backward, to see what God has done for us Endeavorers; second, upward, to ask what God would have us do for Him; and then forward, with strong resolve and purpose true, to new victories.

Looking backward then, let us inquire for a brief moment, What has been God's design in the Christian Endeavor movement? Christian Endeavor is no longer an experiment. Its jubilee year is not far away. This much we can at least say: Christian Endeavor means certain principles and methods which God has used in practically every land, and in every Protestant denomination, and for nearly half a century, in training young people for His service. Let us ask, then, What are these underlying principles?

We answer: Its basic principles were long ago defined as

>   Confession of Christ,
>   Service for Christ,
>   Fellowship with Christ's people,
>   Loyalty to Christ's church.

Training by Doing

While our society puts great emphasis upon *training* young Christians for service by serving and by self-expression, because such training has been largely neglected in the past, it also provides abundant room for intellectual development in Bible-study and mission lore. It encourages clean and wholesome recreations and happy, sprightly, social intercourse.

Through its plans for graded societies it reaches all ages of youth, from the youngest Junior through the period of adolescence to adult manhood and womanhood. At the same time, no Endeavorer can be so old as to outlive his usefulness as an Alumnus, advising, encouraging, and cheering his younger brethren.

It unites all ages in a pledge to Christ and His church, without which in some form of *serious obligation* we believe no society of Christian Endeavor can prosper or long exist.

The society also places much stress on the Quiet Hour of

Personal Devotion, on responsibility for Christian stewardship of time and money and personal influence. It seeks to promote these multifarious forms of Christian activity largely through
  Its religious meetings for prayer and testimony,
  Its committees for service,
  Its unions for fellowship and inspiration.

You will notice that, in my opinion at least, Christian Endeavor glories in being distinctly, avowedly, rejoicingly, a religious society. It does not seek to camouflage its religion with worldly attractions; it does not bait its hook with doubtful amusements.

Terrible wails are heard on all sides about the youth of today. Says the critic, "They are vain, self-conceited, frivolous, morally callous; their hip-pockets bulge; the 'cigarette with fire at one end and a young fool at the other' is typical of our boys." I am quoting what others say. I do not believe it myself.

Of course what the cynic says is true of some; but I believe that religion and religious service are supremely attractive to most young people, when rightly presented. The whole history of Christian Endeavor proves it.

Then let us rejoice in a society that *majors* not in social life, or in athletics, or anything but religion, using all these other things as minors, as means to an end, and that end a worthy character, rooted in religion.

If you agree with me that religion and religious service are the things for which Christian Endeavor stands, what shall be our watchword? How shall we make these aims effective?

I answer,

By Fidelity, Fidelity to Principles

Let us make this not only our watchword, but the objective of our campaign for the two years to come. *Fidelity* is a big word. Adopted and lived up to, it would arouse, enlarge, and energize every society; it would quicken every church; it would fire every soul with new zeal. Dry bones would live again; formality would disappear; and new life would pulse through every society and union.

Historically this word belongs in a peculiar way to Christian Endeavor. The first society was formed to increase and promote the fidelity of young men and maidens to Jesus Christ and His church. The very word endeavor, from the French *en devoir*, means literally "on duty." This has been the high ideal of every true Christian Endeavor society formed in all these two score years and four of our history. We are back to first principles when we adopt *Fidelity* for our watchword, and at the same time we are reaching forward to the highest possible goal.

Let us consider it in the largest way. We think of the word too often simply as allegiance to an organization, to a society, to a church, to a denomination, to a cause. Christian Endeavor loyalty is all this, but it is more. It is hearty, loving adherence to great Christian principles of action that should dominate our lives. Of course Christian Endeavor means, as it always has, special fealty to our own church, our denomination and its work, to the mission cause of our church, to the Sabbath, to good citizenship, in a word, to Jesus Christ and His way of living. The many different methods of Christian Endeavor are simply plans to promote this fidelity.

Our Pledge

Our pledge, for instance, is one great means of promoting loyalty. It increases our sense of obligation, of personal responsibility for the performance of duty. No organization can endure without a pledge of fidelity, expressed or understood. The President of the United States, on the fourth of March last, before a great concourse of his fellow citizens, raised his right hand, and, with a Bible at his side, took a pledge, a pledge of loyalty to the country which he was to serve as its chief magistrate; and then he kissed the book to seal his vow.

The blushing bride and the manly groom stand before the altar, and make a pledge of loyalty to each other before Almighty God. I go to the income-tax office and swear that I have made a correct return, to the best of my knowledge and belief, so help me God! It is another pledge of loyalty to my country. The Christian joins the church of his choice; and joining it involves a pledge of fidelity to that church, its services, and its work.

The Christian Endeavor pledge is no novelty; but it is definite and stringent, and it largely accounts for the society's success. It is a declaration of fidelity to the things for which Christian Endeavor stands. Life is made up of pledges and obligations, assumed and gloried in—obligations of parents to children, of children to parents, of citizens to country. He is a weak and flabby human being who shrinks from definite obligations, who fears a pledge. God Himself has set us the example. "I will be their God and they shall be my people," saith the Lord God of hosts. "I will never leave thee nor forsake thee. Lo, I am with thee alway." This is Jesus Christ's own pledge of fidelity to His people.

Our Weekly Meetings

Christian Endeavor has always made much of its weekly meetings for prayer and testimony. It demands a promise of faithfulness to them. From its very first day it has done this. Please God, it always will. Why? Because such meetings are necessary to spiritual growth. Christianity is not a solitary religion. It is social in its very nature. We have obligations to others. We meet these obligations whenever we come together. St. Simeon Stylites on his lonely pillar was not the best type of

Christian. Robinson Crusoe may have been a Christian when he first landed on his island; he was a better Christian when his man Friday joined him. When the weekly Christian Endeavor meeting dies, the society dies, just as the fire goes out when the embers fall apart.

One of the most ominous signs of the decline of spiritual life in these days is the decline of the church prayer meeting. In many churches the Christian Endeavor meeting is the only one left for united prayer and testimony. Let us treasure the heritage which our pledge of fidelity in attendance and participation has given us.

Practical Service for Others

Again, practical service for every one through our system of committees is essential to a Christian Endeavor society. This too, is no fad, no peculiar doctrine of Christian Endeavor. Service for others is an imperative law of growth, and therefore a law of God. For training in this practical service for God and our fellow men Christian Endeavor exists. There are some things which must be learned, but which cannot be taught us by others. They can be made our own only by practice. *Learning by doing* is the law of life. The fondest mother cannot teach her baby to walk by telling him how to walk while he lies in the cradle.

Yet that is just the way some religious leaders think they are teaching young people to serve God. They give wise counsel; they offer eloquent prayers; they teach and preach; but the babes in Christ remain babes because they are kept in their cradles, because they are never allowed to stand upon their own feet; because they never have the privilege of falling down and getting up again.

A director of religious work for young people who does all the work himself is worse than none. To learn to walk in the paths of righteousness is a great adventure. Our youth will never learn "to run and not be weary," or to "walk and not faint," in God's highway unless allowed to take the first baby steps themselves. A religious boss, though meaning well, is as obnoxious as a political boss.

These are days when too much is done for our youth, and when they do too little for themselves. An indictment lately brought against moving pictures is that they hinder self-development. Everything is done for us in the picture-show. It leaves no room for self-expression. So with some games. Too many people are content to sit upon the bleachers all their lives. They never get into the game. The child-labor amendment forbidding certain kinds of work up to eighteen years of age, does not apply to religious work for God and our fellow men.

Freedom for self-expression allows flowers to bloom on their own stems, and birds to sing on their own boughs. The young

Christian must have practice as well as precept, training as well as teaching, or he will always be a religious moron.

Getting Together

Once more, Christian Endeavor has a blessed mission in bringing young Christians together. Never before in all the history of our movement has this God-given fellowship been so signally prospered as during this past year. Never before have so many millions of Endeavorers met in local and State union meetings, and in national and international conventions, the world around. Especially have the State conventions exceeded in numbers and power anything in the past. Many of them have taken on the proportions of national gatherings.

Can we believe that these interdenominational and international gatherings are not a part of God's plan? Sectarians have opposed our fellowship, and are still opposing it. They have failed to see God's purpose, and have tried to build higher denominational barriers to keep their young people from union gatherings. Loyalty to our own churches and our own denominations has not grown less, but more, during these years of Christian Endeavor; yet there is also a loyalty to universal Christian fellowship which we must cultivate, without which God's kingdom cannot come or His will be done in earth as it is in heaven. When this is established, then will bickerings cease, and small enmities be outgrown, while each church will be a generous rival of every other in charity and good works, and each will be stronger because of the good will of all.

Great Conventions

The late war, the mother of legions of devils, has done its sad work in promoting divisions and jealousies and hatreds throughout much of the world. Christian Endeavor has quietly striven to do its work of healing and reuniting. This last year it brought together twelve thousand young people and their leaders from twenty-one of the recently warring nations of Europe, in a wonderful fellowship meeting in Germany. The Endeavorers of the five Baltic countries, which have not always loved each other, have united to carry the gospel of peace and good will to others. Fifteen hundred Christian Endeavor unions in America have held thousands of fellowship meetings, in which members of nearly one hundred denominations have joined in song and prayer and service. Surely this blessed Christian unity is of God.

Said one of the highest authorities in the land on religious education the other day, in my hearing, one who is not connected in any way with our work. "The two greatest perils that America faces to-day are secularism and sectarianism, secularism in public-school education, sectarianism in religious education."

The Protestant church has been confessing its divisions, longing for Christian unity, singing about it, praying for it, for a hundred years. Here it is, so far as Christian Endeavor can promote it, among millions of young people in scores of denominations and in scores of nations. Some professing Christians still know little about it, and apparently care less. Brethern of all denominations, why not accept this measure of fellowship which Christian Endeavor offers your young people? Allow it to help answer your prayers for spiritual Christian union, and also the prayer of Jesus that all may be one. Give it your benediction, we pray. At least, let it have a fair chance.

Our Foundation Principles

To sum up again in few words, what are the great principles which God has called upon Christian Endeavorers to be faithful to, as judged by our history? They are
United public prayer and testimony;
United service for Christ and His church and our fellow men;
A united fellowship which is bounded by no rivers or oceans or custom-houses abroad, and by no small religious isms at home. In other words,
Christian testimony from every one; practical service by every one; Christian fellowship with every one.

These are vital Christian Endeavor principles, to which we believe God calls us to be faithful. Fellow Endeavorers, I have never asked you to be loyal to myself or to any form of words, but in this my last address as president of the United Society of Christian Endeavor I ask you to be true to the great ideals for which Christian Endeavor stands.

A Yearly Gain of Twenty-Five Per Cent

Let us strive for a definite percentage goal of steady increase and gain all along the loyalty line. Percentages are not everything, and sometimes they are misleading; but I know of no fairer way of promoting and testing real growth. If our societies and unions make a strong resolve at the beginning of this new biennium that, "trusting in the Lord Jesus Christ for strength, we will strive for a net gain of twenty-five per cent, not only in numbers, but in evidence of loyalty to our principles," how glorious would be the history of the next two years!

This campaign would require stock-taking at the beginning. I will suppose that your society to-day has thirty-two active and associate members, which is about the average number throughout the country. To make a *permanent net* gain of eight members in two years is certainly not too much to ask, but in the aggregate it would mean a gain of hundreds of thousands to the ranks of Christian Endeavor.

I would not advise a spasmodic "red-and-blue contest," with

a dinner to the winners, for the sake of mere numbers. Such contests sometimes bring in at the same time careless members and disaster to the societies. Steady and true is the best kind of gain.

If every average local union of a dozen societies should add above all losses three new societies to its roll-call, and keep them, it would mean thousands of new societies.

Steady and True

If every society should add during the biennium one-fourth more to its active participants in the meetings, one-fourth more to its Quiet Hour Comrades, one-fourth to its Tenth Legion of givers (*net gains* in every case), and so for all its activities, the aggregate of zeal, devotion, and service throughout the land would be enormous.

It would be a nation-wide revival of religion, accomplishing far more than many a widely advertised sensational revival. It would mean the steady advance of the kingdom of God in our hearts, in our societies, and in our churches.

The mere review of their present standing and activities, our religious stock-taking, would immensely quicken many of our societies. Some do not know whether they are losing or gaining, whether they are more or less true to the things for which Christian Endeavor stands. A business soon runs down that does not know its financial standing, that never takes stock of its resources, nor systematically endeavors to add to them. So will a society or church.

I Press On

Be willing to face the truth. Then set a definite goal of advance; and thus fidelity to Christian Endeavor principles will not be a mere empty sentiment, but a campaign of tremendous immediate results, and also of results which can be fully comprehended only in the far ages of eternity.

The other day I saw on Charles River Basin in Boston two racing shells practising for a great boat-race. Each of the stalwart contestants had his oar poised, waiting eagerly for the word of action. The coxswain took his place, and after some maneuvering he shouted: "Ready, all. Go!" Brothers, there is a great campaign before us, a campaign that will last, please God, for two full years, a campaign for greater fidelity to Christ and the church and to the principles of Christian Endeavor. Fellow Endeavorers, to you I shout: "Ready, all. Go!"

Allow me to suggest as one motto for our Fidelity Campaign, "I press on." It is St. Paul's own motto. "Forgetting the things which are behind, and stretching forward to the things which are before, *I press on* toward the goal," he said. These are strong and glorious words. Could we have a better motto?

Pressing on to greater fidelity, pressing on to a larger fellowship, pressing on to new victories in every line of Christian Endeavor, in the name of our Lord and Saviour Jesus Christ.

Then, each doing our best, we together will confidently pray, "Let the favor of the Lord our God be upon us, and establish thou the work of our hands upon us; yea, the work of our hands establish thou it."

$100,000 Fund

The nominating committee's recommendation to elect Dr. Clark as president emeritus of the United Society of Christian Endeavor was adopted with acclaim. At the same time it was announced that a $100,000 fund, to be known as the Dr. Francis E. Clark Recognition Fund, had been started, and this declaration was received with a perfect fury of applause and commendation.

Paul, and Others

General Secretary Gates did not make his report. Instead, he gave the credit to the workers in the field for the fine work done. He called Paul Brown to stand, and how the house applauded Paul and all the other field-secretaries as well, as they, too, were asked to rise and made their bow.

Prizes That Were and Were Not

It is impossible to reproduce in print the enthusiasm of the period given to the distribution of the various prizes for contests conducted during the year.

General Secretary Gates presented banners to the winning States in the registration campaign, but the list is too long to put into the record. A whole host of States had outdone themselves in this campaign, whose success meant much for the success of the Convention.

Mr. Vandersall distributed the prizes in the finance and Alumni campaign. The winning States are Florida, Louisiana, Pennsylvania, Massachusetts, New Hampshire, Washington, and Montana. These States met one hundred per cent of their financial quota to the United Society.

Mr. Vandersall also presented to Pennsylvania a beautiful loving-cup, which the union will hold for one year.

The prizes in *The Christian Endeavor World* subscription campaign were handed out by Mr. C. C. Hamilton. Eighty dollars went to Florida for having attained its goal first of all the States, and a second prize of $40 went to Alabama. To both of these States banners were also awarded, while recognition banners were given to New York, Kansas, Washington, Maryland, and Delaware. Prizes of banners were also given to Massachusetts, Indiana, Connecticut, Delaware, and Louisiana.

Editorial Secretary Anderson announced the publicity prizes and the army and navy prizes, and brought down the house when he declared that, while he had been asked to present the cash and other prizes, the prizes themselves had not been intrusted to him, probably because he was a Scotchman. The situation called forth a great deal of good-humored merriment, and was thoroughly enjoyed by everybody, and not least by Mr. Anderson himself. He announced the award of a loving-cup offered to the union which made the best showing during the year. The cup went to the Dallas, Tex., Christian Endeavor Union.

He also announced the award of army and navy prizes offered by the army and navy superintendent, Chaplain Ramsden. The first prize of $100 went to the California Christian Endeavor Union, while Pennsylvania won the second prize of $50, and New York State union the third prize of $25.

A COLORFUL PAGEANT
"If"—"Christ Exalted"

Miss Catherine A. Miller's beautiful Christian Endeavor pageant, "If," or "Christ Exalted," was presented under exceedingly adverse circumstances. There was no time for more than one rehearsal, obviously too little to produce a piece of finished work. A group of Maryland, Delaware, Massachusetts, and Ohio delegates took the parts on short notice, and did wonders with them. The dresses were wonderful and colorful. Evidently there were not men enough for the male parts, but the girls did nobly, even if their voices betrayed them. "Mary" especially put a bit of poignant realism into the scene when she passed across the stage "on the road from Golgotha," weeping and calling with moving realism, "My Son, my Son."

But honor should be given to all the young people who took part in these scenes. It is characteristic of Christian Endeavor that it attempts great things and does not even turn back from the impossible. The speakers did not mumble their words, but spoke out clearly; and if there was hesitation at times, and if the scenes moved a trifle slowly, this was overlooked in the light of the circumstances.

Some of the scenes were especially well staged and impressive, the children's scene, for example. Another scene deserves mention, the one in which was presented the organization of the first society. While this was going on in front, in an opening behind stood the Spirit of Christian Endeavor with Dr. Clark on one side and Mrs. Clark on the other, making a decidedly effective picture.

The pageant was reproduced under the direction of Miss Miller, the author, to whose indomitable energy its success must be ascribed. It will be available for societies and unions, and will certainly make a favorable impression wherever it is presented.

As the curtain rises, we are transported to the days of Jesus and are on the road to Jerusalem among a milling throng of picturesquely garbed Orientals. We see men, women, and children, and recognize in some of them typical Pharisees, who are talking with blind hatred in their hearts about Jesus, while the common people tell how He has helped and healed them.

The next scene takes us to the road from Golgotha. Jesus is dead, and we see His friends smitten with hopeless sorrow.

Then in an interlude we see symbolical characters, Doubt, Experience, Faith, Hope, Love, and the Spirit of Christian Endeavor.

The next scene shows us the parsonage of Williston Church, where the first Christian Endeavor society was formed. Familiar figures are now before us, Dr. Clark, the young minister, his wife, and a group of boys and girls.

The following scene shows a group going to a convention, and in the next episode we are "At the Crossroads," where we again meet symbolical figures and see the search for happiness and the temptations that come to youth.

In the following scenes the author has worked in the Junior society, the Intermediate and his joys, the consecration meeting, and a stirring epilogue that presents groups from all lands.

Yes, the pageant was a success. It presented in pictorial form something of what the society is and what it is trying to do.

Overflow Meetings

After Sunday was over and the sessions began to be held in the Auditorium, which seats 5,600, provision had to be made to take care of delegates who could not get a seat in the main hall, or who might be seated so far back that they could not hear the speakers. For them overflow meetings were prepared in the evenings. The principal speakers in the main hall were taken to the churches where the overflow was gathered, so that all might hear the principal addresses.

These meetings were not large, two or three hundred persons, but they took care of some who otherwise might have missed the inspiration of the Convention. They were held on three evenings only.

Broadcasting the Convention

The three great meetings in Multnomah Field and the meeting in the main auditorium on Monday night, when Dr. Clark delivered his last address as President of the United Society of Christian Endeavor, were broadcast free by the Portland Oregonian, one of the great newspapers of the West. This is only a part of the many courtesies received at the hands of the people and city of Portland.

THE FOURTH DAY

TUESDAY, JULY 7, 1925

The Day of the Parade

In spite of late hours in the evening and meetings at an early hour in the morning the main hall was filled, and the galleries partly filled, with a crowd that manifested sustained interest in a remarkable way, when the forenoon session opened on Tuesday morning.

The first speaker was Rev. J. Christie Wilson, missionary to Tabriz, Persia. He told of some of the things he saw when on his journey from Persia to the United States; the tomb of Queen Esther, for instance, and cuneiform inscriptions carved in rock that tell of the great deeds of King Darius of Bible times. Persia was once a great nation, but now it is a nation in great need.

The country is inhabited by three races, the Assyrians, the Armenians, and the Persians, who are Mohammedans. At the beginning of the war the Armenians took up arms on the side of the Allies. They fought the Turks, and were almost always victorious, until their provisions gave out, and they were driven from home and country, or shot down like dogs.

In spite of the fact that according to the law every Persian shall be killed if he becomes a Christian, Persian Mohammedans are everywhere turning to Christ, and churches have been formed among them. Christian Endeavor is also establishing itself in these Persian churches, and Mr. Wilson stated that they expect in time to form a Persian Christian Endeavor union and come into the great fellowship of the Christian Endeavor movement.

Mr. Wilson told of the poverty of the people and the hunger of the refugees. He described his attempt to reach a district where the people were dying of starvation. He tried to buy grain for the starving population, but no grain was to be had. He found some in Russia, however, and bought it, only to discover that it was against the law to export grain from that country. However, people were dying, and had to be fed, law or no law; and the grain was shipped across the border, a river, at night.

Mr. Wilson relieved the darkness of the picture by strokes of humor. The Kurds, he said, are fighters. They are never happier than when they are in a scrap. They are the Irishmen of the East. Speaking of them, one man remarked that it is time that somebody licked the whey out of the curds. Another story delighted the audience. It was of an Armenian girl who was immensely proud when she received some old new clothes from America. The clothes she received were a suit of men's underwear and a woman's blue georgette evening dress. The dress was cut low, but the underwear was not; and the combination produced an amazing effect.

Christian Endeavor is new in that part of Persia, and communications are difficult. But Mr. Wilson is enthusiastic about the prospects for Christian Endeavor in this ancient Bible land.

C. C. Hamilton, publication-manager, took the floor with a snappy talk on "You Ought to Know," when he showed some caps, books, banners, and so forth, and introduced a Christian Endeavor Bible—the first we have had in years—with articles by Dr. Clark, Dr. Wells, and Mr. Anderson. It is not generally known that Christian Endeavor has a full line of literature to meet the need of every society.

The big thing that Mr. Hamilton presented was the new Christian Endeavor Society Standards chart, which outlines a magnificent programme of Christian Endeavor work. Entirely new, too.*

Peace and the World Court

Rev. Robert P. Anderson, chairman of the resolutions committee, offered two resolutions which were unanimously adopted. The first was a peace resolution. It denounced the evils of war, which settles nothing it sets out to settle, and unsettles practically everything, and called on the Government of the United States to take whatever practical steps may be possible to bring about an international reduction of armaments, and by fair dealing, truth-speaking, and wise generosity remove much of the suspicion and misunderstanding that has often been the cause of war in the past.

The second resolution called for the establishment of an International Court of Justice based on the international acceptance of a code of laws, to which disputes between nations may be brought for fair and just settlement based on law. The world has no hope if the machinery of international justice cannot be set up in the earth.

Another fine talk, here condensed, was on

THE FELLOWSHIP OF CHRISTIAN ENDEAVOR
By E. W. Praetorius, General Secretary of the Evangelical League of Christian Endeavor

Fellowship is one of those fundamental words that are found in the Bible and in life. It implies association, co-operation, participation, comradeship, companionship, communion, conversation, friendship,

---
*See page 147 for an account of it.

love. It is based upon mutual trust, self-giving, and helpfulness.

It is no wonder that it is a fundamental word in Christian Endeavor, for Christian Endeavor concerns itself with the things of the Book, of life, and of helpfulness.

Fellowship has been the genius, spirit, and soul of Christian Endeavor because Christian Endeavor is essentially a Christian Youth Movement. Christian youth movements know no boundaries, castes, colors, sects, or racial distinctions, but are universal in possibility and intent. America has had her youth movement—a Christian Youth Movement beginning in 1881—it is the Young People's Society Movement.

Fellowship has been the history of Christian Endeavor from the day that saw the first society formed and has grown from the day that the second was organized until to-day when it has crossed the lives of every denomination, of every State and Province, and of every nation and race.

Fellowship will continue to be the story of Christian Endeavor, an ever-widening fellowship until all young Christian movements shall be embraced in her fellowship.

Fellowship has been and must continue to be one of the greatest contributions that Christian Endeavor makes to the kingdom of God, to the nations, and to the races. Born in a day when sectarian strife had rent and divided the church, and baptized in a day when the nations and races of the earth are torn by jealousies and hatreds, Christian Endeavor came and comes to build into a Christian brotherhood and unity of purpose and action the youthful forces of the Churches. This large fellowship is necessary to save denominationalism from the sense of smallness and detachment and to give to them the sense of being a vital part of the whole great, glorious army of the Christ.

To remain vital, the fellowship of Christian Endeavor must continue to build loyalties—loyalty to Jesus Christ and loyalty to Christ's Church in general and in particular as represented in the local Church.

CHRISTIAN ENDEAVOR TO-MORROW

The topic of Alvin J. Shartle's address was "Christian Endeavor To-morrow." His introduction was a spledid one—calling to the platform four Pima Indians of Arizona to whom he presented a beautiful Christian Endeavor banner. One of these men is the treasurer of the Arizona Christian Endeavor Union, clear evidence of the education and efficiency of our Indian brothers.

Mr. Shartle turned his topic into an acrostic, as follows:

*M*arvellous
*O*pportunities
*N*otwithstanding
*E*ndeavor
*Y*outh

He told how Christian Endeavor in the past has been supported largely by gifts from the publication department; but our needs are greater to-day, and larger funds are necessary to carry on the work. He urged individual contributions for Christian Endeavor, and explained various ways in which large gifts may be made without undue burdens on the giver. He explained what are called annuities or life-annuity bonds, by which the buyer of a bond receives interest on his bond as long as he lives, while the capital becomes the property of the United Society of Christian Endeavor on the death of the bondholder. Others insure their lives, paying the premiums, but making the United Society of Christian Endeavor the beneficiary when they die. Mr. Shartle has this work in charge, and will be glad to give full information as to how gifts may be made to Christian Endeavor by means of annuities, insurance, wills, or direct gifts.

THE ENDEAVOR PARADE
A Colorful Spectacle.—The Missouri Mule in Line.— Montana in a Baby-Buggy

Portland certainly kept her promise, and gave good weather to the delegates. We were told we should be cool and comfortable; and we were, even on the day of the parade, Tuesday, July 7, although the sun was hot at noontide. Nevertheless, it was an ideal day for a Christian Endeavor parade. The sun shone brightly on masses of brilliant color as the young people marched in step to the stirring strains of music and under the inspiration of their own singing.

Portland is used to conventions, and welcomes them. There is no rude staring at the stranger. Even the flashy dress of the paraders as they walked to the starting-place awoke no comment. Portlanders everywhere showed rare courtesy. To be recognized as a visitor was to be ensured of instant and willing service, not by fellow Endeavorers merely, but by all the citizens as well.

The order in which the various State delegations marched in the parade had significance. They marched in the order in which they had succeeded in attaining their assigned goal of registrations for the Convention. This is why Arizona, a small State so far as Christian Endeavor is concerned, led the van. She had first reached her quota of registrations.

But now down the sun-bathed street float the strains of music, and we know the parade is coming. Flags flutter all the way along, as far as one can see. These flags are part of the city's decorations in honor of Christian Endeavor.

They come! General Secretary Gates of the United Society of Christian Endeavor marched at the head of the procession, preceded only by half-a-dozen motorcycle policemen to clear the way.

Then came officials, Judge Jacob Kanzler, and the officers of the United Society of Christian Endeavor. The commanding figure of Mayor Baker of Portland, who is not afraid to identify himself with the Christian Endeavor cause, was in the foremost line. There were Boy Scouts, too, at the head of the procession, carrying the United States flag, and then the Elks' Band, which rendered excellent service.

The White Car

A beautiful white automobile with Dr. and Mrs. Clark came next in line, and they received a long-drawn-out ovation as spectators on the sidewalks recognized them. Half-a-dozen other automobiles followed with other members of the official party; and then came a group of girls, all in white, red, and blue sashes, from the District of Columbia.

When the parade reached the reviewing-stand, the mayor, Dr. and Mrs. Clark, the officers of the United Society, and the civic authorities took their places to watch the Endeavorers march past. It took exactly an hour and a quarter, quick marching, to pass a given point.

It was a great parade, probably numbering about five thousand. Practically every State in the Union was represented, and at least two foreign countries were in the march. The current talk of youth's decadence seems ridiculous in view of a parade like this. Here was an army, and a very attractive one, marshaling its hosts in an appeal for better citizenship and higher ideals and firmer Christian faith. One need not fear for the future of the country when it can muster such splendid, clear-eyed youth as this.

Arizona, having won the registration prize, was first in the march, carrying a banner reading, "Arizona Leads the Nation." The delegation made a pretty picture with the big straw hats with red balls hanging from the rims. A group of Pima Indians, accompanied by their missionary, Rev. Dirk Lay, D. D., marched with this delegation.

Oklahoma, having won second place in the registration contest, came next in line, all in white, with red sashes and white umbrellas. Harold Singer, their field-secretary, led the procession, carrying a banner.

Utah, having won the third banner, came next with feathered hats and carrying a banner that read, "Utah Is Not All Mormon."

A great host of Endeavorers from Pennsylvania, all of them in white, and wearing white caps with red borders, came next in line, marching splendidly and singing lustily.

The large delegation from Massachusetts wore red middies with white trimmings, white bands on the head, with red and white feathers. An interesting touch was Priscilla and John Alden at the head of the procession, interesting, too, from the fact that those taking these parts were Mr. and Mrs. Edwin Wells, who were on their honeymoon trip.

Following Maine came Missouri with a Missouri mule and three horses. The Missouri delegates wore white hats and blue ties, and formed a picturesque group.

Maryland and Delaware marched together, more than sixty delegates, who made a fine impression with their Mephistopheles cloaks slung over one shoulder, and wearing red-and-white caps with the names of the States in silver on them.

The parade was arranged in divisions. Following a band, Ohio led the second division, a great host of young people with red bellhop hats, the slogan emblazoned on their banner being, "Bring the World to Ohio, Cleveland, 1927." With the delegation was an automobile carrying an immense football with the map of the world painted on it. Working out the idea of bringing the world to Ohio, some of the delegates were garbed in the national dress of different nations.

After Ohio came Idaho with red caps, and after them Washington and northern Idaho. The leader of this delegation had a piercing whistle, with which he marked time. This was one of the largest delegations, all of them in yellow and wearing golden-brown overseas caps. There were delegates from every district in the State, and there was a delegation of Juniors that brought up the rear.

A Boy Scout and soldier marshal led the next division with California in the van. Field-Secretary Allan marched in front of a magnificent delegation wearing purple and gold caps, and sashes of the same color. One striking fact about this delegation was the large number of men that were in it.

Wisconsin came next, the leader carrying a banner with the name of the State on it. The members of the delegation had red bands around the brow, with red feathers in their hair.

Dixie marched next with the Juniors in front and Southern Secretary Evans in the front row. They carried red umbrellas, and wore white dresses with their characteristic red fezes. This great delegation marched in perfect order, and won more than a little admiration as they passed.

"Columbia, S. C., the Golden Rule City of America," were the words printed on a large sign carried by half a dozen delegates from the State. The sign was too broad to be carried straight across the street, and was broken in the centre so that it came forward in the centre like the prow of a ship.

The Texas delegation made a splendid impression as they marched past, their field-secretary in front, carrying white umbrellas with the Christian Endeavor monogram on them.

A division of Boy Scouts carrying a United States flag led the Connecticut delegation, along with Field-Secretary Hicks. This delegation wore blue-and-white sailor hats, and the delegates were linked together with colored streamers.

The New York State delegation wore gold bands and imposing purple capes. In the midst of them in an automobile stood a living Statue of Liberty.

A good-sized delegation from New Jersey wore orange-and-black caps and long capes. They carried on their banners the slogan, "We Invite You to Atlantic City in 1927." The last group in this division consisted of delegates from Canada, who made an excellent impression with maple-leaves pinned to the dresses.

A soldier marshal again led the next division, accompanied by Boy Scouts carrying the flag. The De Molay Band headed the group. The first State to march in this division was Illinois, the leader of which twirled his marshal's staff with extraordinary dexterity. The members wore white pie-plates with "Illinois Christian Endeavor" on them in red as part of the head-dress, and some of the girls had formed an orchestra playing toy instruments.

Indiana with red hats next appeared in line, and behind them an immense crowd of Iowa delegates with sailor caps in red, and wearing red blouses and white trousers or dresses. The Iowa group never fails to make an impression in a parade.

Nebraska delegates wore red caps and capes, sashes and bandanna handkerchiefs, while Kansas, next in line, wore red-and-white sashes.

Then came Wyoming, Colorado, and Michigan, the latter delegation wearing rubber caps and red-and-white overblouses, and carrying toy balloons. The Minnesota delegates wore large farm hats with yellow bands, and made a striking appearance.

Montana is one of the youngest Christian Endeavor unions in the country, and this fact was brought out by a boy marching in front of the delegation pulling a small express-wagon in which a little girl was seated. A banner announced the fact that this was the Montana union, two years old. After them came North Dakota wearing sashes and carrying sticks with roses entwined around them.

The last group in the parade was naturally Oregon. The great army of Oregon Endeavorers wore yellow and white caps, and carried banners telling of various things that the State has done. One group lustily sang a ditty to the tune of "Clementine," and a large placard told of one girl that had driven her car 4,500 miles in Christian Endeavor work. In this delegation was a large group of Finnish Endeavorers resident in the State. A picturesque touch was a covered wagon, suggesting the early days of Oregon, and a young man marched in Indian dress. The Intermediates of Portland were present in large numbers wearing caps of green made in the shape of large flowers. There was a large delegation of African Methodist Allen Christian Endeavor leaguers present, and a tiny automobile brought up the rear.

Prizes had been offered to the delegations that made the best showing. It was difficult for the judges to decide which delegations were the best, all of them having reached a high standard. However, the first prize was given to Ohio, the second to Dixie, and the third to Iowa.

Cleveland Wins the Next Convention

At the Tuesday afternoon meeting of the Trustees of the United Society, it was voted that the International Convention of 1927 be held in Cleveland, Ohio. Atlantic City put in a strong claim, but Cleveland won out.

Trustees Make Pledges

There followed a period for the consideration of raising the budget for Christian Endeavor work. Dr. Poling started the ball rolling by telling what his church and he himself are doing and purpose to do, which was promptly followed by Dr. Foulkes, who pledged himself to match the giving of Dr. Poling's church; and Mr. John T. Sproull promised to match that too. Others of the trustees made pledges of similar import, the significance of which does not lie so much in the amounts pledged as in the fact that the trustees are increasingly feeling their responsibility to support Christian Endeavor, and with increasing and joyous liberality are giving to this cause. The trustees surely appreciated the situation when, as Dr. Clark himself promised to give $250 a year for the next two years, Mrs. Clark added, "I think I can manage to save $50 more, so as to make it $300." Which is, after all, a very good way to show what one thinks of Christian Endeavor.

FORWARD, MARCH!
The Sparkling Wit of Landrith

The fact that a great host of Endeavorers were at the Alumni banquet in the Multnomah Hotel seemed to make no difference at all in the mass-meeting in the main hall on Tuesday evening. The hall was packed with a glorious and happy company of youth. After the period of song led by Percy Foster the people were in the right spirit to absorb the addresses to be delivered later, and they were also in the mood to hear the report of the judges who had been appointed to award prizes to the States that had the best delegations in the afternoon parade. The announcement that Ohio had won first prize brought a great salvo of applause, as did also the announcement that Dixie had won the second prize and Iowa the third.

The air was tense with expectation to hear the result of the vote as to which city should get the 1927 Convention. Like a spring released came the applause when General Secretary Gates declared that the International Christian Endeavor Convention in 1927 would be held in the city of Cleveland, O. Of course the Ohio delegation broke into song, "We're from Ohio"; and then Mr. George C. Southwell, leader of the Ohio delegation, gave warm credit to the sportsmanship of New Jersey in generously proposing to make the Cleveland motion unanimous. "If I had a hat on," he said, "I'd take it off to them." For New Jersey had promised to accept loyally the decision of the trustees to go to Cleveland for the next Convention.

Dr. Ira Landrith, extension secretary of the United Society of Christian Endeavor, was the first speaker, his topic being "A Life or a Livelihood: Which?"

Big and commanding of presence, calm, self-controlled, and abundantly adequate, Dr. Landrith spoke with easy deliberation and with his usual eloquence and force. He has few peers on the platform and none in his own style. The strength of his addresses lies in a peculiarly delightful commingling of wit and wisdom; his aim, of course, is to impart wisdom. To use a radio expression, his wit is the carrier wave.

Dr. Landrith's address follows:

A LIFE OR A LIVELIHOOD—WHICH?

By Ira Landrith, D. D., Extension Secretary of the United Society of Christian Endeavor

"He who would hoard his wealth like the man that would save his life, will lose it, in the death chamber, if not sooner. This is no communistic arraignment of honorable wealth or honest money getting. He who does that is either a fool or a fraud. Why praise a gift for music or poetry or oratory, and condemn a native capacity for successful business? He who buries a money-earning talent when he might use it for the glory of the Lord, is as reprehensible as would be the youth who, divinely called upon to preach, disobediently elects instead to become a bank teller or a wild-cat oil discoverer. Nor does this mean that either of these avocations is inherently wrong, or that any legitimate business, however prosperous, renders impossible, though it often does make difficult, the greatest business in the world, the making of a life. What incomparable opportunity great wealth offers for true life-making, not to the possessor only, but to the multitude of others, living and yet to be. He who gives to deserving causes contributes to his own immortality; literally he lays up treasures in heaven.

"'I wish,' plaintively cried an Eastern philanthropist to me the other day—'I wish I had given all my money away, for what I did give is all I now have,' and there was humble pride in his voice as we stood together about the college he had helped, the church he had chiefly erected, and in the midst of the city he had richly befriended.

"That greatest orgy of murder since the morning stars sang together, that yet incomprehensible earthquake of international butchery, that terrible tidal wave of blood and bestial fury, which in horrified whispers and with bated breath, we call the World War, was ended alone by appeal to soldierly unselfishness, an idealistic, manse-trained President's petition that all generations might be free and safe in self-determining governments. War is all Sherman called it, and we must henceforth find a better way, but try as they may, greed and blind partisanship can never erase America's altruism from this unspeakable war, and they shall not pollute with unhallowed feet the graves of our heroes over-seas while they shout the devilish heresy, 'These dead have died in vain.' No unselfish servant of God and others ever died in vain. These died for their country that many times more might live better lives in better countries. Yours is the task tremendous of seeing to it that they shall not have died in vain; and this you can do alone by

The Massachusetts Court of State Presidents Johnson and Mr. and Mrs. Edwin Webb, costumed as Priscilla and John Alden, are standing together in the front row

interpreting your education in the terms of a life rather than a livelihood.

"Verily, no day in world history was so good as this day. Doubt that and you enthrone Satan over the Kingdom of Christ. Doubt that and you make the Lord's prayer a divinely taught petition for the unattainable, and the church an institution which belies Him who is pledged that the gates of hell shall not prevail against it. Doubt that and every drop of victorious blood will have been criminally wasted from Calvary and down to this sacrificial hour.

"In one of those Main Streets so prolifically spawned across the map of the United States, where everybody lives in a show window and unwillingly broadcasts his most secret and sacred meditations; where even domestic privacy is but an ancient tradition—there live three people, all college graduates, by the way who are more than normally surrounded by other titulary burden-bearers of degrees that are either cherished acquisitions or gratefully accepted, mayhap sought gratuities.

"One of them knows all about his neighbors, and shares everything he knows, or thinks he knows, adding for good measure, pressed down and running over, whatever he imagines about them, their conversation, their conduct, their motives, which only God knows enough to judge. He is a very busy man who would be less harmful and despicable if he had not gone to college. Had he lived in an earlier era, probably he would have been acquainted with the ardor-dampening, scandal-monger-cooling ducking-stool. Why not now? Why hang murderers and provide no capital punishment for slanderers? He makes a poor livelihood and a complete mess of life.

"Another of these educated Main Street dwellers is a heresy hunter, who devotes an otherwise all-but-fruitless ministry to seeing to it that nobody in the town wears anything more attractive to unsaved youth than the baggy, ostentatiously darned, age-old, and faded garments of primitive theology. His is not necessary orthodoxy of life, but the most exact terminology of medieval credalism. In spite of all this he ekes out a poor livelihood and crushes out a worse life. Youth flees his fanaticism, rejecting even the truth that mingles with the errors of his faith.

"In that same village a profound scholar pursues his unobtrusive study of blind fish, concerning whose origin, development, habitat, and varieties he is said to be the world's leading authority. He has written immense illustrated theses, and printed heavy tomes about blind fish. The village gossip sneers at him and prattles against him, but the professor goes on angling for new species of blind fish, answering back no self-defensive word, sure the while that at least blind fish will know enough to attend to their own business. The militant contender for the faith, long since crystallized in himself, is sorely harrassed, too, by this original investigator of eyeless piscatorial cave-dwellers. He is probably already beginning to wonder, this heresy hunter, if the scientific student of the erratic ways of blind fish should not be either ecclesiastically excised or required to renew his early church vows. Meanwhile, the professor reverently goes right on making a life, a pioneer light-bearer to rayless waters, letting his livelihood take care of itself.

"Which several near-fables teach that religious education should not only show us how to think, but how to quit thinking in chains. No man who dresses his mind in second-hand clothes, and subjects all his mental processes to straight-jacket conventionality, ever discovered a truth or a continent, invented a kite or a flying machine, emancipated a galley slave or a generation. The line of least resistance leads from ease to cowardice by way of uselessness, but it is a very broad way and many indolent and afraid there be that walk therein. The benefactors of mankind have dared to do their own thinking, allowing other minds to help, with no dogmatist to hinder them. When they found a dim path they made it into a highway and went right on road-building even after the path disappeared. God loves the pioneers; it is only some of his misguided followers who take panic when ox-carts are crowded out into mudholes where they are most efficient, by distance-spurning, time-annihilating automobiles. Add something if you can to the sum of world comfort, helpfulness, and knowledge. If you cannot, be big enough in a lessening world to accept gratefully what the more gifted, daring, and industrious are contributing. God is no enemy of progress. Who made man's mind? Who but God may limit its achievements? Ever since the tower of Babel, the idolaters of things as they have been vainly praying for a new confusion of tongues. The answer will never come, no matter what towers are builded, nor how high, so long as the builders do not try to usurp the divine prorogatives nor crowd God from the throne, as, alas! the clamorers against progress are constantly doing to the hurt alone of their own babblings.

"Know what to think and think it, whether or not anybody else ever before thought it. Live your own life even if it does reduce your livelihood. Do not be a freak for the sake of freakishness; a heretic for the sake of notoriety; but do not be so afraid of sincerity and individuality that you will paralyze your usefulness by imitation. What *is* does not need always *to be*. The good is never sacred if it is enemy to the best. Popularity is desirable, but it is never necessary, and it should be sacrificed ruthlessly on the altar of duty whenever the Phoenix, that arises from its ashes, is likely to be the public weal. John Greenleaf Whittier once sagely wrote a young friend, 'Attach yourself while you are young to some great cause and you will grow to victory and greatness with it.' The men and women of all the generations who have made lives, and not merely livings, believe every word of wise counsel.

"In all this, I have said no pedantic, sermonic, nor paternalistic word about callings and avocations and the clanking machinery of life for any of you Christian Endeavorers. Where you labor, or how, or in what, is your business and God's, not mine. I might suggest that whatever your work is, pegging shoes or making tents, it should all be done so earnestly as is implied by Charles H. Spurgeon's sublime, if doggeral, life motto—

"'If I were a cobbler I'd make it my pride
The best of all cobblers to be,
If I were a tinker no tinker beside
Should mend an old kettle like me.'"

After some songs by the chorus came a strong address on

The Evangelism of Jesus

Rev. J. Whitcomb Brougher, D. D., pastor of the Baptist Temple, Los Angeles, Cal., is a name to conjure with on the Pacific coast. He is both able and eloquent, and he possesses the gift of quickly getting a grip on his audience. Racy anecdotes flow from his lips with ease and aptness.

The topic Dr. Brougher dealt with in the Tuesday evening meeting was "Evangelism," and he started with the evangelism of Jesus.

Jesus had the secret of success, he said. Sometimes we find books on finding the key to success; but when we look up the authors, we discover that if they have the key to success they have never found the keyhole.

Jesus is our *example* in all the relations of life. He has the key to success. It is said that the Japanese are efficient because they *adopt* the best things in other nations, then *adapt* them to their needs, and by practice they become *adepts* in the use of them. This is what we must do with Christ—adopt His way of life and apply it patiently to our daily problems.

"*Education*" was another word the speaker used. He argued that education does not really change human nature. It cannot. A circus woman had a tame panther, and used to walk down the street with the animal on a leash. Some girls, remarked Dr. Brougher, will walk with anything. One day, in the tent, an ostrich put its head out to look at the panther, when suddenly the panther leaped, and bit off the head of the ostrich. Its nature was not changed by education. The savage nature only slumbered within, and only a very little was needed to call the brute to life.

Dr. Brougher made a passionate appeal for a new birth through Christ Jesus and for personal dedication to soul-winning. This must be our purpose. If a salesman does not find new customers, how long will he hold his job? Of what use are we to the Kingdom? Are we bringing others in?

Dr. Brougher, like Dr. Landrith, can be witty; and there were many happy sallies. "I was brought up on a farm where my father used a thrashing-machine," he said; then in an aside, "Not the kind that are used nowadays. I worked on the farm, and tended mules, and got my training to be pastor of a big church."

He gave us also the secret of his method. When his little girl was sick and would not eat solid food, he played a game with her to make her eat. He told her that her mouth was a railroad station, the spoon was the train, and the food was the passengers, and Dr. Brougher said, "Choo-choo," and got the child to open her mouth, the imaginary railroad station, and let in the train and passengers. Men and women are like the child. Truth must be coaxed into them. So Dr. Brougher's humor has a purpose. It is the game of a choo-choo train intended to get the people to take divine nourishment.

Dr. Brougher's sermons are not entirely made up of witticisms. There is but a short step between laughter and tears, and Dr. Brougher can easily turn from smile to seriousness, as he did at the close of this address, when he told the story of a modern prodigal son.

The Convention adopted a resolution in favor of strict law-enforcement, and as a closing number listened to a quartette singing "Old Black Joe" while a series of beautiful Western mountain scenes were projected on the screen.

Alumni Banquet Hilarity

Seven hundred echoing State songs and yells at the tables in

Assembly Hall of Multnomah Hotel, gay with flags, Christian Endeavor monograms, roses, colorful State caps and regalia—it certainly was an eyeful, earful, to say nothing of mouthfuls. This was the Alumni Banquet held Tuesday evening at the same time as the general session in the main auditorium.

Then that delicious tingle of mystery when the State field-secretaries were asked to step outside. While it simmered, yells and songs ran:

> Two, four, six, eight;
> Whom do we appreciate?
> Dr. Cla-a-a-rk!

And:

> We love you, Dr. Clark.
> We love you every morning;
> We love you every night;
> We love you every minute—
> You're all right!

Toastmaster Poling made two thrilling announcements: the 1927 Convention was Cleveland's.

> Cleveland will be heaven
> In nineteen twenty-seven,

sang Ohio. George Southwell ejaculated "Amen!" and presented a check for $400, completing Cleveland's $1,000 Alumni pledge. And Ohio won first honors in the parade; Dixie, second; Iowa, third.

Mr. John T. Sproull, seventeen years New Jersey's president, closed his response to the toast "East and West" by leading in "Blest be the tie"; and Jersey's sixty, who had worked for Atlantic City, sporting losers, sang lustily.

Judge Jacob Kanzler, Convention committee chairman (brand-new trustee at large), responding to "Many Years," told how he had found his wife in Christian Endeavor, had drifted away, was glad to get back, and proposed organizing the two thousand Portland workers for the Convention into an Alumni association.

Dr. Tenny, treasurer of the Japan Christian Endeavor Union, appealed to Endeavorers to make Christianity ring so true internationally that no other young Japanese, like him who committed suicide on the steps of the United States legation in protest against our exclusion law, would have to say: "I thought Christianity meant brotherhood. I was mistaken; I am disappointed."

Treasurer Alvin J. Shartle reported that a lady had said: "You made a five-hundred-dollar speech this morning. I am going to buy an annuity bond for that sum."

Alumni Superintendent Vandersall boosted future Convention attendance by calling on Miss Clara Dohme of Baltimore to stand while he exhibited a score or more of badges she had accumulated at as many International Conventions as an unofficial delegate.

Intensely interesting were the presentations by President Poling of the daughter of his first Oregon school principal, Mrs. Mabel Baker Maybell, who sang a group of delightful songs; also "my blessed mother," who rose by the side of her honored son.

Then the mystery of the field-secretaries' disappearance was solved. The twenty-one, led by Secretary Freet of Ohio, made a big hit as song entertainers.

Mrs. Clark was introduced for experiences "Under Many Flags." Lifted to a chair, she announced that she intended taking the veil of "The Silent Sisters"; but her laughable reminiscences of travel in Chinese wheelbarrows, and of customs officials who made her own her age, made all wish she might revoke the cruel decision.

Mr. Fred L. Ball of Cleveland, under the head "Now for the Future," proposed chartering a ship to take a thousand "Yanks" to London. He announced that Cleveland has five thousand advance registrations, with hope of twenty thousand.

Mr. James Kelly was so pleased with the Alumni spirit that he invited these "antediluvians" and "relics" to invade London in 1926.

The appeal for the biennial budget was made by Dr. William Hiram Foulkes, who headed the raising of so many millions in the Presbyterian New Era Movement. One could understand how he succeeded so phenomenally.

The climax of this evening of dramatic climaxes was the farewell of Christian Endeavor's beloved leader for forty-four years. Here, as all through the Convention, he was greeted with prolonged and affectionate applause. Hearts swelled with tenderness; eyes moistened; words could give no picture of the deep abounding love for him. This richest feast could not be printed on the slab of Oregon fir that served as a unique menu-card. There never was an Alumni banquet just like it; there never will be another.

Open-Air Evangelism

On several days during the Convention Christian Endeavor carried its message to the people of Portland, on Monday, for example, in three great street meetings conducted on prominent corners in the City of Roses.

The Dixie delegation, with young people from eleven Southern States, held a meeting at Festival Centre. The meeting was conducted by Rev. R. F. Kirkpatrick, D. D., chairman of the All-South Christian Endeavor Extension Committee.

At Plaza Block the meeting was led by Harry Allan of San Francisco, field-secretary for California, and a group of enthusiastic California Christian Endeavorers. This was the largest of the three meetings held, and a fervent evangelistic spirit permeated it. Evangelism is characteristic of Christian Endeavor in California.

Texas, Oklahoma, and Arizona delegates were led by Harold Singer of Oklahoma City, field-secretary of the Oklahoma Christian Endeavor Union, one of the most interesting speakers of the Convention. Prominent among those participating were a group of Pima Indians of Arizona.

These street meetings, conducted as a part of the Christian Endeavor Convention, are a valuable feature in the International Christian Endeavor meetings, and in recent years as a result of the very successful meetings of this type conducted for many years as a part of the State Christian Endeavor conventions in California and the All-South Christian Endeavor conventions among the Dixie States.

The Field-Secretaries' Meeting

The Christian Endeavor field-secretaries in their meeting decided to hold their annual mid-winter conference in Boston, Mass., from December 9 to 12. The gathering will be followed with a pilgrimage on December 13 to Williston Church, Portland, Me., the birthplace of Christian Endeavor.

General Secretary Gates of the United Society of Christian Endeavor addressed the field-workers on the new programme.

Dr. Poling addressed the gathering on several subjects of general interest to the field-force.

THE FIFTH DAY

WEDNESDAY, JULY 8, 1925

INTERMEDIATES HAVE THEIR DAY

They Show Their Powers of Oratory

With his usual vivacity Percy Foster conducted the song service preceding the forenoon session on Wednesday, when the Intermediates had their day. The hall was full and the colored caps of both women and men gave the meeting an exotic appearance, like an Oriental flower-garden. On the platform sat the Intermediate orchestra of 125 pieces (when all were present) under the splendid leadership of Mr. William M. Schunke and Mrs. J. Hunter Wells, Intermediate chairman. The members of the orchestra were recruited from the societies of the city of Portland. The orchestra was started originally as an Intermediate orchestra, but the work done proved so excellent that it was appointed to be "Convention orchestra." And, indeed, the orchestra deserved this distinction, for its performance compared favorably with that of many professional groups. It played with feeling and understanding, and showed what young people are capable of under proper leadership.

The Convention adopted at the opening of this meeting resolutions on world fellowship, interdenominational fellowship, and the family altar, urging a forward movement along all lines.

A Feast of Oratory

The big feature of the session was the national Intermediate Christian Endeavor oratorical contest, so far as we know the first of its kind at an International Christian Endeavor Convention. Four States entered the race, Oregon, Washington, Idaho, and California. These States had had local-union contests, leading up to a State contest, the winner of the State contest being selected for the honor of representing the State at the national contest in the Convention.

The participants were all typical Intermediates in their teens, bright, clean-cut young people, representative of the best in our nation. They made a beautiful picture for any one with imagination as they sat on the platform. Before they began their speeches Mr. Gates introduced Mrs. Wells, head of the Intermediate department at the Convention, and Margery Young, an Intermediate from Hollywood, Cal., who sang beautifully some typical Intermediate Christian Endeavor songs set to popular tunes.

Oregon Begins

The subject of the orations was "The Value of Intermediate Christian Endeavor," and Miss Lois Tuttle of Oregon was first called upon. She began in a clear, carrying voice by saying that Intermediate Christian Endeavor renders to its members two great services, worship and service. She told of a dying boy who asked his father to pray for him, and the father could not. Miss Tuttle made a keen and clear application of her point, which was that Christian Endeavor helps us to meet the crises of life.

The speaker dwelt with enthusiasm and grace on worship, or the relation of man to God, and on service, the relation of man to man. Intermediate Christian Endeavor is an artist that paints a beautiful picture of what Intermediates may become. In the fluid age it molds us for the best. The speech was delivered with ease and confidence, and the illustrations Miss Tuttle used were always to the point. It was a splendid speech, demonstrating the wonderful ability that Intermediates possess.

Washington Tries

Miss Estelle Baldwin, representing the State of Washington, was the next speaker. Miss Baldwin is a real Intermediate in appearance, just the kind of girl whom foolish people blame for being interested only in jazz. She also spoke with ease and simplicity, and with real seriousness. The basis of her talk was the Christian Endeavor principles of Christian Endeavor as enunciated by Dr. F. B. Meyer of London. After describing these principles she told of the things that Christian Endeavor does for Intermediates, placing especial emphasis on the spiritual values in the movement.

Christian Endeavor has educational value, she pointed out, and also social value, providing clean recreation for young people. Her talk was direct and to the point, short, plain, and decidedly pithy.

Idaho Takes the Floor

Next came David Taylor, the only boy in the contest, speaking for Idaho. The motto of Intermediate Christian Endeavor, he said, is, "Put Christ first," and the value of the society to the individual depends on the extent to which the Intermediate gives himself to the work. He illustrated his point by telling of a boy who was so timid that he never dared to open his mouth in public until one day a discussion in the society arose, which interested him so that he could not remain silent. He spoke, and the barrier of timidity melted away. Mr. Taylor told effectively of the training received in Intermediate societies, training in speaking, in executive work, in finance, in co-operation, and so on. It was a well-delivered, eloquent speech.

Golden California

Next on the programme was Irene Reynolds of California, another typical Intermediate in the midst of her teens. In a few brief words she sketched the beginnings of Christian Endeavor, and went on to describe the ideals of the pledge. The society is of value because it is so great a teacher, she said, and outlined the ways in which its teaching comes to us. She indicated that she knew that there is a difference between Intermediates, that to some the spiritual makes a strong appeal, but that the social ideal is the thing that reaches others. "The Christian Endeavor social is very important," she said, "for some of us can be reached only in that way." She told of the work done in her own society, of the organization of an orchestra, of participation in many benevolences, sending candy to prisoners in State prison, and she mentioned one touching feature, the bringing of some of the old men from the county home to attend the church services.

Miss Reynolds made a gripping speech, concluding with the well-known poem, "Somebody said it couldn't be done," a real Intermediate poem, spoken in real Intermediate style that brought a mighty burst of applause.

The ease with which these young people spoke was a revelation to many. Not only so, the talks revealed a multitude of ways in which Intermediates are not only willing, but are really able, to do a surprising amount of religious work. If any believed that Intermediates are light-minded to-day, this meeting would have disillusioned them. The talks showed an understanding truly astounding and an ability that captured the audience.

Paul Speaks

While the judges were at their task of deciding which of the four contestants was the winner, Paul C. Brown delivered a telling address on "The Value of Christian Endeavor." In fact, his address was made before he began, for these four splendid speeches by Intermediates were an irrefutable demonstration of the value of Christian Endeavor. Which one wins the prize is immaterial, he said; the great thing is that these four teen-age speakers have had a wonderful opportunity to "sell" Intermediate Christian Endeavor to the audience.

What can Intermediates do? In a little town there was a church that needed an Intermediate society, but did not know it. The church people did not think that there were enough boys and girls in the place to make a society. Yet a year or two later the Intermediate society from this church was the biggest and most enthusiastic society at the local convention. When the president was asked how it was done, she replied, "Oh, we just went out and got them."

Mr. Brown made a winning and convincing plea for the Intermediate society, which gives absolutely essential training in a period when training is not only needed, but is most effectual.

"Shame on you, Life-Work Recruits," he cried, "if your vision is so filled with India, Africa, China, or other distant lands, that you cannot see the Intermediates and opportunities at your very doors." His talk was a challenge. He aimed at results. He sought to inspire his audience to do something to give the Intermediates a chance. On his call a large number of Intermediate superintendents rose to their feet. But he wanted others to decide to go back home and organize Intermediate societies or help Intermediate work in some way, perhaps set in motion the wheels or give the encouragement that will result in the forming of Intermediate societies. Many rose to his appeal, mostly young people fired with a fine enthusiasm to do something in the field at their own doors.

The Judgment

There was tense interest in the minds of the audience when the judges, Mr. A. J. Shartle, Mr. Roy Breg, and Miss Catherine Miller, delivered to Mr. Gates their decision. The judgment was to be based on English, delivery, subject-matter, and general presentation. The contest was manifestly so evenly balanced that most of the onlookers were glad that they did not need to decide which speaker was best, and many felt that, no matter which way the decision went, all four Intermediates had done noble work. The first prize was a gold medal; the second, a silver medal; and Mr. Gates announced that gold Christian Endeavor pins would in any case be given to the two contestants who could not get medals.

The first prize was awarded to Miss Irene Reynolds of California, and the second to Lois Tuttle of Oregon.

A helpful devotional meditation by Dr. William Hiram Foulkes closed a most unusual meeting.

Trustees Once More

The trustees met on Wednesday afternoon to hear the reports of officers and conduct some business.

Mr. Charles F. Evans, Southern secretary, gave a most encouraging report of the work in Dixie. It means not a little to say that Dixie has now the best set of State officers that she has ever had. It was a pleasure also to learn that one lady from Columbia, S. C., was in the Convention as a guest of the Near East Relief as a result of the fine work done by Columbia and the Endeavorers of the State for Golden Rule Sunday. Another sign of Dixie's interest is the fact that 121 Endeavorers from

Dixie were in the Portland Convention. This is the first time in the history of Dixie that she has had a special train to carry Endeavorers to a convention. Dixie is now training leaders, and there is growing up a spirit of co-operation which will result in Dixie's being developed as a unit.

Extension-Secretary Landrith told briefly of the work he had done in the Fifty-fifty campaign and in visiting various conventions.

Publication-Manager Hamilton made his first report to the board of trustees after eight months of service in his new position. It was a report that told of readjustment and of plans for the future as well as of new publication work done in the past months.

Alumni Secretary Vandersall gave a glowing account of his work and its possibilities.

Paul Brown, Pacific coast secretary, was happy in telling of the work on the coast, which is progressing in every way. Great blessing is coming out of this Convention. The young people of the Northwest are getting a new thrill. The work in this great territory, which they will do when they get back home, will abundantly justify every bit of effort that has been put into this Convention. Think of Montana, where two years ago there was no organization whatever! But her twenty-five delegates to the Convention, when they go back home, will be a centre of energy in the State, and their efforts will give a great lift to the movement.

Dr. Clark $100,000 Recognition Fund

The trustees and field-secretaries of the United Society at an informal dinner effected an organization to turn into cash the idea of a one-hundred-thousand-dollar recognition fund for Dr. Clark. They appointed a committee to consider carefully and prayerfully plans to secure this amount as soon as possible. The members of this committee are Fred L. Ball, chairman; Charles Baumgart, John T. Sproull, Miss G. Stephen, Carlton M. Sherwood, W. G. Hoopes, and Rev. Stanley Addison. Dr Poling, as president of the United Society, and Dr. William Hiram Foulkes, as chairman of the finance committee, will be members of the committee, *ex officiis*.

The First Check

The first check for the $100,000 fund came from a totally unexpected source. The president of the Multnomah Hotel Company, Eric Y. Hauser, called on Dr. Poling in his room, and in the course of conversation remarked upon the high quality of the delegations that were living in the hotel, "the finest delegations that have ever lived in the Multnomah." He spoke of the esteem and reverence in which the people of Portland held

Dr. Clark, and added, "I'd like myself to do a little something to help the cause of Christian Endeavor." Dr. Poling told him of the new $100,000 fund, and Mr. Hauser said: "That's it. I cannot do an awful lot, but I want to do something"; and he wrote out a check for $200 on the spot, becoming the first actual contributor to the fund. So Portland scored again without intending it.

Denominational Rallies

In the afternoon many denominational rallies were held where the programmes of young people's work for the coming year were presented and inspirational addresses were delivered.

A LOYAL HOUSE
A Message from President Coolidge

The theme of the Wednesday-evening meeting in the main auditorium was illustrated in the meeting itself. The theme was "Loyalty," and in loyalty a mighty host had assembled for the occasion. The singing doubtless had something to do with it. Young people enjoy singing, and under so wonderful a songleader as Percy Foster singing becomes a perfect delight.

No convention has ever had more faithful audiences. The Portland people and the thousands of visiting Endeavorers have been inspired in these meetings. They have been getting a new thrill. These young people have seen good conventions, but never anything like this. It is an absolutely new experience, and what it will mean for the future only God knows, but it will mean much. It will remain a sweet memory for half a century and more. It will start many on the higher life. It will lead many to the Saviour. It will lead thousands into new ways of service. Some of us have been in convention work for many years, but even we get the thrill of these meetings and of this meeting in particular.

President Coolidge Speaks

Dr. Clark opened the meeting with a new gavel, made of California wood, the gift of Mr. William Jenkins of Oakland, Cal., a loyal old-time Endeavorer. It will be treasured at headquarters in Boston as a memento of our Convention.

Every convention has its surprises, little touches that prove deeply impressive. Something of this nature occurred when Dr. Clark called on the congregation to rise and listen to a message from the President of the United States. President Coolidge wrote:

"The biennial and International Convention of the United Society of Christian Endeavor, at Portland, Or., to which you have so graciously invited my attention and interest, will be, of course, one of the notable gatherings of the year. I am sorry that it is impossible for me personally to participate, but I gladly embrace the opportunity which your invitation affords to assure you of my hearty and approving interest in the splendid purposes of this great international body of Christian workers. To you, as its founder and leader, I know the occasion will be one of especial gratification, and I express to both you and the delegates who will gather at Portland my felicitations and heartiest wishes for the continued expansion of the organization and the increase of its usefulness."

Dr. John F. Cowan, D. D., former associate editor of *The Christian Endeavor World,* then offered a deeply spiritual prayer of gratitude and thanksgiving and supplication.

What a burst of applause came as Dr. Clark called to the platform Dr. Poling's family with the statement that the members belong to six societies in the Marble Collegiate Church, New York City. Dr. Poling belongs to the Senior society, and the other members belong to other societies down the line to the Kindergarten society. It made a splendid picture to have the whole family of father, mother, and seven children lined up on the platform, and the audience enjoyed Dr. Clark's reference to the fact that Dr. Poling had enough Endeavorers in his home to make a Christian Endeavor union.

Make the Whole World Dry

A new note was struck in this meeting by Ernest H. Cherrington, general secretary of the World League against Alcoholism, whose magic words brought before the audience a new vision of world prohibition. Mr. Cherrington is a powerful and convincing speaker, and he has the facts. He started his talk by an expression of increased confidence in the ultimate victory of prohibition, not only in the United States, but in all the world, when he looked into the faces of this great Christian audience.

SOLVING THE WORLD'S LIQUOR PROBLEM

By Ernest H. Cherrington, Litt. D., LL. D., General Secretary of the World League Against Alcoholism

The liquor problem is more than an individual, county, State, or national problem. It is a world problem.

The Eighteenth Amendement received the strongest official sanction ever given a constitutional provision; yet never before has there been arrayed against any such provision such a powerful and aggressive minority as that which to-day opposes national prohibition. That minority, moreover, is being supported and re-enforced not merely by State and national liquor organizations as in the past, but also by a gigantic, closely organized, wealthy, politically influential international liquor traffic, the size and vitality of which are suggested by the world's annual drink bill of approximately twenty billion dollars.

Township and village prohibition efforts required county and State co-operation. State prohibition laws made necessary the co-operation of surrounding States and that of the Federal Government. Just so to-day the unfinished task of national prohibition requires co-opera*ion of other countries.

An American international boundary line more than seventeen thousand miles in length, along which operate millions of high-powered automobiles, thousands of fast rum-running vessels, and numerous aeroplanes, directed by radio, together with the fact that through the modern revolutionizing of communication and transportation the world has become a great neighborhood of nations, all tend to make prohibition a great international problem.

Knowledge of the truth will eventually make beverage alcohol an impossibility in modern civilization, because it is at variance with the inexorable economic law of the new age. The unskilled laborers of yesterday have to-day become a vast army of skilled workmen whose tasks demand clear eyes, steady nerves, and unclouded brains. Railroad wrecks are no longer chargeable to drunken engineers. Half-drunken miners are no longer tolerated in American mines. Laborers with alcohol-soaked brains no longer operate great American industries. Seventeen million automobiles in America cannot be driven by alcoholized drivers.

The liquor traffic may have been possible in the old age of unskilled workmen—the age of the stage-coach, the ox-team, and the water-mill; but it is not possible in the new age of skilled workmen, employers' liability, and workmen's compensation, the new age of the automobile, the airship, and the electric dynamo.

The moral and religious forces of America must take the gospel of prohibition to the rest of the world, in order to make permanent American prohibition at home, in order to keep the liquor interests of other countries defending themselves there instead of concentrating on breaking down American prohibition here, and in order to lessen one of the greatest menaces to the foreign-missionary work of American churches, thus multiplying the efficiency of America's eighteen thousand foreign missionaries and protecting our vast annual investment of forty million dollars in foreign-missionary enterprises.

The great prohibition missionary project must be undertaken, moreover, because we must prevent the overrunning by Western liquor interests of those countries where 800,000,000 people for centuries have lived under the influence of total-abstinence religions; because it will enable the leaders of the great prohibition religions of the East to meet on a common platform and unite in a common moral welfare programme with Christian leaders of the West, thus making for international and interracial good will; because of the inherent character of the temperance movement itself, which from its inception has been to help "the other fellow," whether he be an individual victim, a community, a county, a State, a nation, or a continent.

A Singing Episode

The Swiss singers, now introduced, all men, stood in two long rows across the platform, and rendered two vocal selections, "On the Sea" and "Memories." It was a beautiful exhibition of male-voice choral singing, perfect in expression, rich and thrilling in tone, tender as a prayer, joyous at times as morning, and like a subtle, unseen hand that touched hidden and unsuspected chords in the heart.

Then followed a choir of Swiss ladies, all in Swiss dress. "Spring song" was their first song, and was followed by "On the Alps," rendered with taste and feeling.

Our Own Chorus

The large platform was filled in this evening hour with our own Convention chorus under the leadership of Dr. McMichael, whose work, faithful and delightful, must not go without its meed of praise. They were always on hand, and their singing was both beautiful and inspiring.

Listening in on Africa

Dr. Royal J. Dye, of Bolenge, Africa, was introduced by Dr. Clark as one of the outstanding missionaries to Africa today. Dr. Dye, with that energy which made him the success he was in Africa, plunged at once into his subject, his trip to Africa and his work there.

Dr. Dye has the faculty of sticking to concrete fact and personal experiences. His talk was full of native wit. Of course he brought down the house with his sallies. He told of his journey up the river, where the hippopotamus swims about like an enemy submarine. You have to zigzag when you see one of them, and you have to "zig" at the right time, or you get upset.

The crocodile, too, is a terrible source of danger. In fact, danger lurks everywhere in the jungle and the rivers. One crocodile the speaker had shot had in its stomach the bracelets of eight persons.

Dr. Dye told of having trouble with a witch-doctor. The witch-doctor had cursed a stone, and threatened with death any one that touched it. Dr. Dye had to take the curse off this stone, or he never could make progress against the influence of the witch-doctor. He forced one of the "boys" to lift the stone and cast it into the river Everybody expected, and the "boy" believed, that he would die.

As fate would have it, the man came down with pneumonia. He felt that he was going to die. The curse was working! The witch-doctor rejoiced, and the whole village watched the struggle between the missionary and the witch-doctor with terror in their eyes.

Dr. Dye said to the patient, "You take my food and medicine, and I'll pull you through." But the man said, "I am going to die." Dr. Dye said, "An evil spirit has entered into you, but my medicine can take it out." He put on three blisters, and the people watched to see whether they would work. They did. When the serum was removed from the sores the blisters caused, the man shouted, "See, the evil spirit is out; I shall live," and he did live.

Some time afterwards the witch-doctor came running to the missionary, and cried; "Come and help me. My wife is dying." She was the woman he had paid most money for. Here was the missionary's worst enemy calling for help. Dr. Dye went with him, and the woman's life was saved. The witch-doctor said: "This is not my town any more. It is your town"; and he quit.

Not many years later Dr. Dye visited one of these out-of-the-way places, and the man who met him was this old witch-doctor's son, who had become pastor of the great church in Bolenge.

Before the war Great Britain provided half the missionaries of the world, said Dr. Dye. But Great Britain can no longer do this. God is calling on us, sending to us the challenge of the world's redemption. Do we hear the call? Shall we go?

Dr. Clark at this point made the award of the Dixie banners, the prizes offered to Dixie societies for the best record of work done by Junior, Intermediate, and Senior societies. The banners were all won by Florida, the first time that one State has captured them all. North Carolina was second and South Carolina was third for the Senior banner, while Georgia stood second and Virginia third for both the Junior and Intermediate banners.

Hosanna!

Mrs. Edith Collais Evans of Portland rendered the beautiful solo, "The Holy City," by Stephen Adams, singing the solo part while the choir joined in the chorus. This was wonderfully well done, perhaps one of the best musical numbers of the entire Convention. If our chorus could sing "Hosanna in the highest, hosanna to our King" as they sang it, one wonders what the music of heaven will be. The song stirred us in the deep places of our hearts, and we saw indeed the new Jerusalem that would not pass away.

A Whirlwind Preacher

The next speaker was Rev. Mark A. Matthews, D. D., of Seattle, Wash., tall, spare, with leonine head, obviously of the nervous temperament, positive in his statements, and terribly, vehemently in earnest, a perfect Western whirlwind.

Dr. Matthews began by saying that many of his own Endeavorers were in the audience. Seattle is not far away. He has twenty odd Christian Endeavor societies in his church, he said, and they have a Christian Endeavor union of their own, which meets at stated periods to discuss the problems of their Christian Endeavor work.

Evangelism was the speaker's theme. If the young people of to-day are to be evangelized, he insisted, it must be by young people themselves. "We have been challenged," he said, "to evangelize the world; but America cannot evangelize the world until she herself is evangelized."

A few quotations will give a faint idea of Dr. Matthews' incisive style, but cannot reproduce the nervous force of the preacher's utterances.

"A depleted treasury of a church is a mark of spiritual poverty," he cried. "I don't want the money of the world to evangelize the world. I want the money of consecrated men who are aflame with a passion for souls."

"I am not interested in Jesus Christ as an example. I am not interested in Jesus as a teacher. He is the Son of God or He

The Shoshones and a Delegation.

Iowa delegates in red and white shown make an impression in a two-tone bluegrass parade.

is nothing. We must be loyal to Jesus Christ as the Son of God if we are to evangelize the world. And we must be loyal to the Holy Ghost as the third person of the Trinity. The Holy Spirit is not an influence, but a person; and it is through the leadership of the Holy Spirit that we must evangelize mankind.''

''I wonder if we are conscious of the fact that the Holy Spirit is speaking to us. He is in the world to reveal the truth of God, and He is in us, over us, guiding and directing us.''

''We must be loyal to the Bible as God's infallible word. It is the word of God. You don't need to defend the Bible. It does not need your defence. It is self-defended. The Bible is the power of God.''

''To evangelize the world we must give ourselves to prayer. Prayer is the true preparation for preaching. It is the arm that reaches up to God and the ladder by which He comes down to us. Prayer does not move the pray-er; it moves God. There is no unanswered prayer. Sometimes God says, 'No'; sometimes He says, 'Yes'; and sometimes He says, 'Wait.' Listen to God, and talk to Him all the while.''

''Then you must insist on incessant work. I am not talking about the periodical revival, but about the unceasing effort of the individual to try to save souls. If I could kill a preacher by hard work, I'd do it and give him a free funeral. I have never known a preacher to die by reason of too much work. I have known them to die because of worry caused by the pew. But nobody is hurt by good hard labor.''

Speaking of some persons who take to golf as an excuse for getting away from work, he said: ''I don't see any necessity for wasting a whole day in chasing a ball. I'd rather chase the devil. It is work that crowns us with success.''

The earnestness of the man was abundantly evident. He spoke with a passion of conviction. His sentences are flaming thrusts. There is no doubt in his mind as to the truth of his message. He does not argue. He does not reason. He asserts, vehemently, the items of his faith. Dr. Matthews sees no gray color, nothing but black or white, no middle way, nothing but a broad road that leads to destruction or a narrow one that leads to life eternal.

He is a man of strong personality, a dynamo of power. He has tremendous driving-force, a man untiring in his labors, fervent in spirit, serving the Lord according to his light and his conscience.

THE SIXTH DAY

THURSDAY, JULY 9, 1925

THE LAST DAY IN THE MORNING
A Blind Man's Talk.—Oratory.—Snappy Greetings from Field-Secretaries

On the last day of the Convention, in the morning, the meeting in the main hall was opened by Mr. Gates' introducing Mr. Carson Mateer, field-secretary of the Ontario Christian Endeavor Union, who was the representative of our great sister nation across the border. Mr. Mateer glowingly told of an increase of thirty-eight per cent in Christian Endeavor in Canada in the last two years. The outlook is now particularly bright in all the great Provinces of Canada. Five of the seven denominations in Ontario have officially recognized Christian Endeavor as the young people's programme of the church.

Mr. Gates then displayed one of the most wonderful Christian Endeavor banners he had ever seen. It came from Winnipeg, and is probably thirty years old. It belongs to a Christian Endeavor union which year by year for thirty years sewed on the banner the pennant of the society, that had made the best record each year, so that the banner resembles a patchwork quilt of many-colored banners, and presents a unique appearance.

Then in recognition of the work of Canadian Christian Endeavor Mr. Gates in the presence of the Convention presented to Mr. Mateer a small medal, remarking that the work of Christian Endeavor in Canada is second to none anywhere.

A Blind Editor

It was a touching sight to see, on Mr. Gates's introduction, Mr. B. F. Irvine, editor of *The Oregon Journal*, who is blind, but who has met life with this limitation in a spirit of enduring and triumphant courage that will not own defeat, come to the front of the platform to deliver a brief speech. Mr. Irvine was seeing visions of the future of the young people. He asserted that if some of the young men and women who have committed crimes in recent times had been sincere Endeavorers their crimes would never have been committed. Young people do not learn bad habits in Christian Endeavor. It is a great steadying force in adolescent life.

"Listen to the statement of a Brooklyn judge," said the

speaker. "Of the hundreds of juvenile offenders who were brought into his court only three had attended Sunday school, and their offences were trivial and technical.

"All I am," continued Mr. Irvine, "and all I hope to be, I owe to Christian parents. I was taken twice each Sunday to church. I knew when I was a boy that the preachers were on the right side and the saloon-keeper was on the wrong side." In simple, eloquent words the speaker urged the young people to live the higher life. All that ever followed other gods have ended in failure. But Endeavorers are under the right leader, and are taking orders from the right commander. Listening to Him all is well.

An Oratorical Winner

Mr. Gates announced that a national oratorical contest had been suggested two years ago; but only Iowa had carried out the plan, and her contestant, Mr. Jack Finnigan, was in the Convention to do his part, and incidentally to claim the prize. Mr. Finnigan is not quite seventeen, but he is acting pastor of a church while he studies at Drake University. He is said to be the youngest pastor in his home State. He is a tall young man, mature for his age; and he speaks with natural ease and simplicity. Again was demonstrated the value of Christian Endeavor as a training organization. Both in matter and delivery this young man's address on young people, and their relation to the church, and on what Christian Endeavor is doing, could very well bear comparison with the speeches of many older speakers. He held the audience to close attention throughout.

Field-Secretaries' Greetings

Mr. Shartle then took charge of the meeting, and in his encouraging, inspiring, and friendly way introduced Harold Singer, who introduced in turn the field-force of Christian Endeavor.

Mamie Gene Cole, Jr., field-secretary of Dixie, brought greetings from eight hundred Junior societies and 15,000 Junior boys and girls in Dixie.

Louella Dyer of Washington was the next on the list. She maintained that hers is the finest State in the United States— "except *your* State, of course," she charmingly said. She stated that Washington had caught a new vision and is going to make good in the coming year.

Mrs. J. Q. Hook of Idaho brought greetings from Idaho, which is on forward-moving lines, and has one hundred Endeavorers at this Convention. A year ago there were 125 societies in the State; now there are nearly two hundred, and the State is learning the power of union in Christian Endeavor work.

W. Roy Breg, formerly of Texas, now of Kansas, expects the next two years to be the greatest that have ever dawned upon

Kansas Christian Endeavor. The leaders are trying to put graded Christian Endeavor into the church programme and to put Kansas increasingly plainly on the map.

Harry Allan of California said that no one in one minute could even begin to tell the good things done in California. Three hundred and fifty-nine new societies were added in the last year. There are 452 Intermediate societies in the State, 325 Junior societies, and 498 Senior. Nineteen hundred were won to Christ in Christian Endeavor. The societies gave $29,000 to missions. Seven hundred Endeavorers were in mission-study classes, and 350 California Endeavorers are now on the foreign-missionary field.

Alfred Crouch of Missouri spoke, too, of gains in all departments. All the goals have been smashed in the State work; 65 new societies have been organized; and there are about 1,400 societies in the State.

E. F. Huppertz of Texas spoke of the immensity of his field in comparison with other States. "We are behind the United Society one hundred per cent in all the plans of the future."

From Nebraska came Thelma Crawford to speak for the six hundred societies of the State. There is no field-secretary in that State, but there are seventy-five Life-Work Recruits, who are a promise of big things to be done in the future, and who are even now doing fine work for Christian Endeavor all over the State.

Illinois and F. D. G. Walker belong together. He said that there are 2,000 societies in the State, three hundred of them new, all ready for any task and eager to follow the plan of campaign for the next two years.

Ohio and Frank L. Freet also belong together. In the last State convention 3,058 delegates registered. Two years ago Ohio promised to bring two hundred delegates to Portland, and she has made good. How many will Oregon send to Cleveland in 1927?

C. E. Hetzler brought from Pennsylvania this motto: "Remember Jesus Christ. He's your friend." In Pennsylvania, as elsewhere, there has been good progress, and there will be more in the coming year because of the uplift of this Convention.

From New Jersey F. L. Mintel, the field-secretary, brought greetings and also from the sixty delegates who crossed the continent to come to Portland. The New Jersey convention registered just about three thousand; county organizations have been strengthened, and the leaders have gone on record in favor of the United Society's Fidelity campaign for the next two years.

Herbert W. Hicks spoke for little Connecticut, happy to say that after a meeting anywhere in the State the field-secretary can get home to breakfast, provided the Ford continues to operate. In Connecticut Christian Endeavor is showing encouraging advance.

Maryland spoke through Carroll M. Wright. It is a small State in territory, but not in Christian Endeavor work. Mr. Wright had reason to be proud of the fact that his party from Maryland and Delaware numbered sixty-one persons, a fine showing for these States.

Carlton M. Sherwood of New York spoke for the 2,800 societies in the State and the five thousand delegates at the recent State convention. In the past year 295 new societies have been organized in New York, and strong leaders have come to the front in Christian Endeavor work.

For Massachusetts and New Hampshire Russell J. Blair spoke greetings. About sixty delegates have come from the Atlantic to the Pacific, and Mr. Blair promised that Massachusetts and New Hampshire will do their share to help to raise the $100,000 recognition fund for Dr. Clark.

Carson Mateer of Toronto, who had spoken before, said that for the coming year Canada's watchword would be "Fidelity."

From old Kentucky came Georgia Dunn, who spoke of Kentucky's work, which resulted in the organization of 116 new societies last year. In this State, too, prospects are exceedingly promising.

Charles F. Evans spoke vigorously of Dixie. Dixie, he said, owes its existence to the United Society. Ten years ago it was not on the map. The States are now organized and new societies are being formed all the time. The work has never been in better form than at the present moment, and it never had better prospects.

Pacific Coast Secretary Paul Brown got a wonderful ovation, showing the esteem in which he is held by the group of States that form his field. He made the various Pacific coast State delegations rise. They were a great host. They were his speech.

Alumni Work

Now came Stanley B. Vandersall with a speech on Alumni work. He used a stereopticon, throwing on the screen five slides, each slide containing five suggestions for Alumni work which Mr. Vandersall briefly explained.

Mr. Gates announced a tour next year to the London World's Convention, and C. C. Hamilton made a clever presentation of *The Christian Endeavor World*, the best-loved paper in the world, urging every one to remember to subscribe for the paper and also to buy the literature of Christian Endeavor.

The closing meditation by Dr. Foulkes brought a splendid and interesting meeting to a close.

THE MINISTRY AND MUSIC

The afternoon session was begun, apart from the song service, by the passage of resolutions commending Golden Rule Sunday and President Coolidge for his action in refusing to sanction the use of Armistice Day as Mobilization Day, keeping Armistice Day associated with thoughts of peace.

A New Form of Church

"Christian Endeavor and the Community Church" was the subject chosen for his talk by Rev. L. F. Jordan, D. D., executive secretary of the Community Church Workers of America. The community church is a new movement. It is a church organized by the community to meet its own peculiar needs, and the organization varies according to circumstances.

There are therefore different kinds of community churches. There is the denominational community church, which affiliates with a definite denomination, Presbyterian, for instance; but the members who join the church do not therefore become Presbyterians. The federated form of community church is also common. It is brought about by the amalgamation of several churches into one, without the members' losing their denominational affiliations. Then there are independent community churches that are not connected with any outside group at all.

No church can long exist without coming face to face with the problem of the young people. Christian Endeavor has been found to possess all the qualifications necessary to meet the needs of such churches. It is democratic; it has that continuity of idea and of programme which the community church needs. To these churches, therefore, Christian Endeavor is wonderfully well fitted. They may have the ordinary pledge, or an alternative pledge, or sometimes no pledge at all; but the young people's society of the Christian Endeavor type is found practically everywhere.

The community church movement is definitely religious. It knows that it cannot hold young people merely by keeping them amused. It needs a religious organization for its young people, and it finds that Christian Endeavor eminently meets its requirements. There is a growing sense of the necessity of fellowship which cannot be found except in great conventions such as these. The Christian Endeavor motto is, "For Christ and the Church," and must not be changed.

Some of Dr. Jordan's sentences are significant. He said, speaking of the community churches which are increasing in numbers:

"If I read the signs of the times among the community churches, these signs indicate that the churches will utilize an organization that seems most providentially prepared for just such a situation as the community church finds itself in. It would be of no use to invent a brand new airplane nowadays to fly in the air. A better attitude is to take one of the airplanes already built and try to improve it in detail if that is possible. Many of the community church pastors think it is easier to use Christian Endeavor for their young people than to try to invent something brand new.

"The people of the independent community churches are growing a little hungry for fellowship. Only a year ago a national organization to give fellowship to all sorts of community enterprises in religion was set up called the Community Church Workers of the U. S. A. It is a symbol of the hunger for fellowship which people always have in religion. If twelve hundred community churches had twelve hundred different kinds of local clubs for their young people, they would miss for their young life the contact with great religious conventions and the sense of unity with the great evangelical movement in America. The young people of these churches want to meet each other and they want to meet all the religious young people of every sort of church in America. In Park Ridge we spend from a hundred to two hundred dollars every year to send our people away to great Christian gatherings, and this is the best spent money there is in the church budget. My society has four representatives at this great convention two thousand miles away from home. That is what the larger fellowship means to us.

"We in the community churches will seek to guard Christian Endeavor against its chief perils. We want it to be a genuinely youth movement and not refuge of the middle-aged who are not willing to admit they are growing old. We want it to be fresh and vital in the past, and never dogmatic and theological. Theology has its place in the world but there is not room for much of it in a young people's movement. We want Christian Endeavor to keep aloft its banner of interdenominational fellowship, never fearing that such an attitude cannot win. Christian Endeavor has never had any dogma of church union, but it has had a practice of Christian fellowship feared by all who would corral segments of the church of God into high fence pastures.

"So here we come as one of your latest additions to the ranks of Christian Endeavor. We come with the fresh enthusiasm of a new religious movement. We are exuberant, and sometimes boyish. But we beg that you will believe of us that at heart we are with you in the great things you have been doing for forty years and which please God you will continue to do. We want to take our place in your councils. Where the hardest fighting is to be found against the spirit of an age that is not friendly to the church, we want to be placed."

The Lure of the Ministry

"The Challenge of the Ministry" was the subject of Dr. Edgar DeWitt Jones' address. Dr. Jones is the successful pastor of the Central Christian Church, Detroit, Mich. He told of a picture of Joan of Arc in the New York Metropolitan Art Museum. Joan is looking raptly upward. She is seeing the invisible and hearing that which is unheard.

There are those who hear the call to-day, and who, like Joan, can see the unseen. There are four elements in the call that challenges us. The first is the fellowship of a common cause, the sense of a brotherly interest. Young painters love to meet with other painters and talk of the masters of the past. But how majestic the fraternity of the ministry is! How the great men of God lift us up before the throne of grace in moments of unforgettable prayer! The preacher belongs to a high brotherhood, and should feel inspired because of it.

Then there are the charm and the responsibility of the teaching career. How challenging this is, too! Our Lord Himself was a teacher sent from God, throwing floods of light on the mystery of life. It is great to teach, to have a message, to open the Scriptures, and to talk with people about God.

Then there is the witchery of the speaking vocation. The magic of human speech never dies. Think of the influences of voices in the wilderness, in rural church or city church, of men who bring to the people their vision of God. Think of the eloquence of the pulpit, the evangelistic trumpet tone! To be a minister is to he a man of power, swinging the lives of men into new and holy paths.

Again, there is the lure of the shepherding ministry. Think of a shepherd caring for his sheep and seeking the lost. That is the picture. There is nothing more beautiful in the life of Jesus than His own shepherding ministry with His disciples, when He lost only one. It was a ministry of love. That is the marvel of the shepherd heart that wants to take all in, and cannot rest content if any wanderer be lost.

With skill and pleading-power the speaker painted in glowing colors the ministry as the fulfilment of the great dreams of youth. It is to dreaming youth, to daring youth, that the ministry with its magic and its witchery makes its appeals. Perhaps—who knows?—some dreams will crystallize through this address, tender and beautiful and delivered with winning power. It was an appeal hard to resist and a talk that thrilled with new ambitions those of us who are already of the brotherhood of the ministry.

Let the Light Shine

Rev. R. P. Anderson was next on the programme for an address on "Tell It."

This was a straightforward talk on publicity, outlining some of the elements that enter into the proper and effective advertising of the society and the church. The speaker listed a number of practical publicity methods, and gave some helpful suggestions as to things to do and things to avoid doing.

Sing for Joy

Forty minutes of joyous singing is all too short for Endeavorers. Percy Foster is always a treat. He is never stale. He constantly does interesting and unexpected things.

The first thing he suggested in this period was that everybody should shake hands with his or her neighbor, and then with the man or woman behind. That meant a moment or two of real hilarity. For everybody obeyed.

Then he gave the congregation a little action song, the body swaying to the rhythm of the song. It was quite unorthodox as seen from the platform, but nevertheless extraordinary effective. Then he made the rows alternate, one swaying in one direction and the other in the other; and, as the folks reached out across the aisles and held hands while they swayed back and forth, the effect was that of great living ropes pulled in opposite directions.

Then he made one-half of the audience—the half nearest the platform—turn about, face the back of the hall, and sing the chorus "I'm bound for the promised land," while they swayed from side to side. And, yes, the audience enjoyed a good time in doing it.

Some community songs followed. "Mary had a little lamb" was resonantly given, and was turned by Mr. Foster into "Mary had a swarm of bees," and they were "forced to go where Mary went," for "Mary had the hives."

Mr. Foster in happy little asides threw interesting light on how some of our jazz musicians use phrases from some of the great compositions. It was news to most that the music of the phrase, "Yes, we have no bananas," is literally taken from Handel's "Hallelujah Chorus."

THE CLOSING SESSION

Dr. Clark Retires.—Dr. Poling Installed.—An Unforgettable Service

Every seat in the Auditorium was filled at the opening hour for the closing session of the Convention. The delegates sat in groups; and as each group wore differently colored head-dresses or caps, the color scheme of the audience was exceedingly pleasing.

Dr. Clark presided over the great gathering—his last Convention as president of the United Society of Christian Endeavor; and the sense of this change hung over our spirits, not with gloom and sadness, but with gratitude for a life so sweet and noble and a work so beautiful and glorious. And we thought, with equal gratitude to God, of the young man who is to fill his place, Dr. Daniel A. Poling. The method of life is change and renewal, which is the will of God, and therefore our will, too.

At the opening of the meeting Dr. Clark called on Rev. E. D. Mallory of Boston and Rev. R. Wright, an old associate of his student days, to offer prayer for guidance and blessing.

A programme of special music was rendered by the Arion-Philharmonic Society, the singing section of the Portland Turnverein, Professor Lucien E. Becker being the director. The splendid choir sang first in German, then in English, choral music, duet, solo, altogether beautiful, delightful. The voices were highly trained, clear, sure, melodious, perfectly controlled, and perfectly blended. One does not need to be a musician to enjoy singing like this. It was joyous and altogether charming.

More and More Flowers

Just as the singers filed from the platform, two young girls, beautiful as flowers themselves, carried between them a basket four feet high filled with flowers, a gift from the Portland Christian Endeavor Union to Dr. Clark, who thanked Portland, the city of roses, for the wealth of flowers with which the people had deluged them all through the Convention.

Messages from Abroad

Among many messages of greeting was one from the local Christian Endeavor union of Mexico City, Mexico, signed by Mr. Macedonio Platas, wishing blessing on all Christian Endeavor works, and another from the India Christian Endeavor union on behalf of more than two thousand societies and sixty thousand members. This message read as follows:

"We remember that we owe our existence to that first little society started in another Portland, but also in America, by our beloved world's president, Dr. Clark, whose portrait we were delighted to have in the February issue of our *India National Magazine*, for Endeavor Day, to remind us of the achievements of the past and to spur us on to yet greater efforts in the future. We do not forget the enthusiastic work of Rev. F. S. Hatch, so generously lent to us by American Endeavorers, the results of whose work abide with us still, and will abide; we are grateful for the continuous financial help we are receiving from American Endeavorers, without which we could not carry on; we look up to the same Saviour and Master of us all, and pray that you may have new blessings through this Convention through new consecration, and fresh vigor through a fresh outpouring of the power of the Holy Spirit, and greater success still in the days to come, through an even more loyal obedience and an even better-sustained effort for His kingdom. The good time is still in the making, and we have the rare chance of helping it forward; the golden opportunity is yet with us to seize and to use.

"Forward, then, to victory! Steady, then, right to the end!
"There is no leader to compare with our Captain!
"There is no service so good as for Christ and His church.

"Yours sincerely,
"RALPH ROBERTSON,
"Honorary General Secretary."

Parade Prizes

General Secretary Gates called to the platform representatives of Ohio, Dixie, and Iowa to receive silver loving-cups as a reward for having had the first, second, and third best delegations in the parade.

More Prizes

For two years the States have been working on the Friends-of-Christ Campaign, and General Secretary Gates was now ready to award silver loving-cups to those States that stood highest in the number of reported honor societies in this campaign. Ohio had won first prize, California second, and Massachusetts third; and representatives of these States proudly received and carried away the visible emblems of their victory and of the success of long and hard work in the campaign.

A Georgia Half-Dollar

Thomas Moye of Georgia made a lively talk on Stone Mountain in Georgia, where the great Confederate Memorial is being created. The United States Government has coined Stone Mountain half-dollars in connection with this memorial, and in the name of the Dixie Endeavorers Mr. Moye presented to Dr. Clark one of the first of the Stone Mountain Memorial half-dollars that ever came from the mint.

In accepting this coin Dr. Clark said that it would remind him, not of war, but of the fact that all enmities are now forgotten and that we are forever a nation one and indivisible.

Choral Praise

Mr. Percy Foster then led the Dixie delegates and the whole audience in "Dixie," and introduced Dr. McMichael, director of the chorus, Mrs. McMichael, and the two ladies who had presided at the two pianos throughout the Convention.

The chorus outdid itself in this last meeting in the splendid rendering of Gounod's "Unfold, Ye Portals," which was sung with spirit. But the audience was itself an immense choir whose singing made a tremendous volume of harmonious sound that swelled like the voice of many waters.

The Penultimate Address

Dr. Clark introduced Dr. William Hiram Foulkes for one of the closing addresses of the Convention. He took his text from a Chinese visiting-card which described his position in the days of the New Era of the Presbyterian Church, and read, "A New Day Going Forward Together of a Company of (Young) Believers to the Beautiful Land." Dr. Foulkes spoke on the various words in the text, and made a great announcement.

To-day, he said, the Francis E. Clark $100,000 Recognition Fund was launched by the committee in charge of the fund. The plan for the fund is that there shall be given an opportunity (not an appeal) to every Endeavorer in the country in Christian Endeavor Week in 1926 to contribute toward this fund. Some of the great citizens of this country will probably be drawn into the committee which is heading up the work, and their names will appear later as sponsors and supporters of the project.

A library, too, will be given to Dr. and Mrs. Clark when the fund is complete. This will not be an ordinary library, but one that will contain a volume from every State in the Union. Each volume will be composed of loose leaves on which will be written the names of every Endeavorer that has given any sum whatever, from ten cents to a thousand dollars. As we have previously intimated, the first check, for two hundred dollars, has come in toward this fund, which has thus made an auspicious start.

In his reply to this speech Dr. Clark said that the proposal had struck him dumb with surprise at the generosity and interest of the host of friends who are proposing to do this thing for Christian Endeavor.

Introductions and Poling

Mr. Gates introduced in warm and appreciative words Rev. Charles T. Hurd, executive secretary of the Portland Convention committee, who has worked day and night for the Convention, suave, always smiling, courteous, efficient, and effective. Mr. Hurd was largely responsible for the perfection of the arrangements. No detail was overlooked; none was too trivial for painstaking attention. The result was a convention as nearly perfect as anything human may be. All honor to Mr. Hurd.

Dr. Poling Accepts

Another ovation, and a basket of flowers from Portland, came when Dr. Clark introduced Dr. D. A. Poling for the last formal address of the Convention. Out of a full heart Dr. Poling began by expressing his gratitude for all the good that had come to him and to others in Portland.

From this he swung into an earnest talk on success. What is is success? What is my definition of it, and what is yours? he asked.

Some people think, perhaps, that success must be measured by a gold standard. But money is not success, although we must not despise it, but should increasingly seek to understand it and hold it as an investment for God.

Is happiness success? No, not that. Happiness is a by-product of disinterested goodness. A brilliant novelist recently wrote of his quest for the happiest man in the world. He visited the great of the earth, but found that they were not happy. Up in the mountains of eastern Tennessee, however, he found in front of a log cabin a woman who was happy. Asked why, she replied: "Why should I not be happy? I have a home and the love of my children, and I have God." Home, love, God—there lies success.

Success is to live your best, to give your best. And to do that you must find a task worth while. Some go to the ends of the earth with the gospel; others give their best to the business of every-day life, doing their best in the daily round. The man who labors with bowed head and burdened shoulders may be a king among men. God calls us to do our dead level best, in spite of opposition, in spite of difficulties, in spite of weakness—our best for our pastor, our best for our city, our best for our Sunday school, our best for our society. What an opportunity it is! Do your best, trusting in the Lord Jesus Christ for strength.

Dr. Poling's close was a mighty effort that swept the audience with him. He told the story of Sir Ernest Shackleton who in an open boat, fighting in the frozen seas of the South while on his way to rescue members of his marooned crew, felt, as his comrades felt, that there was another, an invisible presence, in the boat with them, as there had been a fourth in the fiery furnace. So in the path of duty there is always with us—Another; and there will always be success when we follow His will.

How marvelous a gift is the oratory of Poling! There is a magic in the witchery of words that weaves a pattern in the tapestry of speech. It is a power that entrances and holds us in rapt attention, like a beautiful vision. For we see visions created by words, and visions uncreated; and our souls are moved to high endeavor.

Consecrated Purpose

"What shall we do, with God's help, in the coming two years?" asked Dr. Clark as he announced and opened a period during which representatives of the States might tell in half-minute speeches the purpose of their States for the coming year.

These talks, the main idea of which we here reproduce, showed that several big items in the Convention had taken hold of the delegates. There were many expressions of loyalty to the Christian Endeavor cause, purposes to stand behind the United Society of Christian Endeavor, to work out its plans, to take up the new society standards, to support the $100,000 Clark Recognition Fund, to come up to the Cleveland, 1927, Convention with a worth-while record, and so on. But it is impossible to reproduce the effect of this meeting. There was a spirit of deep earnestness and consecration in it. The purposes expressed were no idle promises, but pledges made, "trusting in the Lord Jesus Christ for strength." They were not merely the purposes of the individuals that spoke, but of whole delegations speaking for their States. The entire delegation would rise with the spokesman, giving thrilling significance to his words.

The States Become Vocal

The representative of the California union put the States' purpose into a vital phrase: "You can count on California for the new $100,000 Clark Recognition Fund and for working out the new society standards."

"Washington union," said Louella Dyer, the field-secretary, "promises five dollars each toward the fund, and will broadcast 'fidelity' in the Fidelity Campaign."

Idaho said, "This one thing I do: forgetting the things which are behind, and reaching forward to the things which are before, I press on."

Arkansas stands before a new day. She has a name for always going over the top.

"Missouri," said Field-Secretary Crouch, "is going to go across with this campaign." It will adopt the society standards, support the $100,000 campaign, and will come with a train-load of delegates to Cleveland in 1927.

Texas, we were told, can be counted on to stand behind the whole programme of the United Society of Christian Endeavor.

Nebraska said that the union is one hundred per cent strong for the full programme.

Iowa is not only the State where the tall corn grows, it is the State where Christian Endeavor goes. The union's purpose, it was said, is expressed in the word given by Dr. Clark, "Go on!"

Illinois expressed a fourfold purpose: 1. Evangelism. 2. To cultivate a larger Christian life and help young people to avoid the sins of the age. 3. Service in all the world. 4. Fellowship which pushes through all barriers to all good friends of Jesus Christ.

Ohio said: "We come in humility. Our winning first place in the Friend-of-Christ Campaign is a challenge to us for the coming years. Ohio comes here to light its torch that it may carry it back to the State and light other torches there."

Pennsylvania said, "Count on the Keystone State to back up Dr. Clark and the Portland Convention in everything proposed."

New Jersey re-affirmed the old motto, "Trusting in the Lord Jesus Christ for strength, I promise Him."

Connecticut expressed its loyal intention to support the programme of the United Society of Christian Endeavor.

Delaware promised, "We will do the very best we can where we are with what we have."

Maryland stated that good things come in small packages (referring to the size of the State). Watch out for Maryland!

New York declared that she hoped, when the State convention is held in Saratoga Springs next year, to organize more than the three hundred new societies, and that the State will give more money to the Recognition Fund than any other State in the Union.

Massachusetts, we were told, has caught the vision, and will try to bring to Cleveland in 1927 the largest possible volume of subscribers to the Recognition Fund.

New Hampshire pledged anew fidelity to Christian Endeavor.

Kentucky said: "Trusting in the Lord Jesus Christ for strength, we will be true, for there are those that trust us." Kentucky stands foursquare behind the United Society in this campaign.

Canada spoke through Field-Secretary Mateer, who said: "Our watchword is Fidelity. Our slogan, 'Only the best is good enough for Christ and the church.'"

Oklahoma promised to do her level best to serve Christ, to be loyal to Him, and to have fellowship with His people.

Arizona's pledge was given, but could not be heard from the platform.

Utah pledged the fidelity of the Christian Endeavor Union to the programme of Christian Endeavor.

Wisconsin has always been faithful to the plans of the United Society of Christian Endeavor, and will not fail in this now.

Dixie intends to begin work immediately on the new monthly service programme and to make a large volume filled with names of those that love Dr. Clark.

Virginia said that the purposes of the United Society of Christian Endeavor are the purposes of Virginia.

Mamie Gene Cole, Junior superintendent for all Dixie, said, "Count on the fifteen thousand boys and girls of Dixie to do their best for Christ and the church"; and Dr. Kirkpatrick, chairman of the All-South Committee, added: "Count on Dixie for the new fund. Dixie hopes to win first place in the 1927 parade." For the other Dixie States it was said, "Watch our speed to Cleveland."

Indiana stands foursquare for the new campaign.

Colorado will be right on deck with a big delegation to Cleveland.

Wyoming will go whole-heartedly into the new campaign in all its aspects, and will bring a delegation to Cleveland.

For Michigan it was said, "Twenty thousand Endeavorers pledge themselves anew to the idea of Christian Endeavor, and will do their best for all its plans."

The West Virginia delegate could not be heard from the platform.

Minnesota said that she has always been faithful to Christian Endeavor principles, and her delegates are going home to push hard the Recognition Fund and to try to win the 1929 Convention to Minneapolis.

Montana is two years old as a State union, and promises to carry on and carry out her share of the work.

North Dakota could not be heard, but we know her purpose is true.

District of Columbia said, "Twenty-five hundred Endeavorers in the District of Columbia, although they have no power to make Washington a model city, will try to make it a model in backing up the United Society of Christian Endeavor and the Recognition Fund."

Oregon declared herself fortunate in having this Convention, and pledged her young people to back up Christian Endeavor.

Maine had but one delegate present, but the Pine-Tree State is never less than loyal to all the programme outlined.

As the purpose session ended, and before the consecration meeting began, Mr. Foster led the great gathering in that beautiful old hymn, "Just as I am," which melted into "Where He leads me, I will follow," sung with clear-voiced earnestness and the freshness of youth. Then "My Jesus, I love thee" was also sung like a benediction.

Dr. Poling Installed

Dr. Clark proposed at this point a brief service of installation for Dr. Poling. No event of this Convention, said Dr. Clark, had given him greater pleasure than to see Dr. Poling step into the presidency of the United Society of Christian Endeavor. He said:

"My dear brother,—I could almost call you my dear son in the Lord, above all, my dear friend of many years,—all that I need to say to you is, Keep on, keep on as you have begun. You have said, 'Trusting in the Lord Jesus Christ for strength,' you accept this position. There is no further pledge that I would ask of you than this. Fulfill it, and you will do your duty to the United Society of Christian Endeavor in days to come. In this faith I give you the right hand of fellowship.

A Charge to the People

Following the custom at installations of giving a charge to the people, Dr. Clark asked the audience to stand up, raise the right hand, and take a solemn, silent pledge to give to Dan Poling their hearts' allegiance, their love in the Lord Jesus Christ, and their promise of fidelity to him. This was done, and Dr. Clark pronounced the words over the multitude, "God bless you all."

A Father's Prayer

It was a solemn moment when Dr. Poling's father, Rev. Charles C. Poling, D. D., stood forth to offer prayer for the consecration of his son. It was a tender prayer, expressing gratitude for the achievements and victories of the past and supplication for aid in all that lies before; asking for help to yield ourselves to God that the new task may be accomplished. Blessing was asked for Dr. Clark and for "Dan" (the word had a tender ring), on whose shoulders lies the responsibility of carrying on. "Set him apart," prayed the father for his son. "Warm his heart. Keep him true and faithful, loyal to God, loyal to Christian Endeavor, loyal to the word of God and the church of God. Give him strength and wisdom, and may the work of the Lord continue to prosper and His name be glorified."

Dr. Poling's reply was very short and very simple. "The pilot has not left the ship," he said. "The new man stands by the side of the old. So 'trusting in the Lord Jesus Christ for strength,' I accept."

DR. CLARK AND DR. POLING
A lifelike picture "snapped" by *The Oregon Journal*

Consecration

Dr. Clark declared that he had attended many conventions in every part of the world, but never has a convention been more blessed than this. The arrangements have been perfect, and the hospitality of Portland has been of a quality quite unique. No words can express our gratitude for it.

For the closing consecration period Dr. Clark called upon the audience to repeat Psalm 121, the Traveller's Psalm, peculiarly suitable to the occasion because for many days the delegates will be travellers on the way to their home places.

A prayer of consecration followed. It was offered by Dr. Clark, a prayer of devotion, of surrender, of consecration, a prayer that seemed to bring heaven very near, and open up new vistas, and awaken new hope.

"Speak, Lord, for thy servant heareth," the audience audibly prayed with him. There came another short prayer of inquiry and consecration: "Lord, what wilt Thou have me do?" The audience took it up, praying it audibly, and the leader pressed home the solemn meaning of the question. What more can we do in home, in Sunday school, in church, for our society? What? Have we been faithful? Willing to lead? Willing to give?

Then softly the audience again sang, "Just as I am without one plea." The place seemed filled with the presence and the love of God. One more word of exhortation to carry home the Convention and its message. "We are bearers of good news to our home town and our society. Think of your responsibility."

"Jesus, lover of my soul," sang the people softly with evident feeling. It was a moment of mountain-top experience. "Hide me, O my Saviour, hide," they sang, and felt that it was true. Christ was with them and about them.

One more song and then a concluding word of prayer by Dr. Clark, ending with the Aaronic benediction, "The Lord bless thee, and keep thee; the Lord make his face to shine upon thee, and be gracious unto thee; the Lord lift up his countenance upon thee, and give thee peace."

Then the song, "God be with you till we meet again," a farewell song sung with spirit and full volume such as is not often heard. Dr. Clark then requested all to join hands and sing the Christian Endeavor hymn, "Blest be the tie that binds." And so, upon the fall of the gavel the thirtieth International Christian Endeavor Convention came to a close.

TOURING FOR PLEASURE

For five and a half strenuous days, morning, forenoon, afternoon, evening, and often into the wee sma' hours, the delegates had been at work. On Friday, July 10, relaxation was provided. The Convention committee had arranged for various trips, one to loop Mt. Hood, a snow-capped giant, by automobile;

another to climb Mt. Hood; a short trip over the Columbia River Highway; and there were boat rides and other trips according to the taste of the delegates.

The automobile trips were great, and more than two thousand delegates took them in about six hundred automobiles. Not only so, but the Convention committee provided for the delegates who took the trips a fine lunch neatly done up in boxes—abundance of sandwiches, a piece of pie, fruit, and so forth. In each package was a printed message from Judge Jacob Kanzler, expressing the desire of the Convention committee that the delegates might see and enjoy the beauty and grandeur of the Mt. Hood mountain range. This major range is cut in two at sea-level by the mighty Columbia River, forming palisades, promontories, and towering rocks that inspire wonder and awe.

The trip gives an idea of the forest primeval, and suggests thoughts of all the generations of the past that have lived here and worshipped. The scenery is everywhere superb, green-clad hills and towering mountains, beetling cliffs and rocks thrust up into the sky like fingers beckoning on to God. Down the mountain-sides cataracts run and leap for joy, or over high cliffs the water falls to break into mist in the air.

The delegates that took any of these trips were all impressed by the magnificence of nature and the glory of this Oregon country. The courtesy of the people was unparalleled.

Oregon gave good weather to the Convention. Cool at first, it gradually warmed up; but at no time was it to be called oppressive, and the nights were cool.

Friday, July 10, the delegates began to leave the city, and the Elks began to come in.

A great many of the delegates went on tour through the Yellowstone Park; some went down into California; others visited Glacier Park; and two parties went to Alaska. These Alaska parties were organized by W. Roy Breg, one party going to Fairbanks, and the other going to Skagway.

There is only one thing more to say about the Convention, the Convention committee, and everybody in the city, and that is,

Oregon Made Good.

THE MORNING CONFERENCES

The Workshop of Endeavor.—The Workers Get to Their Benches

This was a working convention. At nine o'clock on Monday morning the two large auditoriums presented a busy appearance with many hundreds of Endeavorers moving hither and thither, seeking the conferences of their choice. In the main auditorium four conferences were held, and in Al-Azar Temple, across the street, were four others. After fifty minutes of study and discussion a re-arrangement of the conferences was made, four in each place, making it possible for the delegates to attend two conferences each morning, and giving a choice of sixteen conferences each day.

With such crowds to handle it was inevitable that some time should be lost the first morning while each one found the conference he wished to attend. That difficulty was soon overcome, and the delegates buckled down to work in earnest. The Al-Azar Temple, more limited in space than the main auditorium, was especially congested; but the Endeavorers were as always in the best of good humor and moved about, as conferences were re-arranged, without a hitch.

A Trip around the Conferences

It is nine o'clock, and we begin our tour in the main auditorium. In the main hall General Secretary Gates is on the platform addressing a large congregation that fills the major portion of the floor. His topic is "Progressive Endeavor"; and his conference is based on Dr. Amos R. Well's new book, "Progressive Endeavor." Mr. Gates is a rapid-fire speaker, clear, incisive, positive. He knows Christian Endeavor through and through, and is always ready with snappy replies to questions directed at him from the floor. Rev. Frank Linn Freet, general secretary of the Ohio union, was present, and made an address that was both informational and inspirational. This conference on "Progressive Endeavor" was continued each morning of the Convention week under Mr. Gates' leadership, a different speaker, however, delivering the inspirational talk each day. These speakers were Carroll M. Wright of Maryland, Rev. C. E. Hetzler of Pennsylvania, and Rev. E. W. Prætorius, general secretary of the Evangelical League of Christian Endeavor, besides Mr. Freet. Mr. Hetzler's address was on "Christian Endeavor in Service" and listed a great number of ways in which Christian Endeavor serves the young people, the church, missions, civic life, and so forth. The speech gave a splendid idea of the vast field of service that Christian Endeavor covers, and the great variety of the work that is done.

Intermediate Endeavor

Over the Intermediate room with its exhibits and addresses Miss Edith McDonald, California's Intermediate superintendent, presided. The large hall was well filled, and Miss McDonald had provided a regal programme for all her conference hours. The booths that extended along one side of the room were filled with interesting exhibits of charts, posters, and so forth, giving fruitful and helpful ideas to all who cared to look at them. A full report of all Intermediate activities during the Convention will appear later in another chapter from the pen of Pacific Coast Secretary Paul C. Brown.

The Junior Conferences

Miss Mildreth Haggard was in charge of the entire Junior programme of the Convention, and she had a perfectly splendid set-up. Be it here said that the part which Junior and Intermediate work plays in up-to-date Christian Endeavor conventions is exceedingly important. These departments can no longer be held in the background or subordinated to young people's work. They got only demand, they deserve, all the recognition that can be given to them.

Along one side of the Junior room a series of booths were erected showing the greatly varied work of Junior societies, including posters and hand-work of all kinds. The variety of articles that the Juniors had made and the neatness and quality of them were certainly to many a revelation of the tremendous possibilities that are wrapped up in childhood. The programme for Junior superintendents, leaders, parents, children, and pastors ran without interruption all day; and the Junior sessions were as busy and as helpful as the sessions of the main Convention. A full report of this splendid exhibit will be found in another chapter from the pen of Miss Haggard.

Better Meetings

A great and deeply interested crowd gathered around E. F. Huppertz, field-secretary for Texas, in the basement, to hear his address on "Better Endeavor," and R. A. Walker's talk on "New Tools for Workers." This conference was held where the booths and literature-tables were situated, and talks were given on the following mornings by Mr. Vandersall and Mr. Shartle on some aspect of the exhibits there displayed.

Al-Azar Temple

We cross the street to Al-Azar Temple, where we find activity as abundant as in the main Convention hall, but with less room to take care of it. But the Endeavorers soon find their places, and the conferences settle down to work.

Life-Work Recruits

There was a conference on Life-Work Recruits and all interested in full-time Christian service. Miss Mary Guiley, president of the Oregon union, presided over the meeting, and H. L. Pickerill and others took part in the discussions. There were two addresses, one by Rev. G. W. Haddaway, D. D., on "The Work of the Preacher," and one by Rev. Dirk Lay, D. D., on "The Work of a Home Missionary." At the second conference Dr. Royal J. Dye spoke on "The Work of the Foreign Missionary," and Frank Linn Freet spoke on "Christian Endeavor Field-Work." At the third conference R. A. Walker gave an address on "The Field Secretary."

World Citizenship

A wider phase of Christian Endeavor activity was introduced this year into the conference work, with a conference on world citizenship. The leader for the first morning was Mr. George C. Southwell, president of the Ohio Christian Endeavor Union, Dr. D. A. Poling taking the other three mornings, and the scheme of the conference was outlined in a new book from the United Society of Christian Endeavor, Boston, Mass., entitled "Adventuring in World Co-operation," by Jerome Davis and Daniel A. Poling. This book, selling at twenty-five cents, sets forth some of the vital problems Endeavorers must face in this crucial day, problems of war and peace, child labor and industry, the relations of the races and of America to the world. The conference, which was continued each morning, special speakers giving brief talks on different aspects of the subject, proved exceedingly interesting and decidedly helpful.

Expert Endeavor

In another room we recognize the voice of Charles F. Evans, Southern secretary of the United Society, who was scheduled to lead conferences day by day on "Expert Endeavor," using Dr. Amos R. Wells' text-book as the basis of his talks. Mr. Evans not only knows Christian Endeavor; he knows how to present his subject in such a way as to make it easily remembered. The interest that exists in the subject was seen in the host of bright young people who attended this conference each day. One morning Carson Mateer, Ontario's field-secretary, gave a fine talk on "Rural Christian Endeavor."

Christ and the Young People

And now in another room we find an interested group listening to Rev. Walter Getty, director of young people's work of the Southern Presbyterian Church, whose topic was "Christ and the Young People." Dr. Clark was present the first morning to give a talk on this subject, which was peculiarly fitting, as he is the author of a book that bears this title. Mr. Getty led this conference each morning with great acceptance, bringing out Christ's attitude toward young people both in Bible times and to-day, and what the young people's attitude toward Christ should be."

A New Start

There is a breathing-space of five or ten minutes, enough to allow the Endeavorers to change conferences if they wish; and a new series of eight conferencs begins. In the main auditorium Paul Brown is on the job, leading the new conference on Christian Endeavor problems. Rev. H. F. Shupe, D. D., editor of *The Watchword*, spoke in this meeting on "Why Christian Endeavor Believes in a Pledge," and Walter D. Howell conducted the conference on Christian Endeavor problems that followed. This, Mr. Howell did with great acceptance on three mornings.

Social Endeavor

The interest of Endeavorers in the social side of Christian Endeavor was clearly seen by a visit to Mrs. E. P. Gates' conference on Christian Endeavor socials. It was a crowded meeting, and pencils flew rapidly over the pages of note-books as ideas that were new to many present were thrown out. The first conference was on "The Essentials of a Successful Social"; the second was on recreation methods, and included "A Year's Social Programme" and "An Evening's Social Programme," and an address by Herbert W. Hicks, field-secretary for Connecticut.

On Wednesday morning the topic of this conference was "Pageantry"; and the leader was Miss Catherine A. Miller, author of the pageant "If," presented on Monday night. Miss Miller took up the practical aspect of presenting pageants, and gave many valuable suggestions along these lines.

Pastors Come In

In yet another room there was a heart-to-heart conference for pastors, Mr. Carlton M. Sherwood, field-secretary of the New York State union, being the leader. The pastor's problem with his young people is sometimes felt to be more serious than it really is. At any rate, Christian Endeavor helps very materially to solve it. Mr. Roy Breg, formerly of Texas, now of Kansas, spoke out of his experience on "Christian Endeavor in the City

Church," telling the story of grading Endeavor societies to meet the needs of groups of young people of all ages. The second day's conference considered "Christian Endeavor in the Small Church," the subject being presented by Harold Singer, Oklahoma's genial field-secretary. The third conference considered the pastors' problems in relation to the Juniors; and in a fine address Miss Mildreth Haggard described a practical "Programme for Juniors."

Interest in the Bible

Stanley B. Vandersall's conference on "Why We Believe the Bible," which was based on a book by Dr. Amos R. Wells carrying this title, demonstrated the interest that young people have in getting at real reasons why we accept the Scriptures as the word of God. A large congregation faced the speaker as he came before them morning by morning, and searching and intelligent questions were asked him. He was handicapped the first day by the fact that the text-books had been lost on the way; but this did not prevent his beginning his conference, even if the book could not at first be placed in the hands of those present. The books arrived the following day. This proved a worth-while conference for the upbuilding of faith.

Missions

The large audience that faced Miss Faye Steinmetz in her three conferences on the topic "Missionary Education through Christian Endeavor" was clear evidence of the interest of Endeavorers in missionary work. Miss Steinmetz did not confine herself to foreign missions, or even to what are technically known as home missions. She included all sorts of missionary work of whatever kind, and laid especial emphasis on possessing the missionary spirit which grows through closer knowledge of missions. On the first morning Miss Georgia Dunn of Kentucky, spoke at this conference on "Prison Christian Endeavor," a truly missionary endeavor well developed in her State. There were many questions and answers, and other speakers dealt with various phases of the subject.

In the Exhibit Room

Every morning during the conference hours talks were given in the Convention exhibit room. Monday morning there was a demonstration of Christian Endeavor literature, and Treasurer Alvin J. Shartle spoke on "The World's Christian Endeavor Exhibit." Tuesday and Thursday mornings, Stanley B. Vandersall delivered a lecture on the same subject. Wednesday morning, F. D. G. Walker, Illinois' field-secretary, gave a fine talk on "How to Organize a Christian Endeavor Society," and Alfred Crouch, field-secretary for Missouri, spoke on "Rural Endeavor."

Union Work

Clarence C. Hamilton was scheduled to conduct three conferences on "Methods of Union Work." Again the large number attending gave evidence of the fact that many union officers were in the Convention and were eager to get what help and suggestions they could gather regarding their tasks. Mr. Hamilton is a snappy conference-leader, and he has a wide practical knowledge of this subject gathered from his own work and from personal contact with the field. F. L. Mintel, New Jersey's devoted field-secretary, was present the first morning to address the conference on "What a County Union Can Do." Russell J. Blair of Massachusetts, was the speaker the second morning, his subject being "What One County Union Does." The third morning, Miss Louella Dyer, field-secretary of the Washington union, spoke on the same subject that Mr. Blair had taken.

Annuities and Bequests

There was one morning conference on "Annuities and Bequests," conducted by Alvin J. Shartle, treasurer of the United Society of Christian Endeavor. Mr. Shartle explained the object of such annuities and bequests, namely, to provide an income to be used for the world-wide work of Christian Endeavor, and outlined the methods of making both annuities and bequests and the advantage, both to the giver and the United Society. Annuities are a new feature in Christian Endeavor, providing a safe investment for one's surplus funds and ultimately putting the money into a good cause.

Publicity

Finally, in the exhibit-room a conference was held on "Publicity Suggestions." Harry Allan, field-secretary of the California union, delivered here a talk on this subject. He brought out the fact that Christian Endeavor needs publicity in all its enterprises. If we are to grow, we must let people know what we are trying to do. Our light must be made to shine. The society needs advertising, and various methods were suggested, posters, bulletins, bulletin-boards, newspapers, signs, and so forth.

To say that the conferences were successful is putting it mildly. They were the laboratory of the Convention. Inspiration was gained in the main sessions, but it was in the conferences that much of the real work was done. We may be sure that many of the suggestions that went into the note-books of the Endeavorers will come out in the shape of new work all over the country.

THE INTERMEDIATES LOOM LARGE

Some Features and Events in the Portland Intermediate Programme

[*This fine report is from the pen of Paul C. Brown, Pacific Coast Secretary of the United Society.*]

The cause of Intermediate Christian Endeavor was greatly advanced by a splendid series of meetings, conferences, banquets, and rallies scattered all through the days of the Convention. Local arrangements were in charge of Mrs. J. Hunter Wells of Portland, chairman of the Intermediate committee in the general Convention organization. Programme features were in charge of Miss Edith McDonald of San Francisco, Intermediate superintendent of the California Christian Endeavor Union.

A large room, seating two hundred and fifty or three hundred, on the balcony floor of the auditorium, was used as Intermediate headquarters for exhibit and meeting purposes. The exhibit. consisting of posters, pictures, photographs of Intermediate groups, and other material, drew interested throngs through all the days of the Convention. Very many sections of the country contributed to this exceedingly successful exhibit.

The first actual "get-together" of the Intermediates of the Convention was held in the social hall of the First Presbyterian Church at the close of the great Sunday-afternoon mass-meeting in Multnomah Field. It was a fellowship hour, with "eats" contributed by the hospitable Portlanders in charge of Mrs. Wells. More than four hundred participated in this fine event. Immediately following this in the main auditorum of the church was held the great union Intermediate Christian Endeavor praise and testimony meeting under the leadership of Field-Secretary Roy E. Creighton of Los Angeles County union, Cal. Mr. Creighton brought a great message to the teen-age boys and girls, and at the close led them in scores of splendid decisions for Christ.

Each morning during the "work-days" of the Convention the Intermediates had the special Quiet Hour sessions of their own. The boys and girls gathered in great numbers to listen to the heart-searching messages from Dr. William Hiram Foulkes of Cleveland, Dr. William Ralph Hall of Philadelphia, Dr. Royal J. Dye of Africa, and Dr. R. F. Kirkpatrick of Dixie. Each morning also a fine message in song was brought by Miss Margery Young, an Intermediate from Hollywood, Cal.

Following these Quiet Hour sessions each morning the Intermediates were expected to attend the various conferences offered on the general programme while the Intermediate leaders (superintendents, advisors, etc.) gathered under the leadership of Miss Edith McDonald for a most inspiring and practical series of conference sessions. Thus a total of about six actual hours was spent in study and discussion on the following main topics and sub-topics:

1. CHARACTERISTICS OF THE TEEN AGE. (a) Three distinct periods of development during adolescence, early (12-14), middle (15-17), later (18-24), represented respectively by changes in the physical, social and mental phases of life. (b) Control is through public opinion, influence of older friends and seasoned judgment of leaders. (c) Intermediate Christian Endeavor is particularly concerned with the early and middle periods. (d) The characteristics to be considered are (1) *physical*, (2) *mental*, (3) *social*, (4) *spiritual*, the first of these covering rapid growth and resultant awkwardness, sexual development, desire for violent exercise, appetite stimulation, social-life strain and excitement, and moderation hard to observe. The second of these covers the transition from childhood limitations to the strength and self-mastery of manhood, the growth of will power, lack of judgment, impulsive action, lack of poise, morbid fear of making mistakes, age of extremes in sexuality and criminality, growing vision and no fear of failure, intense cravings for thrills and exciting stories, starting of intemperate habits, increased interest in adult companionship. The third, or social period embodies mostly personal pride, expressed in jealously for reputation, sensitiveness about personal appearance and manners, gang spirit, and interest in the opposite sex. The fourth, or spiritual, deals in definite conceptions of right and wrong, passionate devotion to ideals, hero worship, intellectual doubts as well as conversion, religion necessarily both personal and vital, and signalizes this as the most favorable age for religious impressions in general.

2. INTERMEDIATE LEADERSHIP. (a) Qualifications: Consecration; willingness to pay the price of leadership, sympathetic understanding of teen-age young people; confidence of the Intermediates, and knowledge of general work and principles of Christian Endeavor. (b) Training: learn by doing; study Christian Endeavor literature and denominational helps; and attendance at conventions, conferences, etc. (c) Helps for leaders: "The Intermediate Manual," by R. P. Anderson, "Psychology of Adolescence," by Frederick Tracey, "Religious Education of Adolescents," by Norman E. Richardson, and many other similar books in addition to the usual Christian Endeavor literature used by Young People's societies. (d) Superintendent's relation to the society: chosen by Intermediates with approval of proper authorities, possibly elected along with an Intermediate committee by the older society; title should be either superintendent or advisor; attitude should be friendly and helpful, also vigilant but not dominating, ready to take leadership when necessary but even more willing to let the Intermediates learn even by their mistakes; ready to accept plans and ideas of the Intermediates, also deeply concerned but not obviously so. (e) Relation to individual members: secure confidence, study individual differences, interests, strong points and weaknesses, be ready to help, encourage, and advise; pray much, seek opportunities for personal work.

3. GRADED CHRISTIAN ENDEAVOR. (a) Real necessity for grouping

young people in proper age classification, using three-society plan for small churches and the five-society plan for the larger ones. When there is just one Intermediate society the age covers 13 to 17, but with two, the ages are 12 to 14 for Intermediate and 15 to 17 for Senior Intermediate. Age limits are suggestive rather than compulsory. (b) Graded Christian Endeavor makes possible an Intermediate society for every church, and even many small churches may have two successful societies. Proper grading must be carefully attended to. Right social conditions will develop accordingly. (c) Annual graduation necessary if Intermediate Christian Endeavor is to be continuous in the life of the church. Adequate and impressive graduation programme should be given in connection with evening church service, diplomas and special message from pastor to be included. All grades of societies should participate in graduation service. (d) Christian Endeavor must help build a correlation programme for the church, one that will preserve Christian Endeavor ideals and features. Leaders of young people's activities should be united in a Young People's Cabinet to study the whole programme of work and co-operation in regard to the young people of the church and community.

4. THE LOCAL SOCIETY PROGRAMME. (a) Organization suggestions: survey the field and list all possible members; call a meeting of this group and explain Christian Endeavor pledge and general plan of organization; provide associate as well as active pledges; small group preferable to a large one; effect temporary organization and secure a nominating committee; begin Christian Endeavor prayer meetings at once. (b) The prayer meeting should be built essentially on original Christian Endeavor basis of prayer and testimony, with reverence definitely insisted upon. Make prayer meeting the heart of the society, utilizing both regular Intermediate topics and denominational suggestions. (c) Committee work facilitated by use of the "Big Four Organized Committee Work plan." All work of the society grouped under the four heads, lookout, prayer-meeting, missionary, and social. Plan adapted to small society as well as large. (d) Business meeting should not be "bossed" by the superintendent. Best methods of procedure should be used. The Big Four plan helps make better business meetings. Finances should receive special attention. (e) Social life of Intermediate society meets and solves "gang spirit." Social events should avoid sameness and be extra well planned. Chaperonage a necessity and a problem. Worldly amusement problem ever present. (f) Real evangelism achieved by use of personal work, proper use of the Christian Endeavor pledge, and by prayer circles in the society and in the high school. The Intermediate society should have a real part in the evangelistic programme of the church. (g) Christian Endeavor ideals to be taught by example, by fellowship with other societies, and through Christian Endeavor conventions and conferences. (h) Vocational guidance necessary. Intermediate age ripe for life decisions. Provide inspiring literature, especially regarding lives of great Christian leaders. (i) Christian Endeavor fellowship through rallies, conventions, and conferences helps produce enlarged vision regarding the movement as a whole. (j) The project method in Intermediate Christian Endeavor means purposeful activities carried to completion. Activities suggested: singing in hospitals, packing missionary boxes, assisting in church services by singing, orchestra, ushering, etc. Intermediate Christian Endeavor is itself a "project."

5. COUNTY AND DISTRICT INTERMEDIATE WORK. (a) The union superintendent responsible for special promotion of Intermediate work and should have support of all union officers. Should he assisted by an Intermediate Cabinet of boys and girls elected by the union. This plan preferable to Intermediate unions, especially in counties, districts, and States. Contact with local societies obtained through correct mail-

ing lists, personal visits and through union paper or bulletin. (b) Definite Programme necessary, with not too many details. Awards and prizes should be advertised at beginning of year. Special Intermediate affairs to be scattered through the entire year. (c) Promotion plans should include survey of field, visits to churches and Sunday schools, organizing activities, and assistance from old-time Endeavorers. Visitation plan should cover entire field during year and definite messages should be given. Do a few things extra well. Don't neglect help of Cabinet and other union officers. Insist on reports. Check up frequently regarding accomplishments. (d) Intermediate features in conventions should be full of life and interest and help create Intermediate spirit as well as adult co-operation. These features should include Quiet Hour and Bible Study, presentation before the convention, luncheon or picnic, I. C. E. meeting and rally. Use some means of distinguishing Intermediate delegates, for the boys and girls are themselves the best argument for Intermediate Christian Endeavor.

6. STATE UNION INTERMEDIATE WORK. (a) Organization and work in the hands of the State superintendent and assistants. (b) Programme for the year should include a definite goal for new societies, some aims for union Intermediate workers, a system of banner awards for societies and unions and the promotion of contest features only when well-rounded programme of activity is planned. The individual society should be the unit of consideration when programme is being planned. (c) Promotion plans should feature much correspondence, deputation work and visits in unions and at conventions, and making the most of the columns of the State paper or bulletin. Publish special Intermediate bulletin occasionally if necessary. Sell Intermediate Christian Endeavor through advertising by posters, salesmanship letters, and the help of all possible Intermediate enthusiasts. (d) State convention programme suggestions. Make use of very best convention leaders. Cultivate an Intermediate consciousness. Give plenty of opportunity for Intermediate "pep" demonstrations. Make use of "hero worship" qualities in Intermediates. Don't neglect decision features. General programme should include Intermediate Quiet Hour, Bible study, banquet, rally, Christian Endeavor meeting, and a presentation of the I. C. E. message to the entire convention. The Oratorical Contest on the Value of I. C. E. is a most valuable and convincing feature.

These conferences under Miss McDonald's leadership brought together each morning from two to three hundred Intermediate superintendents and church leaders interested in the teen-age problem, and were certainly of tremendous value to the cause. Tuesday noon this same group met for an enthusiastic luncheon occasion at the First Christian Church, where a fellowship hour of introductions and brief messages was followed by an inspiring and practical address by Rev. William Ralph Hall of Philadelphia, superintendent of young people's work for the Presbyterian Church, U. S. A. His topic was "The Place of the Intermediate Society in the Local Church Programme." This meeting adjourned for the parade. And in this connection it might be mentioned that the Portland Intermediates were responsible for a special parade feature in their bright colors of green and white, and that all through the Convention they were everlastingly helpful as pages and guides.

The high point in the Convention so far as impressing the Intermediate idea on the delegates in general was concerned came in connection with the Intermediate oratorical contest in the main auditorium on Wednesday morning.

On the last day of the Convention the Intermediates held a mass-meeting at half past four and a banquet at the Y. M. C. A. at six. The ever-helpful orchestra furnished music. The Intermediates gave wonderful testimonies on "What Intermediate Christian Endeavor Means to Me." At the close of the banquet twenty-four Intermediates came forward and offered themselves as Life-Work-Recruits.

The Intermediate features were simply wonderful, excellently planned, and splendidly executed.

THE JUNIORS SCORE

A Report of the Junior Programme at Portland

[*This fine report is from the pen of Miss Mildreth Haggard of Minneapolis, Minn., who planned the Junior Programme and was responsible for its great success at Portland. The Junior Programme was one of the great features of the convention.*]

The Junior Programme at Portland really began many weeks before, growing out of the reports and suggestions of the State Junior superintendents. As the plans slowly evolved, Miss Mary Brown of California, Miss Caroline Boyer of Ohio, Miss Ethel Brown of Michigan, and Miss Mamie Gene Cole of Dixie, assumed responsibility for gathering, classifying, and arranging the exhibit material in the Prayer-Meeting, Lookout and Social, Missionary, and State superintendents' booths respectively. When Miss Boyer, having made conscientious preparation for her booths, found it impossible to make the trip, Mrs. W. Y. Seymour of Massachusetts willingly took up her task. During all these weeks, Mrs. William V. Martin of Illinois, was fashioning with her fingers and paint brush the countless decorations, place-cards, nut-cups, and favors--the setting for the luncheons and dinners—which were to turn every meal-time into a social function.

More of the Staff

During our happy days in Portland, the Junior staff was augmented by Mrs. Everette Baker of Minneapolis, and Miss Edna Smith of Pasadena, the tireless secretaries, who devoted themselves with entire abandon to making the programme run smoothly, and to collecting the material so that the Portland Junior Programme could be shared with all the Junior workers who were still at home. Mrs. Carl J. Freeborn, Selah, Wash., formerly an Intermediate superintendent in Minneapolis, Mr. Wilbert Martin, also an artist, who did all of our lettering, Miss Faith Martin, a musician, and Mr. William V. Martin,— these, like all the rest of the staff, worked day and night in the interests of the Junior Programme.

Our entire programme was the result of most generous co-operation on the part of the State superintendents and Junior workers, and the field secretaries of the country, on the part also of the Junior staff, the local Junior Committee, whose chairman was Mrs. B. I. Elliott of Portland, the Portland Junior superintendent, Mrs. R. Ethel George, who presided over the books sent each day by the courtesy of the Portland Public Library, the Portland churches, and on the part of the busy convention speakers, whose "Gifts of Self" made our dreams come true. Without the helpful interest and attention of Rev. Charles Hurd, without the literature, furnished and placed on sale by Mr. C. C. Hamilton and Mr. R. A. Walker for the United Society, without the generous loan of everything we could use by the Presbyterian Board Rooms, without the missionary posters and other material, prepared and loaned by Mrs. Mary Hill (the Band-Box Lady), without the loan by Mrs. Louise Moore Welsh of West Newton, Mass., of her seven large notebooks on Junior Endeavor (carefully classified, and fascinating in their wide range of practical and proven methods), without the material sent by Miss Leavis of *"Everyland"*, and the library and leaflets sent by the Missionary Education Movement, the file and sample copies of *"The International Journal of Religious Education,"* the posters and lists from the Child Welfare Association, the South American curios, loaned by two Presbyterian missionaries in Colombia, Miss McLeod and Miss Doolittle, the Chinese exhibit and costumes loaned by Mrs. David Brack, whose daughter, Ruth, is a Presbyterian missionary in China, the wealth of material from many of the denominational boards and secretaries, and not forgetting the books, pictures, sand-table, Victrola, typewriters, and other equipment borrowed in Portland, nor the tedious hours of typing and other help given gladly by good friends, our enterprise must have fallen far short of its planned helpfulness.

A Staff Dinner

While the field-secretaries and the officers and trustees of the United Society were dining together on the evening of the Fourth, Mrs. Francis E. Clark, Mrs. Daniel A. Poling, Mrs. E. P. Gates, Mrs. B. I. Elliott, Miss Edith McDonald, and Miss Nora Darnall had been invited to meet at dinner with the Junior staff. In the centre of our table was a huge bowl of choice roses, the gift of Mr. and Mrs. Ray Steele of Portland, who brought them in person from their own garden.

The aim of the Junior Programme was fourfold—to provide *Inspiration* through the Parents' Hour and addresses, *Fellowship* through the social opportunities in the Conference Room and at meals, *Methods* through the Conferences, luncheons, and Junior conventions, and *Educational Stimulus* through the exhibits, books, and seminars. It was directed to reach the Juniors, the parents, the Junior workers, the State superintendents, field-secretaries, and denominational secretaries, the pastors, and the main convention.

The First Programme

For the Juniors, three Programmes had been planned. The first, simultaneous with the Parents' Hour and in the same church, was most happy in its presiding officer, Miss Mamie Gene Cole, the Dixie Junior field-secretary, who conducted the worship service, using the theme—"Loyalty,"—"For Christ and the Church I would be true." Just before speaking to the parents, Dr. Daniel A. Poling addressed the Juniors. Then the large and appreciative audience witnessed the prologue, and the fourth and fifth episodes of the sacred pageant, "Tidings of Great Joy," written by Dr. Louise Dorman of Seattle, and presented by a fine group of Seattle Junior delegates, beautifully trained by Mrs. A. M. Dailey, Seattle Junior superintendent. It was through the tireless and self-sacrificing efforts of Mrs. Dailey that the trip had been made possible, and her Juniors entered whole-heartedly into every feature of the convention.

On Monday afternoon a demonstration Junior convention was held in the First Methodist Church under the direction of Miss Mary Brown, Junior superintendent of California. From the far corner of the balcony came the Call to Worship in the beautiful tones of Miss Faith Martin's cornet, and Scripture and prayer were skilfully woven into the musical background of the worship service. The initial of Miss Brown's given name stands for music as well as for Mary—she both plays and sings, and was always ready when we needed her. The theme of this Junior convention was "Ready for Service," and Mrs. Francis E. Clark, to whom Junior Endeavor owes more than to anyone else, gave the Juniors a beautiful message. She told the story of the first society in Portland, Me., and of its adopting the pledge. The aim of the society, she said, was to teach us to love God, to love one another, and to work for God. These three points she developed in her own interesting and gripp'ng way. Her talk will surely be remembered by the Juniors.

Handwork

The third feature of the programme was supervised handwork, timed to occupy just forty minutes, graded, correlated with special topics or society activities, and arranged at twenty-five different tables where the girls and boys found their places by matching small numerals with the larger ones on the tables. The commodious and well-equipped educational building adjoining the auditorium of the First Methodist Church, lent itself admirably to all our expressional activities. While Miss Brown and her helpers made sure that each supervisor lacked nothing, other workers visited about, gathering new ideas to use at home.

Next, several tables were combined so that four groups were ready for committee conferences, lookout, prayer-meeting, social, and missionary. Every Junior was given an opportunity to contribute items out of his own society experience, and plans were made for reporting each conference to the Junior convention when it reassembled. These reports were original demonstrations of the work of the committees. Perhaps the most startling was the Funeral of a Dead Junior Society. The pall-bearers brought in the casket, covered with a black cloth, and the members of the society mourned and sobbed uncontrollably while the superintendent in the robes of the clergy read the service for the "dear departed."

The close of a programme dedicated to "Service" came very fittingly in an address by Dr. Royal J. Dye, missionary from the Congo, Africa.

Another Junior Convention

The Junior convention on Wednesday afternoon opened with Handel's Largo played by Miss Mary Brown, while the two leaders stood with bowed heads until the music died away in a whisper, when Miss Ethel Brown offered a brief, earnest prayer. Confession—"Ye are witnesses"—was the keynote of the Worship Service. The three Junior conventions were planned to emphasize "Fidelity to Christian Endeavor Principles" so that the Juniors will G-R-O-W in Confession, in Service, in Loyalty, and in Fellowship.

After a brief period of general conference when Miss Brown drew from the Juniors a comprehensive outline of the work of the Junior society and would have gone on to suggest new ideas for their notebooks, the busiest person in the whole convention arrived to bring a message to the girls and boys. When our General Secretary, Mr. E. P. Gates, came down the aisle, every person in the room was on his feet, waving vari-colored handkerchiefs in greeting. It was a real privilege, truly appreciated, to hear Mr. Gates in one of our Junior conventions.

Expressional Games

The expressional period of this convention was spent in playing games. Ten groups were formed, each one with an adult supervisor. Each group played one race, one quiet game, and one active game,—no two groups playing the same games. In the meantime, one group gathered with Miss Alta Tochterman, Wisconsin State superintendent, who told the story of the Ten Virgins and directed their dramatization of it—to illustrate to the workers how it could be done. Then the presentation was given before all the children reassembled. The Juniors had been keenly disappointed because there was no place for them in the parade on Tuesday, so, from their convention, they marched two blocks to the car-line and sang some of their songs—when quiet unexpectedly, all of them came back again, begging for more of everything. We took their pictures, and then, at their own suggestion, the boys tied their colored handkerchiefs together corner to corner, and marched to the Y. M. C. A. to "show their colors."

For Parents

The Parents' Hour, already reported by Rev. Robert P. Anderson in another chapter, was announced in all the churches by a handbill of invitation, featuring the speakers and their subjects.

The Busy Conference Room

On Monday, Tuesday, Wednesday, and Thursday mornings, from nine to twelve, the Junior Exhibit and Conference Room over the main lobby in the Auditorium Building engaged the attention of two hundred and more Junior workers. The morning conferences concerned themselves with the three main divisions of the new Junior Programme,—Worship, Expression, and Service, while Thursday morning was devoted to Objectives, when Mr. Gates made very clear our place in a Comprehensive Programme of Religious Education, and Mrs. Clark, speaking on "God's Plan for the Junior," majored on our specific aim to lead the Juniors to Jesus Christ. On Thursday morning, Miss Cole opened the Question Box, and conducted a delightful session. I think I have never seen so interesting a collection of questions so well handled.

Some of the Themes

Our first moments together were spent in prayer, led by Mr. Paul C. Brown, Pacific Coast Secretary for the United Society. Miss Mary Brown, California State superintendent, then opened the Monday morning discussion on "Worship"—"Training the Juniors to worship and to lead worship services." Using the five conclusions of the Commission on Worship of the Religious Education Association at their Buffalo meeting, and concluding with the statement that "Christian worship is fundamental to Christian character," she introduced Miss Ethel Brown, Michigan State president, for the subject of "Personal Devotions." She said in part: "Our first, most important charge must be, consciously and unconsciously, to create in the hearts of the Juniors the desire to know the Father as a personal Friend. Through the witness of our lives, through the quiet individual talk with a boy or girl, we may help. In cultivating the habit of the regular Quiet Hour, in creating the atmosphere, we may perhaps assist with a book, a picture, a personal word from our own experience."

In discussing prayer-meetings that train in worship, music was presented by Miss Brown, and the use of the Bible, prayer, and the offering, by Mrs. William V. Martin, State superintendent for Illinois, both of whom suggested many practical helps for improving the Junior meetings. Miss Mamie Gene Cole said that the steps in "Preparing for Worship" are: "1. Does the child see Jesus in you? 2. Prepare—Be Ready—Know You are Ready. 3. Create the atmosphere for worship immediately. 4. Begin with a worship service (Miss Hooper's 'Delivering the Goods' suggested).''

The next topic was Worship Services, and Miss Mary Brown talked most helpfully about Themes, Orders of Service, Objectives, Variety. Later, during the exhibit period, her points were illustrated with Worship Music played on the Victrola. She then presented Mrs. Dailey, who drew from her rich experience with memory work, discussing also Memorizing Worship Materials. After a brief opportunity for further discussion, Miss Brown closed the conference period with a choice prayer quoted from "The Manual for Training in Worship," by Hartshorne.

Expression

"Expression—Training Juniors to Express Themselves" was the subject of Tuesday's conference, which Mrs. W. Y. Seymour, Massachusetts State superintendent, introduced by outlining the possibilities of supervised participation—how to prevent its becoming stereotyped and formal. Miss Mary Brown, in speaking of "Preparing for Prayer-Meeting Participation," included the meeting with the leaders, the pre-prayer circle, individual thought books, Daily Readings, prayer lists, advance assignments, and the real heart-preparation of the Junior. The next topic, "Making the Topics Live," was considered under three heads,—"For the Primary Endeavorers," by Mrs. Martin, "Through Dramatization," by Miss Tochterman, and "Through Service Activities," by Mr. W. H. Beeman of Seattle. These speakers packed their minutes full of practical help from their own experience—so full that no excerpt can even suggest their value. We were next privileged to have the Publication Manager of the United Society, Mr. C. C. Hamilton, who, in addressing himself to the subject, "Helps in Vitalizing Expression," gave us two splendid messages,— the one in what he said, the other in the books and leaflets he presented, and the copies of *"The Christian Endeavor World"* and *"The Junior Christian Endeavor World,"* placed in our hands. Mrs. Seymour next introduced Miss Hilda Appelbaum, new York State superintendent, to whom had been assigned the subject, "Recruiting for Christ." The need for decision, the age for decision, how recruit, courses in preparation for Church membership, and supplemental lessons, were the subdivisions of her outline.

When Mrs. Clark was introduced she said she had never seen so beautiful a greeting. A number of boys, stationed in the balcony and in the choir-loft above Mrs. Clark's seat on the platform, when she rose to speak tossed into the air hundreds of tissue-paper hearts, birds, butterflies, and flowers of all colors.

Mr. William Ralph Hall, Director of Young People's Work of the Presbyterian Board, spoke on the important topic of "Loyalty to the Church."

Service

On Wednesday morning the key-note was "Service—Training Juniors to serve the world." Miss Ethel Brown, presiding, first introduced Mr. Paul Brown, who had been asked to outline briefly the Big Four Committee Plan.

The Christian Endeavor plan of organization and activity is still approved as educationally sound. Mr. W. H. Beeman, who with Mrs. Beeman superintends the Woodland Park Presbyterian Junior society of Seattle—306 members, 155 of them boys —every member of which is actually working on two committees, told out of their experience about selecting, organizing, installing, training, and encouraging the chairmen and members of the committees.

The district secretary of the Presbyterian Board, Mrs. C. W. Williams, gave every possible hour and everything at her command to assure the success of our project. It was a rare privilege to follow her clear thinking as she presented the subject, "Training the Child in the Right Use of God's Gifts."

Following Mrs. Williams came a concrete illustration of Stewardship for Juniors in Mrs. Beeman's story of their Junior School of Stewardship, a pioneer effort undertaken at the special request of the Presbyterian Board. The notebooks and materials were on display in the missionary booth, and Mrs. Beeman was there to explain and answer questions.

Miss Faye Steinmetz was most helpful to the Junior workers in her plans for the missionary meetings and her introduction of the new home and foreign mission-study books and helps for the Juniors.

In Washington State, Mrs. C. B. Siler is working for more missionary libraries, and gave us some very practical and effective plans.

Missionary interest growing out of missionary meetings and study should always result in Prayer, Giving, Doing, and Going. Miss Hilda C. Appelbaum told the "How" for Prayer and Giving.

A marvelous and challenging list of "The Acts of His Juniors" in the Pasadena First Congregational Church, one of the California Honor societies, was given by Miss Helen Gertmenian, a delegate, whom Miss Mary Brown introduced in her stead. Mrs. Warren G. Hoopes of Pennsylvania, contributed a splendid list of "Sunshine" activities for Juniors.

Exhibits

Supplementing the morning conference hours, the exhibits were open each day until twelve o'clock. In each booth, a committee was on duty to meet the delegates, introduce them, display the materials, learn their problems, and answer questions. Thus opportunity was afforded for the personal contacts which are so vital a part of every convention. Mrs. Seymour was assisted in the Lookout and Social Booths by Miss Tochterman, Miss Elsie Rhodes, Ohio, Miss Agnes Blake, of South Carolina, and Mrs. Elsie McLaughlin, Portland. In the Prayer-Meeting Booth with Miss Mary Brown were Mrs. Hoopes, Mrs. Dailey, Miss Sadie Seaver, and Miss Louise Chambers, Portland. With Miss Ethel Brown in the Missions Booths were Mrs. C. W. Williams, Miss Appelbaum, Mrs. Beeman, Miss Nora Darnall, and Mrs. H. C. Courter of Portland. In the State Superintendents' Booth, Miss Mamie Gene Cole was assisted by Mrs. Siler, Mrs. William M. Tennis, Ohio superintendent, Miss Wolfangle of Pennsylvania, and Mrs. W. R. Gaither, Portland. In this booth were State Programmes, Records, Publicity, Junior Convention Programmes, Promotional Plans and Essays, Posters, Scrap-books and Illustrated Hymns from Contests held,—representative of the entire country—carefully classified and bound in books—in addition to the pictures and charts on the walls, making a very effective display and supplying visitors with many new and unique ideas that are sure to prove helpful in their work.

The exhibit materials were widely varied and were changed each day, making them a part of the Programme. There were invitations, attendance-records, pledge helps, evangelistic suggestions, church-attendance stimuli, honor-rolls, birthday books, posters, social suggestions, a game list, sunshine ideas, scrap-books, cheer books, programme pictures, a model prayer-meeting room, a demonstrative sand-table, Quiet Hour plans, curios, maps, mission-study materials, a marionette show to illustrate the home book, a book house, missionary charts and gifts, memory work, note-books, stewardship display, handwork, and a wonderful index of selected material for Junior dramatization —mostly missionary. (Miss Vorta Walker, formerly missionary superintendent for the Illinois union, did us the priceless service of making an exhaustive canvass of all sources, listing only those of value to Junior superintendents. Her index was accompanied by sample copies, bound and numbered.) Each booth had for distribution a sheet of methods, thus affording another opportunity of effectively supplementing the formal conferences.

On the walls of the Junior room were flags, emblems, posters, and pictures, borrowed from the Junior departments of the Portland churches, besides the banners representing those States, whose State Junior superintendents were present.

Luncheons

Combining pleasure with business, our noons were spent in the First Congregational Church. The ladies of the church provided excellent meals and service, Mrs. Martin and her daughter, Miss Faith, cared for the decorations and seating, while Miss Mary Brown presided over the forty-minute conferences which closed each day with an address from one of the main convention speakers.

With blue and white cut-out shields overhead, Oregon Grape about the room, and tinted letters to spell "J-U-N-I-O-R C-H-R-I-S-T-I-A-N E-N-D-E-A-V-O-R" arranged on blue and white table-runners, with blue and white pansies, baby-breath and ferns, with hand-painted Junior arm-bands across each napkin, about eighty Junior workers sat down to luncheon on Monday noon.

On Tuesday, the decorations were Chinese. Large red dragons, cut from firecracker paper, alternated on the cloth with black Chinese characters for "child," and napkins tied with Chinese cord and sash were at each place.

Wednesday was Christian Endeavor Day, with red and white roses in vases and at each place, Christian Endeavor napkins, and stickups in the ice-cream. Thursday was Latin-America Day. Clusters of silk flags, representing the South American countries, centered the table and small hand-made baskets from Colombia, South America, held nuts.

The conference theme was "Co-operation" and each of the speakers had been asked to report certain features of their own State programme. Mrs. Martin and Mrs. Tennis told of co-operation with the home, Miss Ethel Brown of co-operation with the day-school, and Mrs. Seymour of co-operation with the church-school. The address was given by Mr. Roy Breg, who spoke on "Graded Christian Endeavor."

The luncheon conference of Tuesday considered "Organization." Mrs. C. E. Hetzler's paper on

J. S.—J. C.=a Dead Society
J. S.×J. C.=Continued Life

told "How" it had been accomplished. In Dixie, societies are organized "for keeps" and Miss Mamie Gene Cole gave her very thorough plan for starting a new society. California has over fifty "Junior Marksmen" to show for the second year of the "Friends of Christ" Campaign. Miss Bessie Dunn, of California, had been given the subject, "Expert" training. Massachusetts has the record for the most "Honor" Junior societies, and Mrs. Seymour showed us "Why" in telling of committee activities. The speaker was Rev. James Kelly from Glasgow, President of the European Christian Endeavor Union.

Mrs. E. P. Gates, the "Social" specialist for the whole convention, addressed the luncheon conference of Wednesday. "Planned Recreation" was her topic.

On Thursday noon, Miss Carrie Miller, Junior superintendent of the Quincy District, Ill., was very helpful in her presentation of the "Budget-Pledge Envelope Plan" for training in systematic giving, and Mr. Beeman talked of "Business Meetings and Written Reports."

A fitting close to our luncheons together came in the personal message to the superintendents from Mr. A. J. Shartle, field-secretary for the United Society. His theme was "Partners with Him."

The Seminars

Then there were Seminars for Junior workers in the lovely private dining-room of the Hotel Multnomah. From Dixie, there was Miss Cole with Miss Agnes Blake, South Carolina, Miss Mary Huband, Virginia, Miss Alice Downing, Georgia, and Miss Maisie McClure, Kentucky. The new Texas superintendent, Miss Nina Mae Nowery, came, and Miss Mignon Cordill, representing Miss Stoelzing of Arizona. From the East, there were Mrs. Seymour and Miss Seaver of Massachusetts, Miss Appelbaum of New York, Miss Florentina Coburn, assistant superintendent of Maryland, Mrs. Warren G. Hoopes, representing Miss Wiggins of Pennsylvania and Mrs. C. E. Hetzler. Mrs. John T. Sproul was the official representative from New Jersey. Ohio brought Mrs. Tennis, and Miss Marie Gregson, representing the Junior field-secretary, Miss Caroline Boyer. Miss Ethel Brown represented Michigan, and Illinois boasted Mrs. Martin. Wisconsin sent their State superintendent, Miss Tochterman, Miss Barnstein, a State officer, and two other Junior superintendents. Mrs. Baker and Miss Haggard came from Minnesota, Miss Mary Brown, Miss Dunn and Miss Edna Smith from California, Miss Bessie Facey from Utah, and Mrs. C. B. Siler from Washington. The newest State superintendent was Miss Dulcina Brown of Oregon, elected during the convention.

Some of the field-secretaries honored us with their presence,— Mr. H. Carson Mateer of Canada, one of our speakers, Mr. Paul C. Brown, Mr. Harry C. Allan, Mr. C. E. Hetzler, and Mr. E. F. Huppertz. We appreciated too the interest and helpfulness of the denominational secretaries, Mr. Walter D. Howell, Miss Faye Steinmetz, and Miss Nora Darnall.

These workers discussed in Seminar such subjects as the Junior Christian Endeavor covenant, promotional plans, memory work, records, motivation, leadership-training, and the New Junior programme, which was presented in chart form. The spirit in which they were approached is best epitomized in the opening address by Mr. Walter D. Howell, whose subject was "The Junior Superintendent's Conception of Her Task."

This was a heart-to-heart talk to leaders emphasizing the

destructive features of Christian Endeavor and pointing out that both Sunday-school teachers and Junior superintendents have big enough jobs not to encroach on each other's work. He dealt with some of the things a Junior superintendent should know, such as how to teach and how to train the Juniors. She must know child psychology and a deep conviction that her task is vital and tremendously important. In this spirit we can face the new day in Junior Christian Endeavor.

[In all the above Miss Haggard has kept herself in the background. It should be said here that the entire plan and programme of the Junior section of the Portland Convention are hers alone. She gave time, talent, thought, labor, and money to make the Junior programme the success it was. She gathered Junior leaders of talent from all parts of the country and laid out their work for the convention, thus making available a mass of information based on actual experience and not on theory such as has never before been presented at any convention. The Junior programme was a remarkable feature of a remarkable gathering, and behind it and in it, giving it vitality as well as being, stands Miss Mildreth Haggard of Minneapolis, who does not claim credit for a tremendous success, but who deserves the credit, with her co-workers, just the same. R. P. A.]

THE DENOMINATIONAL RALLIES

The Friends' Rally

One of the rare treats of the recent Portland Convention was the denominational rallies. Of these various gatherings, none was more greatly enjoyed than that of the Friends. About one hundred and fifteen were in attendance from various sections of the country. The president extended a welcome and struck the keynote of the rally by his words, "The question we face is not, 'Is there a need?' but, 'Are we going to meet the need?' " Rev. Edward Mott followed with an address, the theme of which is best expressed in the words of Paul, "O Timothy, keep that which is committed to thy trust." H. W. Cope, president of the Iowa Christian Endeavor Union, next spoke on "Our Contribution." He emphasized the thought that our lives should be ordered by the question, "What have we to contribute?" After these inspirational messages the delegates enjoyed an informal social hour, at which "the ties that bind" were strengthened into cords of lasting friendship.

The Disciples' Rally

Three hundred and fifty youthful members of the Brotherhood of Disciples of Christ met around the banquet-tables in the First Christian Church of Portland. Following an hour of fun and fellowship, the group adjourned to the auditorium, where it was augmented by several more who could not get in for the luncheon.

After a brief devotional service the Endeavor delegates divided into four groups for forty-five minute conferences on the new Fidelity programme of Christian Endeavor. The programme was presented to the various groups by Miss Cynthia Pearl Maus, H. L. Pickerill, Willard Wickizer, and Miss Georgia Parker.

A second general assembly of the group was called at a quarter past three, and brief messages were brought by some of the leaders of the Disciple young people. The session closed with a message from Dr. Royal J. Dye, formerly missionary to Africa, who spoke on "The World Challenge to Christian Endeavor."

Rally of the Presbyterian Church in the United States

The main discussion in the denominational rally of Southern Presbyterians was on the adaptation of the new Christian Endeavor standards to the young people's programme of the denomination. In the Southern Presbyterian Church there is a programme for the whole denomination, known as the Presbyterian Progressive Programme, which has five great divisions or departments of work: Spiritual life, evangelism and missions, Christian training, stewardship of possessions, Christian social service. These departments of work have been grouped under three heads in the young people's programme of the church—worship, instruction, expression.

All of these activities among the young people of the Southern Presbyterian Church are so nearly like the new Christian Endeavor standards that it will take very little change or adjustment to fit the two programmes into each other. The action, therefore, taken at this denominational meeting was to present the Presbyterian Progressive Programme to the Christian Endeavor societies and to show them how this programme fits in with the new programme of Christian Endeavor. By this plan great things are expected of the Christian Endeavor societies in the Southern Presbyterian Church the coming year.

The Union Rally

It was a real live crowd of Endeavorers that gathered in the union rally at the Auditorium. Seventeen different denominations were represented in that gathering.

Brief pointed addresses on the theme, "How Can I Serve My Church?" were given by Dr. Johanson of the Seventh-Day Baptist Church, Rev. Robert Alexander of the Cumberland Presbyterian Church, and Dr. A. B. Kendall of the Christian Church.

The addresses emphasized the value of Christian Endeavor to the small denomination, and set forth some of the plans and some of the gains in Christian Endeavor in these denominations, and also some of the denominational plans for the future.

After these addresses the meeting was thrown open for brief speeches from a representative of any denomination present. Eight other denominations responded as follows: Lutheran, Reformed Church in America, Church of God, Mennonite, Methodist Protestant, Church of the Brethren, Community Church, Methodist Episcopal.

It was estimated that about one hundred and fifty were present. The meeting closed by singing one verse of "Blest be the tie that binds" and repeating the Mizpah benediction.

The Congregational Rally

Two hundred Congregationalists had lunch together at the Y. M. C. A. They were joined by as many more in the First Congregational Church, where the afternoon programme was presented. A feature was the excellent organ recital which preceded the discussions.

Brief talks were made on the general theme, "Congregational Youth Facing Their Tasks." Those who spoke were Rev. H. E. Johnson, on "The Spirit of Congregationalism"; Rev. J. J. Staub, on "Our World Task"; Rev. C. C. Clark, on "Building a New Earth"; Secretary Fred Grey, on "The Young People on the Job."

The concluding address was given by the national secretary for young people's work, Rev. H. T. Stock, on the theme, "What Is Youth Going to Do to the World?" Mr. Stock spoke of the destructive and dangerous elements in our present civilization and challenged Christian young people to build a better civilization.

The United Brethren Rally

An enthusiastic company of one hundred and fifty participated in the United Brethren rally in the First United Brethren Church. Rev. G. K. Hartman presided. Rev. H. F. Shupe, D. D., editor of the *Watchword*, had charge of the introduction feature of the programme, when more then seventy Endeavorers from ten States told who they were and their official relation to Christian Endeavor in their home churches.

Bishop W. H. Washinger, D. D., bishop of the Pacific coast district of the United Brethren Church, gave an address on evangelism. Rev. C. E. Hetzler, secretary of the Pennsylvania State Christian Endeavor Union, related Endeavor experiences, encouraging loyalty to the church. H. Dixon Boughter, president of Philomath College, Philomath, Or., told the young people about that institution. C. E. Ashcraft, president of the Nebraska Christian Endeavor Union and dean of York College, told of the work in his State.

A. M. E. and A. M. E. Zion Rally

The A. M. E. and A. M. E. Zion denominational Christian Endeavor rally was held in the A. M. E. Zion Church. In the absence of Rev. S. S. Morris, general-secretary of the Allen Christian Endeavor League, who was detained on account of the serious illness of his mother, Professor Aaron Brown, the honored general-secretary of the Varick Christian Endeavor Society, was the inspiring leader of the spirited meeting. Welcome was extended by Bishop J. W. Martin, bishop of Pacific Coast conferences, and Rev. Leo H. Johnston, pastor; response by Bishop W. J. Walls. Bishop L. W. Kyles discussed "The New Programme of Christian Endeavor"; Bishop W. J. Walls, "Our Church and Christian Endeavor"; Professor Aaron Brown and Jas. W. Eichelberger, Jr., "The Correlated Religious Education Programme of the A. M. E. Zion Church." Prayer was offered for the mother of the Rev. Dr. Morris and a message sent him.

RESOLUTIONS

Adopted at the Thirtieth International Christian Endeavor
Convention, Portland, Oregon

Thanks to Portland

Resolutions of thanks are so feeble and inadequate in recognition of the incomparable favors received by this convention from the people of Portland, Oregon, that we decline to use a single unnecessary word. For the sake of history, however, and because we are unwilling not to try to voice in some way our great gratitude, we hereby subscribe ourselves forever the debtors of the Committee of 1925, from Chairman Kanzler, Associate-Chairman Carrick, and Executive-Secretary Hurd, to the last and least page who has done his best in his place. Likewise we owe more than we can pay with words or works to the pastors and churches of Portland; to the hospitable homes of the city; to Governor Pierce and his staff; to Mayor Baker and the obliging metropolitan police; and to an efficient press for full and faithful preparatory publicity and daily convention report. At the peril of invidious mention, we are constrained, also, to name among our largest creditors Director McMichael, Song Leader Percy Foster, the great chorus, and other volunteer singers, bands, and orchestras, all of whom have contributed to this convention's unexcelled ministry of music. But naming all our creditors is as impossible as would be the payment of our debts to them; it was characteristic of Oregon hospitality, as fragrant and lovely as the roses that gave Portland the name she bears, and our gratitude shall be as abiding as the mountains that frame this unapproachable urban picture.

On the Resignation of Rev. Francis E. Clark, D. D., LL. D.

[*The following resolution was first adopted by the trustees of the United Society of Christian Endeavor and later by the Convention. It was framed by the Nominating Committee, Fred L. Ball, Stanley H. Addison, and Warren G. Hoopes.*]

The members of the nominating committee, having heard with deep and sincere regret the resignation of Dr. Francis E. Clark, our honored president for thirty-eight years, and his determination not to consider "No" for an answer as presented this afternoon to the corporation of the United Society of Christian Endeavor, wish to offer the following resolutions:

BE IT RESOLVED that we make recognition of the worth and work of our dear Dr. Francis E. Clark, who founded and has served the cause of Christian Endeavor to the glory of God and the moral and spiritual betterment of the young people of the world. We believe that Dr. Clark has been the exemplification of Christian Endeavor ideals as a true man of God. He has brought to Christian Endeavor his wise but kindly executive ability, his splendid mental equipment, and his deep spiritual nature in the long years of tireless, self-sacrificing service in the spirit of the great Master whom he loves and has most faithfully served; and with him we would recognize the invaluable services of his dear companion, Mrs. Clark, whose very life has been an investment in Christian Endeavor. Together they have fostered the growing success of the great organization of Christian Endeavor until it has become to-day one of the greatest spiritual instruments in the hand of God for the building of the Kingdom of God on earth.

BE IT FURTHER RESOLVED, therefore, that we, as a nominating committee, present the name of our beloved Francis E. Clark to be elected for the office of President Emeritus of the United Society of Christian Endeavor.

Be it still further resolved, that we recommend, remembering Dr. Clark's many years of unsalaried service, that a suitable committee consisting of a representative from each State, territorial, and provincial union of Christian Endeavor, including the United States, Canada, and the District of Columbia, be appointed or elected at this meeting to plan and carry out the raising of $100,000, which will be known as the "Dr. Francis E. Clark Recognition Fund," the interest of the investment of which sum shall go to Dr. and Mrs. Francis Clark as long as they live, and after their death said fund shall be kept as a memorial fund to Dr. and Mrs. Clark, the interest from the investment of the fund to be used in the work of Christian Endeavor as the Trustees and the Finance Committee shall see fit.

BE IT FURTHER RESOLVED, that a record of the adoption of this report be spread on the records of the corporation of the United Society of Christian Endeavor, and that a copy of the same shall be given to Dr. Francis E. Clark.

Dr. Daniel A. Poling

Resolved, that the Endeavorers assembled in this Thirtieth International Convention of Christian Endeavor commend and approve the action of the Trustees of the United Society of Christian Endeavor in electing as President of this organization Reverend Daniel A. Poling, D. D., Minister of the Marble Collegiate Church of New York City, one of the oldest and greatest Protestant churches in North America. Dr. Poling steps into the presidency of the United Society from the office of Associate President. His long contact with the movement as an officer in local unions, as field secretary of Ohio, one of the great Christian Endeavor States, as national citizenship superintendent, and as strenuous crusader for the cause of prohibition, has given him a knowledge of Christian Endeavor principles and methods that eminently fit him for his new tasks.

We rejoice in the election of a man whose record in Christian Endeavor and whose civic and church activities have been an unbroken success. He has measured up to the highest and sternest requirements of every office to which he has ever been elected. He has shown that he possesses vision and driving power,—vision to see and driving power to achieve. Dr. Poling is no stranger. Already he has won the love of a great multitude and he has given his services as associate president without stint to the cause we all love.

We pledge ourselves to stand by him and support him in all the work he undertakes. He comes among us as a tried and faithful friend. We hail him as our leader, together with Dr. Clark, in these crucial times when great battles are to be fought, and lost or won. We assure him that we are with him and that he may count on us.

Leaders may change but Christian Endeavor goes on from strength to strength. The world needs service and service calls for leadership. With deepest sincerity, with honest purpose, with holy devotion, with friendly trustfulness and with sacrificial love we welcome Dr. Poling as our leader, promising participation in his plans and co-operation with him in every enterprise he undertakes.

Peace

It is with profound satisfaction that we see a growing sentiment in the United States against the monumental iniquity of war and in favor of world peace. We feel that of all people the Christian Endeavorers of this country have the right to express their feeling on this urgent matter, because in the World War 150,000 Endeavorers went overseas to defend our country's honor. A very large proportion of our members are now of draft age and would again be called in event of war to take up arms. War is no longer a conflict between armed forces. It is a gigantic struggle of whole peoples, and the evils which it brings with it fall indiscriminately upon innocent and guilty, young and old, armed and unarmed, learned and ignorant. It is our belief that with the new weapons of offense which modern science has developed,—poison gas to cover whole cities with a blanket of death, aeroplanes, aerial bombs, long-range guns, and such like,—war has become hideous, indiscriminate, and wholesale slaughter.

Since war settles absolutely nothing it sets out to settle, and unsettles practically everything, Christian Endeavorers call upon the government of the United States to take effective steps to bring about a limitation of danger of war, with the ultimate object of eliminating it entirely.

We ask Congress to support every effort that promises to bring about international limitation of armaments or that will create a spirit of friendliness among the nations of the earth, to the end that by truth speaking and fair dealing and even-handed justice and wise generosity the suspicions and misunderstandings which have so often been the cause of war in the past may vanish forevermore.

The World Court

RESOLVED, that since war has now become so deadly a menace to the development of our civilization, and since the issue is narrowing down to a choice between war on the one hand, and on the other hand, the establishment of a tribunal for the peaceful and judicial settlement of international disputes, we Christian Endeavorers earnestly urge the establishment of a World Court of International Justice, based on international acceptance of law, to the end that there may be provided a tribunal to which international disputes may be referred and settled on a basis of law and justice. And we further lay on the consciences of the Endeavorers of North America the need of studying this great question and adopting for the nation the principle universally adopted for individuals, namely, law, not war.

Naval and Military Maneuvers

RESOLVED, that the millions of Christian Endeavor young people of North America, who stand unequivocally for peace and good will in the relations of the United States with the rest of mankind, deplore naval maneuvers executed at such places and in such ways as to awaken in the minds of other nations as to the peaceful intentions of the United States. It is nothing less than deplorable, if, while we speak sincere words of peace, as we really do, our naval and military activities should even appear to prove our insincerity.

Mobilization Day

RESOLVED, that we heartily commend President Coolidge's action refusing to sanction the use of Armistice Day as a Mobilization Day. We also approve his suggestion to relate Armistice Day definitely with thoughts of peace. We endorse the President's suggestion to mobilize the patriotic sentiment and strength of our people on the Fourth of

July, and are heartily with him in his generous and statesmanlike utterances with regard to the great problems confronting us in the Far East.

Law Enforcement

RESOLVED, that the Endeavorers of North America are earnestly in favor of strict enforcement of all law, especially the Eighteenth Amendment. We see with distress a dangerous tendency on the part of many to disregard and violate laws which do not suit their convenience. We believe if this spirit prevails, our nation cannot endure. We therefore call upon the Governors of the States in which we reside to take the necessary steps to make effective the laws, to see that there is no discrimination, and that all violators of law are punished. We rejoice to see that the Federal Government is willing to place its power behind prohibition enforcement in all its phases.

The Endeavorers of the country, who gave the United States the victorious slogan, "A Saloonless Nation by 1920," pledge again their support of vigorous law enforcement, and will labor to put into office only men who are pledged to uphold the Eighteenth Amendment and the Constitution of the United States. We deplore the fact that in many cases prohibition laws are being openly violated, and that frequently big offenders, the men higher up, go free, while miserable bootleggers are punished, and that in some cases there is truth in the report that some public officials, charged with the administration of the law, violate their oath of office and fail to apply the law with even-handed justice. We call upon the millions of our fellow Endeavorers in other lands to petition their governments to take steps to put a stop to the shipment of liquor to the United States in violation of our basic law, believing, as we do, that the time is fast becoming ripe to wipe the liquor trade off the face of the earth.

The Young People

RESOLVED, that this gathering has confidence in the young people of to-day and in their desire for uprightness of life and character. We deplore the modern tendency to slander youth, convinced that the sins of youth are reproductions of the sins of manhood and womanhood and are in large part due to failure in the leadership and example of the older generation.

We have abundant evidence of the real sincerity of our youth in the fact that six thousand groups voluntarily, in the past year, formed themselves into Christian Endeavor societies, whose aims are pre-eminently spiritual, and in the further fact that Christian Endeavor conventions never have been better attended than they have been this year. With many thousands of young people at this convention, thirty-five hundred of whom have come from the Eastern side of the Rocky Mountains, while hundreds of thousands would gladly have come but for the heavy expense involved, we feel that we need have no fear for the young people of the churches who are to-day as religious and as spiritual as they have been in any age in the past.

The Family Altar

RESOLVED, that the Endeavorers of America commend every effort made to establish in Christian homes the family altar. We call upon our young people and their leaders aggressively to support the campaign launched by the United Society of Christian Endeavor in this convention for Bible reading and Scripture memorizing.

Our country must be supported by religion, and there is no more effective way to build religion into life than by building it into the life of the child. The family altar makes for good citizenship. It helps to develop character by laying deep foundations in the subconsciousness of childhood. It establishes respect for God, the Church, and law, without which we are building on shifting sand. The family altar is the bulwark of the home.

Much of the evil of our day comes from the fact that religion has been neglected in childhood. The modern divorce mill would soon stop grinding if we had more religion in the home. Christian Endeavorers stand foursquare for personal and home religion and for the full application of religion to every sphere of life. We call upon the fathers and mothers of America by example and leadership to give to the youth of this generation those spiritual foundations that have made America great.

Interdenominational Fellowship

RESOLVED, that we express our gratitude to God for the growing acceptance, by the denominations, of Christian Endeavor as a part of the religious training of their children. Experience has shown that young people can be loyal to their own church and denomination while at the same time they participate in the interdenominational movement. This movement is in no sense a governing or law-making agency, but a clearing-house of methods, a spiritual power house, the West Point of the Church. The leadership of the society does not lie in the United Society of Christian Endeavor but in the individual churches and denominations themselves. The United Society of Christian Endeavor has no creed but love, and no policy but service. It aims at no allegiance to itself, but emblazons on its banner the slogan, "Loyalty to Christ and the Church." Our interdenominational fellowship strengthens the hands of the individual societies in the churches of all denominations. It gives the young people through their local-union work immensely valuable experience and training in initiative and in organizing all sorts of campaigns, which no single society could undertake. We rejoice to see that the local leaders of Christian Endeavor seek to extend the usefulness of their unions, and that by kindly fellowship, they contribute something towards the ultimate fulfilment of our Lord's Prayer, "That they all may be one."

World Fellowship

RESOLVED, that we view with gratitude to God every manifestation of the spirit of friendliness and good will between Endeavorers of different races and countries. Christian Endeavor has proved that it meets the needs of widely varying races. It is to be found in every clime. Men and women of all nations meet on its platform of love and service. It was the first organization that brought together in public meeting and in friendship Boer and Briton after the Boer War. It was Christian Endeavor that brought together Frenchmen, Briton, German, Italian, and ten other nationalities besides, in an all-European Christian Endeavor Convention in Hamburg, Germany, after the World War. British Endeavorers even now invite foreign guests to spend two or three weeks' vacation in English Christian Endeavor holiday homes, where ties of international friendship may be more firmly knit. We rejoice in this particular example of that Christian love that sees no male or female, no bond or free, no Greek or barbarian, but looks upon all in the beautiful white light of brotherly Christian love.

Recognition of the Young People

RESOLVED, that this convention give recognition to the multitude of young people in every State in the Union who are generously giving themselves and their talents to the service of the church through Christian Endeavor. The Christian Endeavor society is a unique movement in the church because of the fact that its leadership is in the hands of 350,000 young people serving as volunteer officers of societies and unions. It is fitting that this host of workers should receive our meed of praise, and it is here given, although words are inadequate to express the sense of indebtedness that we all feel for the great things the young people are doing.

Graded Christian Endeavor

RESOLVED, that this convention of Endeavorers of North America warmly approves the steps that have been taken in hundreds of churches to grade the Christian Endeavor society according to the age of the young people. In many churches, no doubt, there is no room for more than one society; in others, there will be room for two, a Junior and a Young People's; while in others, again, there will be room for three or more. We rejoice that the grading of societies is proving eminently successful, and we commend the zeal of all Christian Endeavor workers in putting the grading plan to the acid test of experience. We see with great satisfaction that hundreds of churches are organizing their young men and young women above twenty-four years of age into Christian Endeavor societies, and are so conserving for Christian Endeavor the leadership values developed in the younger societies; and not only so, but these older societies are bringing out gifts of leadership in young people who may not have had Christian Endeavor training in earlier age. We commend this movement and rejoice in its steady extension.

The New World

To build a new world there must be new-world builders. The Christian church alone has the theory, and works out the process, of a new birth. In doing this, and so building a new world, Christian Endeavor, as part of the church, enlists and trains millions of young people in the service activities of their generation. Endeavorers are found everywhere ministering to the physical and spiritual necessities of their fellows. All of Christ for all of life is the heart of Christian Endeavor teaching, and the basis of its policy. It is a fatal fallacy that the words and principles of Jesus, while they may be worthy of thought, are to be forgotten or disregarded in the practical affairs of life. Society must take Jesus Christ in earnest or crucify Him afresh. He is the way, and the only way out of our perplexities: the humanizing of industry, the equalizing of opportunity, the Christianizing of the social order,—these are but the fulfillment of the sermon on the Mount.

Christian Endeavor aims at building a new world by service. Its Holiday Homes for clean and happy vacations; its work for sailors; its efforts to reach and help men and women in prison; its visits and gifts to hospitals; its departments for Christian Endeavor in Army Posts and on vessels of the Navy; its fresh-air-home work, which gives thousands of city children vacations in the summer; its gifts to missions and to churches; and its law-enforcement activities are but a few of the ways in which it is seeking to relieve distress and loneliness, to create a new and more beautiful spirit in the world, and to lead all men to live more fully by the laws of heaven.

The Near East

It is a joy to us to note that the Endeavorers of South Carolina won, two years in succession, the prize offered by the Near East Relief for having put across the best programme for Golden Rule Sunday, while many other States did work almost equally valuable. The terrible sufferings of orphans and children in Bible lands has made a strong appeal to the sympathies of Christian Endeavorers. It was impossible that they could stand idly by and see thousands upon thousands of little children perish. We have heard the call of the little ones, and we hear it still. Having rescued thousands of orphans from death, we realize that now they must be cared for, loved, clothed, fed, and educated. We are grateful for the opportunity now open to us to organize Christian Endeavor societies in the Near East Orphanages. We feel that the work of the Near East Relief is not done. It has only begun. The need for Christian education is as great in its way as the need for food. If these orphans are to be made good citizens, they must be taught to live the Christian life. We rejoice therefore that the opportunity to celebrate Golden Rule Sunday and to contribute to the Near East Relief is not past. We point out to Endeavorers this opportunity and suggest that in greatly increasing numbers campaigns for Golden Rule Sunday may be conducted by them in their communities, that abundant funds may be provided for this work that concerns the salvation of the bodies and souls of multitudes.

Sabbath Observance

RESOLVED, that this Thirtieth International Christian Endeavor Convention assembled in Portland, Oregon, declare itself unequivocally against the commercial use of Sunday amusements and Sunday sports, and that the Endeavorers pledge themselves to better Sabbath observance and to work for such observance. The Endeavorers declare themselves in favor of Sunday-rest laws and call upon the Endeavorers everywhere to use their full influence.to make the Lord's Day a day of rest, worship and home-life.

THE SIZE OF THIS CHART IS 34 BY 22 INCHES. IT MAY BE PROCURED FROM THE UNITED SOCIETY OF CHRISTIAN ENDEAVOR, 41 MT. VERNON STREET, BOSTON, MASS., FOR $1, POSTPAID. THE READING MATTER ON THE CHART WILL BE FOUND ON PAGE 117 AND FOLLOWING PAGES.

CHRISTIAN ENDEAVOR SOCIETY STANDARDS

The New Standards Chart

The following is taken from the new Christian Endeavor Society Standards chart. This chart may be purchased ($1, postpaid) from the United Society of Christian Endeavor, 41 Mt. Vernon Street, Boston, Mass. The printed matter given below does not show the appearance of the chart, which has spaces for marking goals and achievements and so forth. The necessary seals to affix to the chart when definite work is done are supplied with the chart.

These standards are sufficiently general to apply to Christian Endeavor societies everywhere. The executive committee of each society, in consultation with the pastor of the church, should set definite goals adapted to local conditions. In planning the programme careful consideration should be given to the work being done in the Sunday school, day school, and elsewhere, so as to avoid duplication of effort. If the members of the Christian Endeavor society are doing some of the work outlined in these standards under auspices other than Christian Endeavor, the same recognition should be given as if the work were being done by the society.

For service suggestions in connection with this chart write to the United Society of Christian Endeavor, 41 Mt. Vernon Street, Boston, Mass., or your denominational young people's department.

I. WORSHIP
  A. PRIVATE DEVOTIONS
     (Prayer-Meeting Committee, Quiet Hour Committee.)
     Ideal: Every member making it a rule to pray and read the Bible every day.
     Goal: Set a goal for Quiet Hour enrollments, to be reached within six months, and mark the chart as progress is made.
  B. PARTICIPATION IN CHRISTIAN ENDEAVOR MEETINGS
     (Prayer-Meeting Committee, Music Committee, Information Committee, Missionary Committee, and Lookout Committee.)
     Ideal: Every member taking some part, aside from singing.
     Goal: Set as a goal an aggregate number to take part during a period of six months.
  C. ATTENDANCE AT CHURCH SERVICES
     (Lookout Committee, Prayer-Meeting Committee, Publicity Committee.)
     Ideal: Every member attending church services regularly.
     Goal: Set a goal specifying the total number of Endeavorers you expect should attend church services during a period of six months. (For example: One person, attending one service a week for twenty weeks, should score a total attendance at twenty services.)

II. INFORMATION
   The information programme of the society should be planned in relation to the programme of other organizations in the church. Among the subjects which should be considered are: The Bible—

How to Know It and Use It; Church History and Doctrine; Methods of Church Work (including Christian Endeavor principles and methods); Stewardship; Choice of a Life Work; World Christian Citizenship, etc.

A. STUDY CLASSES
(Missionary Committee, Citizenship Committee, Executive Committee.)
Ideal: Every member enrolled in at least one class a year.
Goal: Set as a goal the total number of members you aim to enroll in study classes.

B. WEEKLY MEETINGS
(Prayer-Meeting Committee, Missionary Committee, Citizenship Committee.)
Ideal: Specific questions presented as part of regular society meetings.
Goal: Set as goal the number of meetings during six months when such discussions will be held.

C. CHRISTIAN ENDEAVOR LITERATURE
(Executive Committee, Christian Endeavor World Representative, Good Literature Committee.)
Ideal: Enough readers of "The Christian Endeavor World," other young people's religious papers, and Christian Endeavor books of methods to familiarize officers and members with the principles and methods of Christian Endeavor.
Goal: Set as a goal the number of subscriptions to "The Christian Endeavor World," and other young people's religious papers, to be taken by members of the society or church.

D. CONFERENCES AND CONVENTIONS
(Executive Committee.)
Ideal: One or more delegates to some denominational or interdenominational conference, institute, or convention, where information and inspiration for better work may be secured.
Goal: Set as a goal the total number to be sent to all meetings.

III. RECREATION

A. PERSONAL STANDARDS
(Prayer-Meeting Committee, Social Committee.)
Ideal: One or more Christian Endeavor meetings in which personal standards of recreation will be discussed.
Goal: Set as goal a definite date for such meetings.

B. A SOCIETY PROGRAMME
(Social Committee, Executive Committee.)
Ideal: An adequate number of well-planned indoor and outdoor social events.
Goal: Set as goal the number of social events to be held during a period of six months.

C. GOOD TIMES FOR OTHERS
(Social Committee, Citizenship Committee, Missionary Committee.)
Ideal: Recreation provided for those not members of the society.
Goal: Set as goal the number to be served during a period of six months.

IV. SERVICE

A. WINNING NEW MEMBERS
(Lookout Committee, Publicity Committee, Sunday-School Committee, Social Committee, Evangelistic Committee.)
Ideal: New Members added regularly to church, Christian Endeavor Society, and Sunday school.
Goal: Set as goal the total number to be added during a period of six months.

B. HELPING CHURCH AND PASTOR
   (Executive Committee, Pastor's Aid Committee, Sunday-School Committee, Flower Committee.)
   Ideal: Definite service each month for church and pastor.
   Goal: The executive committee should outline the work to be done, after consultation with the pastor. Mark the chart each month when work is done properly.
C. SERVING THE NEIGHBORHOOD
   (Executive Committee, Missionary Committee, Citizenship Committee.)
   Ideal: Definite service for the community in which the church is located.
   Goal: The executive committee should outline the work to be done, after consultation with the pastor. Mark the chart each month when work is done properly.
D. MISSIONARY SERVICE AT HOME AND ABROAD
   (Missionary Committee, Executive Committee.)

V. FELLOWSHIP
   A. WITH OTHER YOUNG PEOPLE OF THE DENOMINATION
      (Executive Committee, Missionary Committee.)
      Ideal: Correspondence with the denominational young people's secretary, or department secretary, and support of his work.
      Goal: Set goal as suggested by young people's department of the denomination.
   B. WITH YOUNG PEOPLE OF THE COMMUNITY AND STATE
      (Executive Committee.)
      Ideal: Co-operation with local, county, district, and State Christian Endeavor Unions.
      Goal: Set goals for total attendance at Christian Endeavor Union meetings during six months, and contribution to local and State Christian Endeavor work.
   C. WITH YOUNG PEOPLE OF AMERICA AND THE WORLD
      (Executive Committee, Missionary Committee.)
      Ideal: Co-operation with the interdenominational and international Christian Endeavor movement.
      Goals: Set goals for: Observance of Christian Endeavor Week. At least one other meeting each year on world-wide Christian Endeavor. At least one letter a year to the United Society of Christian Endeavor, reporting officers and activities.

VI. ORGANIZATION
   A. OFFICERS AND COMMITTEES
      (Executive Committee.)
      Ideal: Every member in active service.
      Goals: At least the following officers and committees appointed: President, Vice-President, Corresponding Secretary, and Treasurer; Lookout, Prayer-Meeting, Social, and Missionary Committees, or their equivalent. Other committees, such as Information, Publicity, Flower, Sunday-School, Good-Literature, Music, etc., appointed as needed.
      Written reports from every committee.
   B. MEMBERSHIP STANDARDS
      (Executive Committee, Lookout Committee.)
      Ideal: Some form of pledge for active and associate members. Affiliated membership, without membership pledge, open to all young people.
      Goal: Set goal as follows: The pledge hanging on the wall of the society meeting-room; read in concert when new members join; given special consideration in at least one meeting.

C. PARTICIPATION
(Executive Committee, Prayer-Meeting Committee.)
Ideal: Every member trained in expression and leadership.
Goals: Weekly prayer meetings and monthly consecration meeting in which individual participation is encouraged. Committee meetings at least monthly. Business meetings at least bi-monthly. Regular meetings of officers and committee chairmen in executive committee.

D. CO-OPERATION IN CHURCH PROGRAMME
(Executive Committee.)
Ideal: Heartiest co-operation with other organizations in the church.
Goals: Election by society, with approval by church authorities, of an adult to advise in planning and conducting society work. Representation of society by president or counsellor on official church committee, if the church leaders approve.

How to Use This Chart

1. *Study these Standards.* Your society should be doing something under nearly all of these lines of activity. Make a note of what is now being done, and what weak points in your work need strengthening.

2. *Consult Your Pastor.* Get his suggestions as to work that he would like to see your society undertake. Remember that every Christian Endeavor society owes first loyalty to its own church and pastor.

3. *Set Your Goals.* In a meeting of your officers and committee chairmen decide what your society ought to accomplish under each section during the next six months, and set your goals accordingly. Do not set your goals too low, but do not set them so high as to be impossible. Indicate these goals in the proper spaces on the chart.

4. *Assign Committee Work.* Make sure that the attainment of every goal is definitely assigned to some committee. The success of your efforts will depend on the extent to which every member of every committee understands his responsibility for part of the task.

5. *Appoint a Campaign Manager.* Some member, perhaps the vice-president or chairman of the Lookout Committee, should be appointed campaign manager to secure reports from each committee and mark the chart under each head as progress is made toward the goal.

6. *Report Adoption.* Send word to General Secretary, United Society of Christian Endeavor, 41 Mt. Vernon Street, Boston, Mass., that your society has adopted the chart and set definite goals. In reporting, give the name and address of your president and of your campaign booster, together with the name of your church and denomination. This information will make it possible for the United Society of Christian Endeavor to send your society helpful information in regard to your work.

7. *Mark Your Progress* in the spaces provided under each section by filling in the blocks with ink, paint, or crayon. If this is done neatly the chart will present an exceedingly attractive appearance.

8. *Report Success.* At the end of six months' work report your success to the United Society of Christian Endeavor. You do not have to reach every goal in order to be recognized as an Honor Society. If your pastor will certify that for six months your society has done acceptable work, which he believes worthy of recognition, report this fact over his signature, and the Gold Honor Seal will be sent to you to be placed on the large circle at the bottom of this chart.

9. *Inscribe Names of Workers* in the spaces at the bottom of the chart. When the Honor Seal has been affixed, let each officer and committee chairman sign his name in the proper space at the bottom of the chart. The chart will then form a permanent record of six months' worthy achievement.

10. *Start over Again.* Begin work with a new chart. Set new goals and try to make the new record better than the old one. Keep the old chart on the wall of the Christian Endeavor room as a basis of comparison.

11. *Honors and Recognitions.* The names of all Christian Endeavor societies winning honor seals will be inscribed in a permanent record to be kept in the Christian Endeavor Headquarters Building in Boston. A special honor roll will be kept of societies winning seals for two or more six-month periods.

12. *For Service Suggestions* in connection with this chart write to the United Society of Christian Endeavor, 41 Mt. Vernon Street, Boston, Mass., or your denominational young people's department.

CONVENTION SNAP-SHOTS

It was a firecrackerless Fourth of July in Portland, Or. Many delegates remarked on the absence of the noise of exploding crackers. It seems that it is prohibited to set off firecrackers within the city limits, and the law is enforced. It may be hard on the small boy, but it is good for the city. There are no fires caused by firecrackers in Portland.

Edwin Wells of Lowell, Mass., and his pretty bride, who made the trip to Portland, Or., with the Massachusetts delegation as part of their honeymoon, will never forget that rollicking experience; nor will they ever forget their march in the parade at the head of the delegation, when they represented John and Priscilla Alden. They looked the part most charmingly.

Probably the joke of the Convention appeared in one of the local daily newspapers, and was wholly unintentional. Across the top of the front page, in large, bold-faced type, were two head-lines, the one under the other, which read:

ENDEAVORERS ARRIVE
People Flee in Panic

New Jersey had sixty delegates at the Portland Convention, the largest delegation New Jersey ever has sent to any distant convention.

One of the delegates called to one of the cowboys at Medora, N. D., to give a speech. "It would be a rough one," came the reply. And if it was as rough as the riding, it would certainly have been full of pep.

At Logan, Mont., the delegates saw the only trace of the Montana earthquake. It was a schoolhouse, a large brick structure, the roof of which had been pretty thoroughly shaken down. The church near by and the other wooden buildings seemed not to have been harmed.

While the Endeavorers from the Portland special were visiting the North Dakota State convention in Bismarck, General Secretary Gates read a message of greeting from former General Secretary William Shaw.

At the round-up at Medora, N. D., a dozen fine young girls from ranches in the valley attracted attention by their fine riding on beautiful and docile steeds. One of them had a ribbon on her felt hat (which covered a head of adorable curls) on which were printed the words in golden letters, "I am looking for a sweetheart." Unfortunately the train whistle blew, and the available young men had to run for the train. When we pulled out, the little girl was still sitting, lonely, on her horse.

For service and comfort no International Convention group has ever fared better. The Northern Pacific Railway has everything on its trains, practically everything that the traveller's heart can wish. The food in the dining-car is delicious and abundant. The Convention group was fed as no convention delegates ever were fed before.

"Did you see the swimming pool?" one young lady asked her friend while in Helena, Mont. "No," answered the other. "Oh, then you have missed the whole trip," returned the other pityingly. There are no grades of value in young life. Everything is superlative.

It was a pretty girl from the First Baptist society of Minneapolis, who gave to each delegate on the train a friendly kiss from the society. The kisses were of the candy variety, wrapped in paper.

"P. B. M. C." is the title of a bulletin issued by the "Progressive Business Men's Club" of Portland, Or. The issue for July 9 was largely devoted to Christian Endeavor. On the front page was a large Christian Endeavor monogram in red, along with an announcement that Dr. Clark and General Secretary Gates would be the speakers at a meeting of the club. On page 2 was a short article by Dr. Clark, and on page 3 another by Rev. Robert P. Anderson, editorial secretary of the United Society of Christian Endeavor, on "High Points of Christian Endeavor." This is the spirit in which Portland received Christian Endeavor.

The Grand Lodge of Oregon Orangemen not only sent greetings to the Convention, but also a hearty invitation to Endeavorers who might be staying over Saturday, July 11, to attend the Orangemen's annual celebration and picnic. Most of the Endeavorers had left the city before Saturday, but the invitation was greatly appreciated all the same.

Here is a sample of Portland courtesy, not the courtesy of Endeavorers, but of the general public. I had left a Convention supper, and was anxious to reach Multnomah Hotel for another meeting. I inquired of a man on the street-corner the way to the hotel, and found that was about thirteen blocks away, quite too far for me to walk. I inquired whether there was a taxi stand near by. A look of real concern came over the man's face as he said, "Are you feeling unwell?" "No," I replied, "just tired." "Well," he continued, "my car is parked around the corner. Hop in, and I'll run you down to the hotel." And he did, protesting against my thanks, and glad, as he said, to be able in any way to be of use to the Endeavorers. And this is the kind of treatment we got everywhere.

A touch of "internationality" was given to the Convention choir by the presence in it of two Chinese girls who contributed their part to the music.

For the first time in history the picture of a religious leader at a religious convention was sent over the telegraph wires of the United States. Dr. Clark had the honor of being the person whose photograph was broadcast in this way. The method will doubtless be developed in time and applied to scenes as well as photographs.

Assurances of the improved health of Dr. William Shaw were received with much appreciation by a multitude of his friends, and his telegraphic letter of greeting was received by the Convention with great pleasure. His great services for the cause of Christian Endeavor during many years of eminent service as general secretary of the United Society will never be forgotten.

The secular papers since the Convention have frequently emphasized the happy faces and the good spirits of the delegates, as though it were an unusual thing for a great throng of Christian young people to be full of good cheer. But why not? Why should they, of all others, ever be gloomy and long-faced? Christianity is a religion of joy. The "gospel" itself means "good news." Believers have "the promise of the life that now is, and of that which is to come." Brother editors of the secular press, in dealing with the joyous side of the Convention you have been telling a twice-told tale.

The Convention weather for the most part was superb. It was possible to sleep soundly throughout the cool nights, and the midday heat was never oppressive except possibly on one day, while not a single shower marred the out-of-door features of the Convention or spoiled the summer finery of the visitors. The heavens smiled as well as the delegates.

Dr. and Mrs. Clark wish to express their profound thanks to the Endeavorers and other citizens of Portland, Or., for the many kindnesses showered upon them during their stay in that delightful city. Their rooms in the Multnomah Hotel were perfect bowers of roses and other flowers from the beginning to the end of their stay, being decorated by as many as half a dozen large baskets of flowers at one time. Automobiles were constantly at their disposal, with obliging chauffeurs, usually of the fair sex; beautiful young "pages" were always at hand to do their bidding; and magnificient Oregon cherries continually "said it with fruit" in addition to the flowers.

They were also indebted to the proprietor of the Multnomah Hotel and to the managers of the Northern Pacific and Great Northern railway lines for many courtesies.

At the Convention the trustees of the United Society of Christian Endeavor sent telegrams of greeting to Dr. William Shaw, former general secretary of the United Society, and Dr. Howard B. Grose, who has been for many years vice-president of the United Society. It was Dr. Grose who, by the way, designed the Christian Endeavor pin, and he was one of the two men (Dr. Ira Landrith was the other) who coined the great slogan at Atlantic City in 1911, "A Saloonless Nation by 1920."

Some of the little meetings which will be longest remembered will be the parlor-car devotions just before the porters made up the berths. As the train sped through the black night with rumble and roar, many hearts were bowed in gratitude before Him of whom the Psalmist said:

"The Lord shall preserve thee from all evil;
He shall preserve thy soul
The Lord shall preserve thy going out and thy coming in."

Millions and millions of miles were travelled by the delegates. The Dixie Endeavorers alone aggregated more than a million miles of travel; but not a single serious accident, going or coming, has been recorded. Even Mrs. Hetzler of Pennsylvania, who was somewhat injured in an automobile accident, was able to attend most of the Convention exercises.

This Convention was particularly favored with beautiful gavels, though there was little occasion to use them in keeping order, which kept itself. The ever-thoughtful Convention committee provided a lovely gavel made of fourteen different kinds of Oregon wood deftly and artistically joined together. This was presented to the chairman of the Convention on the first evening in an appropriate address by Judge Kanzler, the chairman of the Convention committee. Friends of the Near East work gave the Convention a gavel made of olive-wood from Jerusalem. And Mr. W. N. Jenkins of Oakland, Cal., treasurer of the California Christian Endeavor Union, sent Dr. Clark a beautifully finished and mounted gavel made of California rosewood for his use during the last day of the Convention. These gavels will all be cherished by the United Society and preserved in its Memorial Room for future generations.

Of course the magnificient scenery with which Portland is surrounded added greatly to the joy of the delegates, many of whom had never before seen such a fairy-land of beauty. The majestic Columbia, snow-covered Mt. Hood, fortunately not obscured, as it often is, by the smoke of forest fires, the unequalled highways, the sylvan charms on every side, the magnificent roses and other flowers of the "Rose City," have hung up mental pictures for us which we shall carry to our dying days.

LOOKING BACKWARD
Some Impressions of the Convention

Now that it is all over, I want to say that the International Christian Endeavor Convention held at Portland, Or., July 4-10, 1925, was one of the best International Conventions I have ever attended, and in some respects it was decidedly the best.

In the matter of organization and arrangement, for instance. The local Convention committee had overlooked no detail. The comfort and convenience of the delegates were looked after with a thoughtfulness and careful planning that are beyond all praise. Nothing was wanting. The machinery was set up, and it worked smoothly. From the page at the bottom to Rev. Charles T. Hurd, executive secretary of the Convention committee, and Judge Jacob Kanzler, chairman, courteous, kindly, and generous service was given to all.

Then I should want to register it as a spiritual convention. By that I mean that the dominant note was the devotional. It was struck in those pre-prayer meetings that were held on the opening day of the Convention when hundreds of Endeavorers met to pray for guidance and blessing. It was continued in the morning Quiet Hour sessions, and was carried through most of the inspirational meetings. The speakers were drawn largely from the ranks of pastors, and there seemed to be a deep realization of the fact that our activities are fertilized only as the Spirit of God is in them.

Then, again, it was a working convention. Hours and hours were given to class study or to conference work. And interest was maintained throughout. Among the young people there was a manifest will to learn as well as a will to serve.

I should call it a colorful convention, with a decided tendency to make more of color and spectacle than has been common in the past. Delegations are more and more dressing alike as to color, and when the members of a delegation sit together in the Convention hall, as they do, the mass effect of the great variety of color is pleasing to the eye. The color scheme of head-dresses and caps was especially charming.

Emphasizing the colorful feature were the parade and the pageant. The latter especially, in the nature of the case. It is possible that in future conventions this feature may be used to better advantage, more time being given to preparation and rehearsal.

Burning public questions received attention in the speech delivered by Governor Gifford Pinchot of Pennsylvania; and the social values of the gospel were brought out in Dr. A. Ray Petty's addresses, so that, although there was no glittering array of public men on the programme, wide interests received attention. The world situation in its bearing upon Christian Endeavor was dealt with by Mr. James Kelly.

This was also a convention of power. This was felt by all who attended. Hearts were moved. Resolves were made. Visions were seen. New life was begun. The discouraged were renewed in spirit. The Convention will mean much to the young people of the West. Many of them received a new idea of what Christian Endeavor stands for, and of what it is capable of achieving. Many received a new baptism of enthusiasm. Ideas that were expressed in conference will be seen in operation in many societies and many lives.

The Convention will go down into history as the one in which the career of Rev. Francis E. Clark, D. D., LL. D., as president of the United Society of Christian Endeavor, which began in the East, was closed in Oregon, on the other side of the continent. Dr. Clark retires full of honors. He retires not to idleness, but to increased activity as president of the World's Union of Christian Endeavor. Life is change, and we believe that Dr. Clark's desire to be free of the burden of his one presidency that he may give himself more fully to his other will be justified by events.

For one man especially this Convention has great significance, namely, Dr. Daniel A. Poling, minister of Marble Collegiate Church, New York City, now president of the United Society of Christian Endeavor. He takes up, in this position, a great and noble tradition. He takes it up well aware of its responsibilities and in a humble spirit. The prayers of millions go up for him. The loyalty and love of millions of young people are his to-day. May divine grace be his to sense the divine will and to have the courage and wisdom of leadership. God bless him!

But the Convention is not over. The benediction pronounced by Dr. Clark links the past with the future. The Convention, in its practical influence upon thousands of Endeavorers who could not be present, is just beginning. It is also beginning for many who were present. The value of a convention depends on the way its ideals work out in life. The slogan of the 1911 Atlantic City Convention, "A Saloonless Nation by 1920," swept across the nation, and perpetuated the Convention throughout the years. And although no stirring slogan went out from Portland, unless, perhaps, it be Dr. Clark's great challenge to "Fidelity," the Convention will live on in consecrated lives, in higher aspirations, and in a better-equipped service by the young people "for Christ and the church."

DR. CLARK'S RETIREMENT

Practically the entire religious press and many secular papers commented on the retirement of Dr. Francis E. Clark from the presidency of the United Society of Christian Endeavor. The following editorials are only samples of the character of the press comments.

[Editorial in *The Christian Herald*.]

There are few men better known or more widely beloved than Dr. Francis E. Clark, the founder of Christian Endeavor, who, after a long and phenomenally successful leadership, has resigned the presidency of the United Society of Christian Endeavor. Fourteen years ago he felt that, in view of the rapid growth of the organization, and of the fact that he was also president of the World's Christian Endeavor Union, the increasing duties of both were more than one man should carry, and a change was desirable. He was overruled by a host of loving friends. Now, however, with impaired health, and having reached his seventy-fourth year, he feels that resignation from one of the offices is an important duty.

Dr. Clark's whole career has been one of splendid self-sacrifice. He won the love of people of every class and denomination through his unsparing devotion to the spiritual welfare of others. His life has been literally spent in service, and his field has grown until it has become world-wide. He is beloved in many lands, and his long life of devotion to the spiritual uplift and enlightenment of humanity has won him enduring appreciation.

To *The Christian Herald* family Dr. Clark has long been a familiar figure, and his helpful sermons and letters of travel have appeared in these columns at short intervals for thirty years or more. He has proposed as his successor in the presidency of the United Society of Christian Endeavor Rev. Dr. Daniel A. Poling, who is one of the most popular contributors to *The Christian Herald*. Dr. Clark's choice of a successor already trained to the work of the organization and splendidly equipped should receive cordial indorsement.

Meanwhile the Christian veteran, who loves the work of which he was the founder, will not be wholly detached from it, even though he has surrendered the helm to younger hands. Revered by all, he will stand by them in spirit, if not in active leadership—a safe guide, a wise counsellor, a lover of souls, a man among men!

Endeavor under New Leadership

[Rev. Orvis F. Jordan in *Zion's Herald*.]

Without doubt one of the most interesting features of the Portland

Convention was the retirement of Dr. Francis E. Clark from the presidency of the organization, which he has held for thirty-eight years. He is now almost seventy-four years of age, and the infirmities of years seem to make it necessary for him to have a quieter life than heretofore. Every courtesy that could be paid the veteran leader was his. The Convention authorized the raising of $100,000, the interest from which will go to Dr. and Mrs. Clark during the remainder of their lives. Then the fund will be a special named endowment fund to continue the work of Christian Endeavor.

Portland was made conscious of an unusual experience on Tuesday when the annual parade was staged. The young people, arranged by States, marched through the streets in brilliant uniforms of various kinds, singing Christian songs and full of the joy of youth. Such a demonstration helps to dissipate the general pessimism of publicists about the young life of to-day. Four million young people banded together for Christ and the church are a force that must be reckoned with. The youth movement is not a movement toward radicalism and atheism. So far as there is any youth movement in America worth noting, it is a movement toward a more vital relationship with Jesus Christ.

Leader of Youth Since 1881

[Editorial from *The Continent.*]

Many hearts will be sad, especially the hearts of those who once were active Christian Endeavorers but have now passed middle life, to learn that Dr. Francis E. Clark—long affectionately known as "Father Endeavor" Clark—has retired from the presidency of the United Society of Christian Endeavor. His successor is Dr. Daniel A. Poling, who for ten years, as associate president, has assisted in bearing the burdens and shaping the policies of this worldwide organization of Christian youth. And Dr. Poling has proved his capacity for the task. Nevertheless, there is keen regret that the weight of years has led Dr. Clark to conclude that his official relationship should be terminated.

A rare record attaches to the name of Francis E. Clark. In 1881 he organized the first Christian Endeavor society in the church of which he was pastor at Portland, Maine, and from that date until his resignation at Portland, Oregon, this month, he headed the movement which has extended to the ends of the earth and given birth to numerous other powerful organizations of Christian young people. From the beginning until now the keynote not only of Christian Endeavor but of other denominational movements has been that of loyalty to Christ and his church, and the method emphasized has been that of self-expression as essential to the development of a vigorous and effective Christian life.

Dr. Clark was a pioneer. He was one of the first to see what is now generally admitted, that the appeal of the church had been almost altogether to the adult mind and that its general attitude toward youth had been an attitude of neglect and suppression. The young pastor, making no particular effort to introduce a new theory into the minds of men, started in to give a practical demonstration of what he thought could be done. And he succeeded where mere theorists would have failed. While they were writing about what ought to be done, he quietly went ahead and did it. The outcome affords a striking illustration of how concentration upon the opportunities nearest at hand may be the most effective way to influence the whole world.

Instead of neglect and suppression, Dr. Clark provided for the young Christians of Portland cultivation and expression. He suggested to them a method by which they might learn for themselves the will of their Lord and Master, and then do the Father's will in their own way. He gave his young people a chance, and they grasped it eagerly—as young people always will. Others saw what was happening and insisted on having the same chance. Thus the movement spread—in spite of the intense opposition of a good number of pastors and other church leaders.

Dr. Clark will be known for generations to come as one who was called of God to lead in utilizing for Christ the tremendous power of virile, idealistic youth. The whole Christian church owes a great debt of gratitude to this quiet, faithful, wise leader—a true father of Christian youth.

Dr. Francis E. Clark's Retirement
[Frederick Lynch in *Christian Work*.]

I have just seen the notice of Dr. Clark's retirement from the presidency of the United Society of Christian Endeavor, and I cannot let pass this opportunity of saying just a word of tribute to one who is not only one of the most outstanding figures in the religious history of the last fifty years, but who has always been the wise counselor to me and a very highly cherished friend. I do not suppose that one can overestimate what Dr. Clark has done for the religious life of youth, not only in America but throughout the whole world. The Christian Endeavor Society is but an illustration of what great things can come from small beginnings, when the small beginnings are in the hands of a prophetically minded statesman. Our readers will remember the Christian Endeavor movement grew out of a little organization which Dr. Clark started years ago in his own church in Portland, Maine. He felt that somehow or other the church was not sufficiently ministering to the life of the young people in the parish and so he brought them together into an organization where he as pastor could not only meet them personally but could lead them in finding expression for their religious thought and feeling and finding opportunity for Christian service. The movement was such a success in Dr. Clark's own parish that he soon got the vision of its expansion throughout the nation and afterwards the world. Out of this little parochial beginning grew the world organization.

The Society grew by leaps and bounds until it was not many years before practically every Protestant church in the United States had a Christian Endeavor Society or some young peoples' organization which corresponded to it. For a time the movement met with some criticism on the ground that Dr. Clark was forcing religious expression on the boys and girls. Critics said boys and girls had practically no religious experience and therefore their taking part in prayer meetings or even repeating phrases of Scripture tended to mere routine, but Dr. Clark was wiser than the critics as time has proven. He knew, moreover, that the attempt to express it gave it form and shape. There was criticism of the movement because it demanded of youth the signing of a pledge. It was a very simple pledge: simply that boys and girls would read the Bible every day and would pray every day and would take some active part in the meetings of the Society. Here again Dr. Clark was wiser than the critics. He understood the psychology of habit. Furthermore, he had the long and universal experience of the Roman Catholic Church behind him. Perhaps one of the greatest factors in the development of Roman Catholicism has been its realization that the soul needs daily exercise for its healthful functioning as much as the body needs physical exercise. In all this Dr. Clark was wiser than his generation.

Neither can one overestimate what the Christian Endeavor movement has done for the Church. At a time when the Church seemed to be losing its hold upon the youth of the land, this movement not only held the young people to the Church but became the great preparatory and fitting school. It was only a few years after the organization of the Christian Endeavor Society that the Church began to realize its helpfulness. Not only did it hold innumerable youth to the Church but it brought them into its fellowship and service at a much earlier age than had been common in previous years. The Church of Christ in America should rise up and call Dr. Clark blessed.

I should not be telling the whole truth if I did not take this opportunity of saying what the Christian Endeavor movement has meant for the peace of the world. In his later years Dr. Clark became an active worker for international peace. He was an officer in several peace organizations and has been a valued trustee in the Church Peace Union, the endowment for international peace through the churches, founded by Andrew Carnegie. I remember at the time when Mr. Carnegie was considering this endowment, we were talking over together one day the composition of the board of trustees, and the two men whom Mr. Carnegie at once mentioned were Dr. Francis E. Clark and Dr. John R. Mott; for, he said, no one has done more than these men to bring the youth of all the world into the consciousness of their own needs. Mr. Carnegie was right. Under Dr. Clark's remarkable leadership Christian Endeavor societies have come into being in every country of the world and all these young people have felt their kinship with one another. In the great world conventions they have met face to face and realized that their loyalty to Christ was higher than even their loyalty to the nation; that among the true disciples of Jesus Christ boundary lines do not exist. In the great addresses which Dr. Clark has made both as president of the world organization and of the national society, he has again and again stressed this thought. He has been one of the great peace makers of the world.

Dr. Clark has written much. For years he was a weekly contributor to *The Christian Endeavor World*. Again and again he has gone around the globe, visiting all peoples and all countries and he has written articles to the papers of America and incorporated them in books. These articles have always been instrumental in interpreting the best of the different peoples and races to America and in interpreting the best in America to the peoples of the world. His last important book was the story of his own life, work and travels. It reads like a romance. Perhaps no single American, unless it is Dr. Mott or Sherwood Eddy, knows all the peoples of the world as does Dr. Clark, and in this story of his life one finds the keenest insight and the most brotherly comprehension of all peoples such as one can hardly find elsewhere. This book also contains two or three chapters which throw light upon the beauty and simplicity of Dr. Clark's character. With all his travelling and adventure he is a home loving spirit and there are few more beautiful pictures in recent literature than that he makes of his country home on the shores of Massachusetts Bay not far from the rock where his forefathers landed on our shores.

INDEX

Topical, Addresses

A
Adventuring in World Co-operation 117
Alaska 45
Alumni Banquet 83
Alumni Work 100
Amusement Question 43
Annuities and Bequests 120

B
Basement, The 42
Bismarck 10
Booths 42
Broadcasting the Convention 71

C
Challenge of the Ministry 103
China 45
Chorus, Convention 22, 94
Christ and the Young People.... 118
Christian Endeavor 22
Christian Endeavor and the Community Church 102
Christian Endeavor Field Work.. 117
Christian Endeavor, How to Organize 119
Christian Endeavor in the City Church 118
Christian Endeavor in the Small Church 119
Christian Endeavor Is Growing.. 49
Christian Endeavor To-Morrow.. 74
Clark, Dr. Resigns 57, 60, 105
Clark Recognition Fund......... 58, 69, 91, 107, 140, 158, 159, 160
Cleveland, 1927 79
Closing Session 105
Columbia 46, 77
Community for Christ, The 29
Consecration Service 113
Convention Snapshots 152
Coolidge, Letter from President.. 92
Count for Your Country 17

D
Denominational Rallies ......92, 137; Friends, 137; Disciples, 137; Presbyterian, 137; Union Rally, 138; Congregational, 138; United Brethren, 139; A. M. E. and A. M. E. Zion, 139.
Dixie Prizes 96

E
Evangelism 28, 82, 96
Exhibits, Christian Endeavor 119, 133
Expert Endeavor 117
Expression, Junior 131

F
Fellowship of Christian Endeavor 73

Fidelity Campaign (Dr. Clark's Message) 60
Field-Secretaries' Greetings 99
Field-Secretaries' Meetings 86
Field-Secretary, The 117
First Check, The 91
For Christ and the Church 33
Forbid Them Not 33
Friends of Christ Prizes 106

G
Games, Junior 129
Graded Christian Endeavor ..122, 145
Greetings from Abroad 106

H
Handwork, Junior 128
Helena 11
Home God Meant, The 32

I
Indians 10, 44, 74, 76, 86
Interdenominational Fellowship 37, 144
Intermediate Characteristics ... 122
Intermediate County Programme 123
Intermediate Leadership 122
Intermediate Oratory 87
Intermediate Society Programme 123
Intermediate Society, The Place of the 124
Intermediate State Programme .. 134
Intermediates Have Their Day .. 87
International Fellowship 34
Interracial Fellowship 36

J
Japan 45
Junior Conferences 130
Junior Convention 33
Junior Superintendent's Conception of Her Task 56, 135

L
Life or a Livelihood, Which? 80
Life-Work Recruits' Lunch 55
Loyalty 134
Luncheons, Junior 134

M
Medora 11
Minneapolis 9
Missionary Education through Christian Endeavor 119
Monthly Service Plans 51
More Junior Societies 41
Multnomah Field 15, 28, 34

N
Near East Relief 46, 145

O
Oratorical Contest 99
Oratorical Prizes 90
Orchestra, Convention 87

Our Friends for Christ 29
Overflow Meetings 71

P

Pageant 70
Pageantry 118
Parade 75
Parents' Hour 32
Peace and the World Court 73, 142
Persia, Christian Endeavor in ... 72
Pictures for Dr Clark 59
Place of Christian Endeavor, The 40
Poling Installed 112
Pre-Prayer Meeting 14
Prize Parade Delegations 73, 106
Prizes Awarded 69
Prison Christian Endeavor 119
Programme for Juniors 119
Publicity Suggestions 120
Purpose Period 109

Q

Quiet Hours 39

R

Resolutions 140
Rosarian, Dr. Clark Made a 59
Rural Christian Endeavor 117, 119

S

Seattle 12
Seminars, Junior 134
Service, Junior 132
Sing for Joy 104
Social, Essentials of a Successful 118
Social Programme, An Evening's.. 118

Social Programme, A Year's 118
Solving the World's Liquor Problem 93
Spokane 12
Standards Chart, Christian Endeavor Society 147
Street Meetings 85
Success 103
Syria 46

T

Tell It 104
Tidings of Great Joy 33, 128
Tours, Convention 113
Trustees' Meeting 57, 79, 90

U

Union Work, Methods of 120
United Society Officers 58

V

Value of Christian Endeavor, The 89

W

What a County Union Can Do.. 120
Why Christian Endeavor Believes in a Pledge 113
Why We Believe the Bible 119
Work of a Foreign Missionary... 117
Work of a Home Missionary.... 117
Work of the Preacher 117
World for Christ, The 30
World's Convention 35, 54
Worship, Junior 130

Y

You Ought to Know 73

NAMES

A

Abe, Seizo 45
Allan, Harry 77, 85, 100, 120, 135
Anderson, Robert P. 12, 58, 70, 73, 104
Appelbaum, Hilda 131, 132, 133

B

Baker, Mayor George L. 16, 75
Baker, Mrs. Everette 126
Baldwin, Estelle 88
Ball, Fred L. 85
Beaven, A. W. 30, 39
Beeman, W. H. 131, 132, 133
Blair, Russell J. 101, 116
Blake, Agnes 133
Boyer, Caroline 126, 135
Breg, W. Roy 90, 99, 113, 134
Brougher, J. Whitcomb 39, 82
Brown, Aaron 139
Brown, Ethel 126, 129, 132, 133, 134, 135
Brown, Mary 126, 128, 129, 130, 131, 133, 134
Brown, Paul 15, 55, 58, 69, 89, 91, 101, 113, 130, 135

C

Carrick, Lloyd 59

Chambers, Louisa 133
Cherrington, Ernest H. 93
Clark C. C. 139
Clark, Francis E. 13, 14, 57, 58, 60, 69, 91, 105, 107, 140, 158,159, 160
Clark, Mrs. Francis E. 32, 85, 128, 131
Cole, Mamie Gene 33, 99, 111, 126, 131, 133, 134
Coolidge, President 44, 92
Courter, Mrs. H. C. 133
Cowan, John F. 93
Crawford, Thelma 100
Creighton, Roy E. 121
Crouch, Alfred 100, 10, 119

D

Dailey, Mrs. A. M. 126, 131, 133
Darnall, Nora 127, 133, 135
Dorman, Louisa A. 33, 128
Dunn, Bessie 134, 135
Dunn, Georgia 101, 119
Dye, Royal J. 40, 55, 95, 117, 121, 129
Dyer, Louella 99, 109, 119

E

Eichelberger, Jr., J. W. 139
Elliott, B. I. 127
Evans, Charles F. 58, 90, 101, 117

F

Finnigan, Jack 99
Foster, Percy 15, 34, 40, 55, 79, 87, 92, 104
Foulkes, Wm. Hiram 32, 37, 42, 85, 101, 107, 121
Freeborn, Mrs. Carl J. 126
Freet, Frank Linn ..85, 100, 115, 117

G

Gaither, Mrs. W. R. 133
Gates, E. P. 48, 49, 58, 69, 86, 98, 101, 115, 129, 130
Gates, Mrs. E. P. 118, 134
George, Mrs. R. Ethel 127
Getty, Walter 118
Grey, Fred 139
Grose, Howard B. 58
Grauel, Mrs. James H. 46
Gulley, Mary 117

H

Haddaway, G. W. 117
Haggard Mildreth 32, 116, 119, 135
Hall, Wm. Ralph 40, 121, 124, 132
Hamilton, C. C. 12, 58, 69, 73, 91, 101, 120, 127, 131
Hartman, G. K. 139
Hetzler, C. E. 100, 115, 155
Hetzler, Mrs. C. E. 134, 135
Hicks, Herbert W. 77, 100, 118
Hill, Mrs. Mary 127
Hook, Mrs. J. Q. 99
Hoopes, Mrs. Warren G. 132, 133, 135
Howell, Walter D. 56, 118, 135
Hubbard, George H. 45
Huppertz, E. F. 100, 116, 135
Hurd, Charles T. 108, 127

I

Irvine, B. F. 98

J

Johnson, H. E. 139
Johnston, L. H. 139
Jones, Edgar De Witt 103
Jordan, L. F. 102

K

Kanzler, Jacob 13, 15, 75, 83
Kelly, James 34, 39, 48, 85, 134
Kirkpatrick, R. F. 40, 85, 111
Kyles, Bishop 36, 139

L

Landrith, Ira 58, 80, 91
Lay, Dirk 44, 76, 114

M

Marsden, E. O. 45
Martin, Bishop J. W. 139
Martin, Faith 126, 128, 134
Martin, Mrs. Wm. V. 126, 130, 134, 135
Martin, Wilbert 126
Martin, Wm. V. 126
Mateer, Carson ..98, 101, 110, 117, 135
Matthews, Mark A. 96

McAfee, Lapsley A. 28
McDonald, Edith ...116, 121, 122, 124
McLaughlin, Elsie 133
McMichael, Dr. 107
Miller, Catherine A. 70, 90, 118
Mintel, F. L. 100, 130
Morris, S. S. 139
Moye, Thomas 107

P

Pence, Dr. E. H. 16
Petty, A. Ray 29
Pickerill, H. L. 55, 117
Pierce, Governor Walter M. 16
Pinchot, Gov. Gifford 10, 16
Platas, M. 106
Poling, Daniel A. 22, 32, 39, 41, 83, 86, 108, 112, 141
Poling, Charles C. 16, 112
Praetorius, E. W. 73, 115

R

Ramsden, S. C. 58, 70
Reynolds, Irene 89
Rhodes, Elsie 131

S

Schunke, Wm. M. 87
Seaver, Sadie 133
Seymour, Mrs. W. Y. 126, 131, 133, 134
Shartle, Alvin J. 12, 40, 58, 74, 83, 90, 116, 119, 120, 135
Shaw, Wm. 154
Sherwood, Carlton M. 43, 101, 118
Shupe, H. F. 113, 139
Siler, Mrs. C. B. 132, 133, 135
Singer, Harold 76, 86, 119
Smith, Edna 126
Southwell, George C. 79, 83, 117
Sproull, John T. 79, 83
Sproull, Mrs. John T. 135
Staub, J. J. 139
Steele, Ray 127
Steinmetz, Foye 119, 132, 135

T

Taylor, David 83
Tennis, Mrs. Wm. M. ...133, 134, 135
Tenny, Dr. 83
Tochterman, Alta 129, 131, 133
Tuttle, Lois 88

V

Vandersall, Stanley B. 44, 58, 69, 83, 91, 116, 119

W

Walker, F. D. G. 100, 119
Walker, R. A. 116, 127
Walker, Vorta 133
Wallis, Frederick A. 58
Walls, Bishop W. J. 139
Wells, Mrs. J. Hunter 87, 121
Williams, Mrs. C. W. 132, 133
Wilson, J. Christie 73
Wolfangel, Miss 133
Wright, Carroll M. 101, 115

www.ingramcontent.com/pod-product-compliance
Lightning Source LLC
Chambersburg PA
CBHW031353040426
42444CB00005B/272